NEBRASKA ROOTS

NEBRASKA ROOTS

A Memoir about Coming of Age
in the Nebraska Sandhills

Leah Jesse Lambert

LUMINARE PRESS
WWW.LUMINAREPRESS.COM

Nebraska Roots: A Memoir about Coming of Age in the Nebraska Sandhills
Copyright © 2023 by Leah Jesse Lambert

Printed in the United States of America

Luminare Press
442 Charnelton St.
Eugene, OR 97401
www.luminarepress.com

LCCN: 2023906302
ISBN: 979-8-88679-222-5

*For my mother Virginia, a kind and gentle soul
with a will of iron. Her unwavering support was,
is and will always be my foundation.*

Contents

Acknowledgments

Thanks to my husband Dennis for his unwavering patience and support while I wrote this book; to my children Andrew, Jonathan and Matthew for their encouragement; to Dennis and Matthew for their editing expertise and to my four siblings, Sharyl, Lester R. (Ronnie), Roy and Rick for their reality checks.

To Ronnie, 1942–2023.

Introduction

The Sandhills region covers 20,000 square miles in western Nebraska and southern South Dakota and is the largest area of sand dunes in the western hemisphere. A variety of grasses grow in tufts and bunches across the hills, and their roots stretch down seven feet or more into the fine sand, helping to keep the dunes from returning to bare, blowing sand. Seen from a perch on a high peak, the hills roll away in all directions, folding into one another until the they melt into the sky. On a clear day, the horizon is thirty miles away with only a few isolated ranches and alkali lakes interrupting the endless succession of hills.

It would be easy to imagine that it's a bland, beige environment but color is everywhere. In the early spring, the grasses are bright green, and patches of white, yellow, blue and pink wildflowers cover the hills. The flowers fade and the green grasses become khaki, bronze, lavender and mauve in late summer. The azure blue sky is vast and the sunsets spectacular with red, pink, orange and purple pushing away the azure to make way for navy blue. In the deep blue night sky, millions of stars swirl overhead while the Milky Way, like a sparkling pink ribbon, curls away toward the north.

I was born and raised on a cattle ranch on the southern edge of those Sandhills. My dad had hundreds of Hereford cow-calf pairs, some yearling steers and heifers, a dozen bulls and a lot of horses. The animals roamed through the hills, eating hardy grass and drinking fresh water pumped from the underground aquifer by clanking windmills.

For many years, Nebraska's motto was The Good Life. As a country girl growing up in the Sandhills, it was more than a good life. It was a great life. Like the sandhills grasses, my Nebraska roots are deep. When I left for university, my mom reminded me for the umpteenth time to remember where I came from. This account of my life from birth to young adulthood is my attempt to honor my Nebraska roots and my mother's wishes.

It may seem that some of my stories cannot possibly be true, but I assure you that the events were real and I describe them as I remember them. The people are (or were) real and for the most part I used people's actual names. However, in a few cases I changed someone's name or simply used their initials. I did this to protect the anonymity of individuals because of my not-so-flattering reporting of circumstances and events.

CHAPTER 1

The Beginning

I don't believe there ever was a life more attractive than life on a cattle ranch.

—THEODORE ROOSEVELT

So, there they were on January 1, 1949, stuck in the snow in the middle of a blizzard. The snow swirled in all directions and the fifty-mile-per-hour wind gusts buffeted the car, forcing snow through the cracks around the windows. Everything was moving except the little black car.

The saga began several years earlier when my parents, Lester and Virginia Jesse, and my oldest brother, Ronnie, moved to the Case place after my dad got out of the army at the end of WW II. My grandfather, Frank Jesse, owned the five thousand-acre isolated ranch far back in the Sandhills in Nebraska's Sheridan County and he hired my dad to manage the ranch. My parents lived in a tiny, two-room ranch house on the north side of the property. They had no electricity and no running water. Roy was born in the winter of 1947 and Mom got pregnant with me in the late summer of 1948.

The family of four had been invited to celebrate New Year's Day 1949 with my mother's family, the Woodworth's. It was a beautiful day, 65 degrees and sunny with a mild breeze. In the early afternoon, dark clouds started piling up in the southwest and the warm breeze turned into a cold wind. By three o'clock, clouds were coming in from all directions and it began to snow. My dad was anxious about the weather because it was a long drive home—sixteen miles of paved highway, then ten more through the hills. He told my mom to get ready to go, but my grandmother begged them to stay just a bit longer for sandwiches and cake. Dad reluctantly agreed, so they stayed another hour.

When they finally left the celebration, it was nearly dark and a heavy snow was falling. The temperature was dropping rapidly and the wind was fierce. "This is bad," my father thought. He drove north on the highway in blinding snow before reaching the turnoff onto the gravel road and finally the trail road that led home. By the time they got to the last gate, about a half mile from the house, the road was nearly impassable because of the deep snow. The old snow underneath had thawed during the warm day and then froze solid with the frigid temperatures that evening. New snow was drifting in, covering the ice. Dad was grateful that they were only a half mile from home, and he was confident they would make it. Then the car got stuck. At first, Dad tried rocking the car free: first gear, step on the gas hard, reverse gear, step on the gas, then first, then reverse, over and over. The car shuddered with every gear change—but would not move. Dad got out of the car, grabbed the shovel from the trunk, and started digging. After a while, he got back in the car and tried rocking again, but to no avail. So, it was back into the cold for more digging. The shovel's handle broke so Dad dug with the shovelhead and his hands. Still the car would not move.

Finally, Dad told Mom that he would try one more time to dig the car out, but if it didn't work, they would have to walk through the blizzard to the house. Dad would carry Ronnie and Mom would carry baby Roy. He would tie everyone together with rope so they wouldn't get separated. It was only a half-mile walk and Dad told Mom that they could handle it. In his heart, Dad figured he could make it (if he didn't get lost in the blizzard), but Mom was pregnant and would be carrying a wiggling, screaming baby. It was a risky plan but staying in the car meant sure death. My mother was terrified but she nodded in agreement. She knew they might not survive the half-mile walk, and she had no idea how they could even find the house in the blinding snow.

Dad took a breath, got out of the car one last time, and started digging and chipping at the frozen snow. By some miracle or stroke of luck, he saw the problem. There was a patch of snow and ice about two inches wide under the rear spring. He chipped at that little patch of icy snow until it felt like it moved. He climbed back into the car, started the engine, and hit first gear. The car lurched forward. Neither he nor my mother said a word, and Dad drove forward gingerly that last half mile. He stopped as close as he could to the front door, grabbed Ronnie while Mom pulled the baby close, and covered his head with a blanket. They got out of the car and struggled through the drifts and the blinding whiteness to the front door of the tiny house. Once inside, they sat down on kitchen chairs and my mother cried. It was nearly midnight.

That particular blizzard lasted several days, but there were eighteen different storms in January 1949 with thirteen days of blizzard conditions and over forty-five inches of snow. Temperatures were below zero for weeks and wind gusts blew 65–70 mph. February and March were a bit better but not much. There was very little time between storms to feed the cattle, so Dad enlisted Mom's help. She left six-year-old Ronnie and thirteen-month-old Roy alone in the house with a fire roaring in the stove while she and Dad fed the cattle. She glanced toward the house often while silently reciting prayers.

The family was well-fed through the months of blizzards because they had stocked up on staples in December and Dad hacked meat off cows that died in the storm. They feasted on roast beef or steaks every day. A neighbor who lived several miles away drove a wagon pulled by a team of horses into Alliance every two to three weeks. He loaded the wagon with food supplies for his family and for my parents.

The phone lines were out through January, but by February, a rudimentary phone service was restored. On some days, around noon, Dad's parents would call, but Mom and Dad could never make an outbound call. Every day, Mom and Dad waited for a phone call. Dad told Grandpa how many cattle had been lost, how much hay was left, and what the kids were doing. They talked about getting up every morning and finding a pyramid of snow from the floor to the keyhole by the front door. Grandpa told Dad that hundreds of people and thousands of cattle had died in the blizzards. He said that the Fifth Army was using airplanes to drop hay to stranded cattle in Nebraska, South Dakota, and Colorado.

My grandparents, Frank and Bess Jesse, also survived the 1949 blizzard. They lived on a 3,600-acre ranch, the home place, about eighteen miles south of the Case place.

They bought the ranch in the 1930s and moved a house from the Hoffland ghost town to their new home. Hoffland had been a busy town of about five thousand people during the potash boom before and during World War I. The town was close to both the railroad tracks and the alkali lakes in the Sandhills. Alkali lake water was pumped through pipes to the plant in Hoffland, where the alkali was refined into potash, which was loaded onto railroad cars and transported to factories for processing into fertilizer. In 1916, priorities changed and the potash was processed as a key component of the munitions used during World War I. When the war was over, the demand for domestic potash collapsed. Hoffland shriveled up and the residents were scattered by the restless Nebraska wind. The houses remained vacant and deteriorating until ranchers began moving them to their ranches. My grandparent's ranch in southern Sheridan County was about three miles north of Hoffland, so moving the house only took a day. They chose a well-built, three-bedroom house with a small bathroom. The exterior was stucco, there were green shingles on the hip roof, and the trim around the windows was painted dark green to match the roof.

Grandpa poured a concrete foundation and positioned the house on the western edge of a green meadow. A small lake, surrounded by bulrushes, was about a half mile east of the house. A low hill just behind the house on the north side was the perfect place for a water-pumping windmill and an underground water holding tank. The slope of the hill made an adequate angle for gravity to pull water from the underground tank into the house for running water. The septic tank was installed behind the main house. To the left of the house, Grandpa erected a power-generating windmill next to a small stucco milk house, which housed the electric storage batteries. Finally, he planted dozens of fast-growing American elm trees around the house.

It was a comfortable house, but spending months trapped by winter blizzards was the tipping point for my grandmother. Enough was enough. She had lived on the isolated prairie for years and was ready to move. My grandfather agreed. He wasn't a young man anymore, and he was tired of the hard work and the horrific winters. They moved to a house in Alliance, Nebraska, in late April of 1949. My dad and my grandfather went into a ranch partnership and my parents and the two boys moved from the Case place to the home place in early May 1949.

With the move to this home place, my parents began living a luxurious life. There was a kitchen, living room, dining room, and three bedrooms, but that wasn't the best part. The best parts were that the house had hot and cold running water, an indoor toilet, a forced-air furnace, and wired electricity. It was a far cry from the one- and two-room houses they had shared since they were married in 1941. Mom didn't have to pump water from a well and heat it on the stove for warm water. She didn't have to leave the house and walk to the outhouse when nature called. She didn't have to light a kerosene lamp for light. Everything was wonderful.

The ranch partnership was a fifty-fifty arrangement where Grandpa furnished the land and materials needed to run the ranch while Dad furnished the labor, fed and cared for the livestock, kept the fences and the grounds in good repair, stacked hay in the summer, and fed the cattle in the winter. Dad and Mom bought into the cow herd so their share was one-half of the total. Once they purchased the cattle, the partners registered a company brand. All calves got this brand (jay-tee-jay) from the spring of 1949 forward. Dad was a high school graduate and had attended business college, so he supplied both the brawn and the brains for the operation. He kept the books, monitored expenses, and calculated income potential for scenarios. He was an astute businessman and Grandpa trusted his judgment.

Shortly after my parents moved in early May, the spring calves needed to be branded. Cow-calf pairs were collected on horseback with the help of neighbors and were kept in a holding pen where calves were roped one by one and dragged into the coral. Cowboys tackled the calf and held it down while it was branded on the hip. Calves were vaccinated and de-horned, the males were castrated, and each calf was then released to its frantically mooing mother. The last calf was branded by twelve thirty in the afternoon, so around one o'clock my nine-months pregnant mother and a few other women served a huge meal to the twenty-five cowhands. After the men left the tables, it took the ladies hours to clean the kitchen.

Ten days later my mom went into labor, so Dad drove the family to his parent's house in Alliance. After some waiting, Mom said that it was time to go to the hospital, so they left the boys with the grandparents and drove to St. Joseph's Hospital about five minutes away. When they got to the reception desk, attendants whisked Mom down a hallway, leaving Dad in the waiting room. Mom was starting to deliver, so the nurses quickly poured disinfectant over her and then gave her a drug of some kind. Dad waited while Mom, who said she was "knocked out," gave birth. My mom and I spent the next week in the hospital. Mom was flat on her back, and I was tucked away in the hospital nursery. The nuns carried me to Mom's bed every now and then for feeding and cuddling, but the rest of the time, the nuns took care of feedings and hovered to make sure Mom didn't move. Mom couldn't even walk down the hall to the nursery. Dad visited as often as he could, and various relatives stopped by the hospital to visit Mom and to look through the nursery window at the first female Jesse in the next generation. My brothers weren't allowed to visit.

Mom was relieved when the doctor dismissed us from the hospital. She had spent a week lying on her back in an uncomfortable hospital bed and was so weak she could barely walk, let alone take care of two wild little boys and a newborn baby. Besides, it was mid-May and there was work waiting: the garden needed to be planted, spring cleaning was past due, laundry had surely piled up, bread needed to be baked, and butter needed to be churned. So many things to do besides hug and kiss Roy and Ronnie and get me, baby Leah, settled into the bassinet in the corner of the master bedroom.

When the doctor told Dad that his wife and baby could go home, he drove the old, reliable Chevy, the car that had saved them back in January, into Alliance to retrieve Mom, me, and my brothers. Mom cradled me in her arms in the front seat and the boys clambered around in the back. Eleven miles east on Highway 2 to Hoffland, then over rutted trail roads, through pastures, over hills, past the Bauer house, and finally home. Mom's baby-boom family was perfect—three kids, two boys and a girl. For six years, Dad and Mom were perfectly happy with the little group, and then, things began to change. Sharyl was born in 1955 and two years later, Rick joined our troop. The family was now complete with five kids spread over fifteen years. To us, it seemed perfectly normal for seven people to live in a twelve hundred square-foot, three-bedroom, one-bath house, but friends and relatives secretly thought that Mom and Dad were crazy for having so many kids "in this day and age."

Two Big Brothers

What strange creatures brothers are.

—JANE AUSTEN

Ronnie was six and a half years old and Roy was fifteen months old when I was born. Ronnie was a doting older brother and Roy and I were so close in age that we became nearly inseparable as we grew older. I began walking at thirteen months, but had a hard time keeping my balance. I fell often when big brother Ronnie wasn't holding my hand. One day, Mom left the broom next to the kitchen table. I crawled to the table, pulled myself up onto a chair, and grabbed the broom. Then, like a circus tightrope walker, I began walking, holding the broom at arm's length and parallel to the floor. The broom was just the ticket and provided the balance I needed. Falling was a thing of the past. I proudly walked around the house with my balance broom, much to the delight of everyone who witnessed the little broom walker. I only had trouble navigating through doors or around furniture placed in tight quarters. When that happened, Ronnie swooped in and saved the day. He took my hand, grabbed the broom, and turned me so I was walking in the right direction before giving the broom back.

Roy wasn't talkative but he understood conversations and followed instructions. Relatives thought there was something wrong with Roy, but Mom and Dad knew better. Roy was bright and clever, just not ready to talk. When I started to talk, Roy began to talk. His vocabulary was much larger than mine because he had been listening to conversations for a long time. He taught me everything he knew, and soon the two of us were talking incessantly, which probably drove Mom crazy. She sent us outside when she got sick of the constant chatter.

One morning, Mom left Roy and me alone in the house while she went outside to do some chores. She was gone five minutes and during that short time Roy and I decided we were thirsty and needed to get the tomato juice out of the refrigerator. We opened the refrigerator door and started to pull out the forty-eight-ounce can of juice, but we weren't strong enough or tall enough to haul the can off the shelf. It slipped and fell onto the floor in front of the refrigerator and the juice gushed out of the two holes punched into the top of the can. We panicked because the juice puddle grew quickly before we could set the can upright. We needed to clean up the mess before Mom came back and decided the most practical solution was to lick up the juice. We were thirsty and Mom would be so happy that we cleaned up our own mess.

Mom stepped back into the house and saw us on our hands and knees, lapping up spilled tomato juice. She was not happy. The refrigerator was next to the door, which meant that the floor wasn't even a little bit clean. Everyone walked into the kitchen wearing boots, and boot soles were covered with cow, horse, pig and chicken manure. The thought of licking anything off the floor made Mom gag. She yelled, "Get up, get up, get up! Get off the floor!"

Roy and I stared at Mom because she was mad at us and we didn't know why. We were proud of our solution and confused about her reaction. Mom pushed us out of the kitchen, grabbed a rag and mopped up the juice that was left, and then mopped the floor with soap and water. Roy and I watched from the dining room, still not understanding why Mom was mad when our plan had been so good.

In the summer of 1951, Ronnie got sick. He had always had asthma, but now he had pneumonia and it was getting worse. The family doctor gave Ronnie medicines and told Mom to lay him over the end of the bed for thirty minutes twice a day and pat his back to make him cough. Nothing worked, Ronnie's condition worsened, and Dr. Kennedy told my parents that he couldn't do anything more. He recommended that Ronnie go to a heart-lung specialist, Dr. Claggett, at the Mayo Clinic in Rochester, Minnesota. Kennedy respected Claggett because they had served together in WW II. Mom and Dad agreed and Kennedy made appointments for Ronnie at Mayo. Dad and Mom took Roy and me to Grandpa and Grandma Woodworth for safe keeping and loaded Ronnie into the car for the long drive to Rochester.

When they got to Rochester, there were lots of tests, and the doctors finally told Mom and Dad that Ronnie should have one lobe of one lung removed because he had a condition called bronchiectasis. After the surgery, the doctor brought the lung to Mom and Dad to show them how badly it was damaged. Dad said that instead of being spongey and pink, it looked like liver. During the operation, the surgeons also had to remove one of Ronnie's ribs, but the doctor told my parents that it would grow back.

Ronnie gradually regained his strength and after a few weeks he was discharged. Dad, Mom and Ronnie could finally make the long trip home. Mom's memory of the trip was that of never-ending white paint dashes in the middle of the blacktopped road. At night, the dashes were hypnotizing—flashing up in front of the car, then disappearing beneath the hood. Mom hated that memory but loved leaving Mayo with Ronnie, who was clearly on the mend.

Extended Families

Family faces are magic mirrors. Looking at people who belong to us, we see the past, present and future.

—GAIL BUCKLEY

The Woodworths

My mother's earliest Woodworth ancestor, Walter Woodward Woodworth, arrived around 1632 at Plymouth, Massachusetts. Walter was an indentured servant and a surveyor but eventually earned his freedom. Generation after generation, Walter's descendants moved west seeking land and opportunity. Dorcy and Iva Woodworth, my mother's parents, grew up in eastern Nebraska and were married in Palmyra, Nebraska. Dorcy was drafted into the army in 1917 and took the train to New York for basic training before deployment to Europe, where he would potentially be one of the millions of men fighting in World War I. But during training in New York, he contracted influenza and suffered debilitating pneumonia. He lingered in the infirmary with hundreds of other soldiers for weeks before he was healthy enough to travel. He was discharged and took the train west to Albion, Nebraska, where Iva was waiting. While lucky to have dodged a trip to the trenches of Europe and to have survived the flu that killed millions, Dorcy was left with severe lung complications and asthma. His doctor blamed the flu for the asthma and recommended that Dorcy move to a drier climate to ease the symptoms. The couple decided to leave humid eastern Nebraska and move to the arid high plains of western Nebraska.

In 1928 the economy was booming, so Dorcy and Iva sold their farm outside Albion for top dollar and used the money to buy a small farm just east of Alliance. They sent their livestock and most of their household goods west on the Alliance-bound train before they loaded their kids into a Model T Ford and started the drive west. In 1928, the Woodworths had four children. Their first daughter, Viola was born in 1919 and Merlin was born in 1921. Next came my mom, Virginia, born in 1922, and Lyle in 1925. Lyle was born with the umbilical cord wrapped around his neck and he was disabled because of a lack of oxygen. Baby Verna was born just weeks after the Woodworths arrived at their new farm, and Wayne arrived a few years later.

Before the family left Albion, Iva's mother, Sarah Rogers Russell, gave Iva her set of treasured Austrian dinnerware that she had purchased just after Iva was born in 1896. Sarah also gave Iva a few china teacups and some fine linens for the new home. The Baptist Ladies Aid Society in Albion quilted a red and white quilt for the Woodworths to honor their service to the church and to be a remembrance of their lives in Albion. The Woodworths and their children left Albion, knowing they would likely never see friends and family again. There would be no extended family in Alliance, but, over time, they developed strong ties with fellow parishioners at the First Baptist Church. That church became their extended family.

Mom was five years old when she left Albion with her family, and had no memory of her life in Albion and no memory of her grandparents. While Iva and her mother Sarah exchanged letters, they never saw each other again.

At first, everything was wonderful on the new farm. The family had chickens, hogs, and a few dairy cows, and Dorcy planted corn and potatoes. It was a happy life until October 1929 when the stock market crashed and the country was plunged into the Great Depression. The Woodworths considered themselves lucky because they owned their farm. Beginning in 1930 there were droughts in the Great Plains and the Dust Bowl was upon them. A light wind gained strength and the sky darkened as the dust began to spin in the sky. People ran to their homes to escape the coming choking dust. During the worst storms visibility was nearly zero in the gritty, black blizzard. At the first hint of a storm, Iva hung wet sheets over doors and windows to keep out as much dust as possible to protect Dorcy's lungs. In just a few hours, the bright white sheets turned into gritty brown sheets as the dust filtered into the house through small cracks around windows and doors.

Through the Dust Bowl years, Dorcy kept a few cows and hogs alive and Iva kept chickens, so they had food. During those lean years, hobos, dressed in tattered, filthy clothes, jumped off trains that were slowly making their way into Alliance and walked the half mile or so to the Woodworth back door. They begged for something to eat and Iva told the men to wait outside. She fried eggs, put the eggs between slices of homemade bread, and handed the sandwiches to the men through the narrowly opened back door. Tears welled up in their eyes when they accepted the gift, saying, "God bless you, ma'am. God bless you and your fine family." Grandma hoped the men could find work, but she knew it was unlikely. She was just happy that she had food to share.

Mom and her siblings caught scarlet fever during the depression, probably through contact with other children in their small, rural school. The children had classic symptoms: sore throat and bright red skin on their torsos and limbs. Scarlet fever was a devastating diagnosis because many children died and others developed heart ailments or lost their hearing because of the infection. The doctor quarantined the Woodworth household and hammered a large QUARANTINE sign next to the front door. While quarantined, the kids could not leave the house and my grandmother fed them hot tea and toast. My mother dutifully drank the tea but started to loathe the taste. Drinking tea morning, noon and night destroyed her ability to enjoy—or even tolerate—the smell and taste of tea. Fortunately, beyond having an aversion to tea, none of the Woodworth children had long-term effects after their bout with scarlet fever.

Franklin Roosevelt was elected president in 1932, and in 1935 the Works Projects Administration (WPA) started projects big and small across the country. The WPA made its way to Alliance and Dorcy was hired to help build a golf course east of Alliance. The project was fairly close to the farm, being just south on the service road to airport. Dorcy often took Lyle to the jobsite, and even though Lyle wasn't paid for his work, he worked hard. Both were very proud of their efforts to make the golf course beautiful.

The Woodworth house was a small three-bedroom bungalow with a combined living and dining room and a tiny U-shaped kitchen just to the left of the dining room. The house was initially heated by a coal furnace, but Grandpa later converted it to fuel oil. There was a single two- by three-foot floor vent between the kitchen and living room that warmed the entire house. While the kitchen, living room, and dining room were warm in the winter, the bedrooms were frigid. There was a small mudroom next to the kitchen on the north side of the house. The family used the mudroom door as an entrance to the house, leaving their muddy boots, coats and coveralls in the mudroom before walking into the kitchen. In the summer, the outside door was always open but insects were kept at bay by a screened door that slammed shut when anyone went in or out.

When they first moved into the house there was no indoor toilet, but in the mid-1940s Grandpa installed a bathroom in an addition on the north side of the mudroom. It was only eight- by-eight feet, but included a tiny shower, a toilet, and a sink. There was a little electric heater inserted into one of the walls, but my grandparents only turned on the heater a few times each day during the winter; just long enough to keep the pipes from freezing.

My mother and her siblings attended a one-room school a half mile from their house, and after graduating eighth grade, all but Lyle went to high school in Alliance. When my mother was in tenth grade, she met my father, a senior who was about to graduate. He was walking down the stairs when his eyes met my mother's. She was a small, pretty girl wearing wire-rimmed glasses. He was a handsome cowboy with black, wavy hair and hazel/gray eyes. They dated a while but Lester went away to business school after graduation. When he returned, the two dated more seriously. My mother graduated in 1940 and they were married in the spring of 1941.

My mother's oldest brother Merlin served in the Navy during WW II. After he was discharged, he married Eileen and they farmed and ranched around Alliance. They had three children: Winona was born in 1939, and Dan and Don were born in the mid-1950s. Mom said that Merlin and Eileen were having marriage problems and they had the little ones to keep the marriage together. Mom said that it was not the best idea to bring babies into a rocky marriage, but it's what Merlin and Eileen chose to do and, by all accounts, it worked for their family.

Uncle Merlin was a prankster who was famous for his practical jokes. When Mom and Dad were dating and Dad took Mom home, she always asked Dad to walk her to the corner of the house so she could run to the outhouse before going inside the house. She wanted a guard because if he wasn't there, Merlin often jumped out of the shadows, yelling and terrifying her.

Mom's older sister, Viola (Vi) married Harvey Gray and they had two children. The Grays ran a diner, Gray's Café, on the west side of Alliance for many years. We didn't eat out often, but as a special treat we went to Gray's Café, sat in a booth, ate burgers and fries, and drank chocolate milkshakes. The Gray children and their families moved to Denver for work and when Harvey died, Vi moved to Denver to be close to her kids. She later fell in love with a man named Les, a bachelor who had never been married. Vi and Les married and they lived in a tiny cottage close to the airport, Stapleton Field, for many years.

Verna, Mom's younger sister, married a local farm boy, Bob Schefcik. Farming wasn't his career choice and he became a builder. They had three children: Jerry was a year younger than me, Vicky was Sharyl's age, and Marlene was

Rick's age. Bob and Verna had a fourth child, a girl, a couple of years after Marlene was born, but the baby girl died suddenly. Mom said that the doctors didn't know why the baby died. "It was crib death and just one of those things," she said. "It was God's will."

After the baby died, we visited the grieving Schefciks. It was evening when we walked into a dark living room. The only light came from a small lamp with a single bulb on a table near the sofa, and Uncle Bob was stoically sitting alone on the sofa. Dad walked up to him and they shook hands but didn't exchange a word. The only sound in the house came from the dining room where Aunt Verna, Aunt Vi, and Grandma were quietly talking. Mom and I walked into the dining room and I saw tears in Mom's eyes. I began crying too because Mom was crying.

Shortly after the baby was buried, the Schefciks moved to Las Vegas, Nevada. They came back to Alliance every year after that, but Aunt Verna never visited her baby's grave because she just couldn't bear reliving the heart break.

In Las Vegas, Uncle Bob was very busy with the building boom and Aunt Verna got a secretarial job, working for the FBI. This was in the '50s and '60s, when organized crime supposedly owned Las Vegas. One can only imagine the information Aunt Verna might have been privy to at the FBI but she never said a word. When asked what she did at the FBI, she just said, "I can't talk about it."

Wayne, Mom's youngest brother lived in Alliance and married a local girl named Patricia but everyone called her Patsy. She was full of energy, talkative, and she made everyone laugh. I don't think I ever saw her when she wasn't smiling or laughing. Wayne and Patsy had a couple of kids and built a basement house on the west side of Grandpa's property. Grandpa said that he sold the land for the house to Wayne on the condition that he never sell it. That land was to stay in the family. It was a cute little underground house, complete with two bedrooms, a bathroom, a kitchen and a living room. Patsy told Mom that as soon as they had paid for the basement house, they would build their real house on top of the basement and move out of the dungeon. Mom and Patsy laughed at the comment. Those plans were never realized. Wayne and Patsy sold the basement house to an outsider, much to Grandpa's disappointment. They moved to Washington State for work and, like Verna, only came back to Alliance to visit.

Mom's brother Lyle, who was disabled, was Grandpa Woodworth's partner on the farm. He couldn't speak clearly, but Grandma and Grandpa could understand him. Vi was the oldest girl and when Lyle was born, she became his primary caregiver. The two had a special bond and even as adults, held hands when sitting side by side.

Lyle learned small engine repair and carpentry from Grandpa Woodworth, but Lyle's specialty was building birdhouses. He was always in the midst of creating birdhouses out of scraps of found lumber. Each birdhouse was carefully crafted, and houses in various stages of completion were lined up in Grandpa's milk house. Lyle painted each one in bright colors, and when we visited our grandparents, Lyle led Roy and me to the milk house and proudly showed us his creations.

When we were young, Roy and I spent a lot of time with Grandpa and Grandma Woodworth. Whenever Mom needed a break from us, she dropped us off at our grandparents' house for some family time. Grandma was a good cook and prepared huge meals for Grandpa, Lyle, Roy and me.

Breakfast was bacon or ham and eggs, home-baked bread, jam, and coffee. For me, the coffee was three-quarters cream, one-quarter coffee with three teaspoons of sugar. "You have to learn to drink coffee," Grandma said. Over time, there was less cream and more coffee, and in the end landed at about fifty-fifty but always had three teaspoons of sugar.

Dinner, in the middle of the day, was the largest meal of the day, and just like at home, we had meat or chicken, potatoes, a vegetable or two, bread, butter and jam, and milk to drink. There was always homemade cookies, cake, or pie for dessert. Supper was a lighter meal, often leftovers from the main meal at noon.

In the 1950s, Grandpa had a small dairy operation, and he and Lyle milked fifteen to twenty cows every morning and every evening. I was fascinated with the milking process because Grandpa had an electric milking machine. He and Lyle herded the cows into the milking barn, the cows lined up in their assigned stanchions and started munching on their oats. Instead of milking each cow by hand, Grandpa and Lyle attached clear tubes to each teat. These tubes were in turn attached to long, clear overhead hoses that attached to a stainless-steel collection tank at the end of the stanchions. Lyle flicked a switch that turned on the machine, and milk magically flowed from the cows' teats, through the hose, to the collection tank. Roy and I watched with wonder as the foamy, white milk flowed through the hoses to the tank. The milking was completed in just a few minutes. Grandpa and Lyle poured the milk from the tank into large milk cans and sold the milk to the dairy in Alliance where it was processed for local customers.

I loved the idea of automation and told Dad that he should buy a milking machine like Grandpa's. We could milk all the cows at once, which would be so much faster, but Dad said he didn't have an operation big enough to justify a milking machine. "No, for our few cows, milking by hand is just fine," he said. So that was that. No milking machines for the Jesses.

Grandma kept chickens and sold eggs to the markets in Alliance. When we stayed over, Roy and I helped gather eggs and helped feed the chickens, just as we did at home. When Grandma slaughtered the chickens, she wrung their necks. This method of dispatching chickens was a little revolting to me because it looked cruel, but the method was effective. After the chicken was killed, Grandma dipped the carcass into hot water and Roy and I plucked off the feathers. We created a blizzard of white feathers flying in every direction. Grandma singed off the pin feathers, chopped off the heads, removed the inner organs, and washed the chickens under the outdoor faucet. She wrapped each chicken in freezer paper, tucking the neck, heart, and gizzard inside the bird. She secured the package with string, labeled the package, and stashed the chickens in her chest freezer.

Grandma's chicken and noodles were my favorite meal, so she always made this when we visited. She dropped pieces of chicken, carrots, and onions into a large pot of water, and after a couple of hours she removed the bones, strained the cooking liquid, and put the chicken pieces and the liquid back in the pot for continued simmering. While the chicken simmered, Grandma made the egg noodles. She sifted a mound of flour onto the table, made a small well in the middle, and dropped egg yolks into the well. She added a little salt and a little lard and mixed the dough with her hands until it was just right. Next, she rolled the dough into a thin rectangle, sprinkled flour on top and cut strips of noodles with a sharp knife. She placed the noodles in a single layer on newspaper and sat them on the dining room table to dry. In the winter, Grandma put a newspaper covered with noodles on the big floor heating grate in the dining room, reminding us to be careful and not step on the noodles. Just before dinner, Grandma thickened the chicken liquid and added the dried noodles. After five minutes or so she served the chicken and noodles over mashed potatoes. It was perfect.

One summer when I was six or seven, Lyle told Grandpa that there was a wasps' nest in the milk house. Roy and I peered into the milk house to look at the nest. It was huge, close to the ceiling in the corner by the door. Since the insects were bothering Lyle when he was working on his birdhouses or when he went in and out for his other chores, the nest needed to go. Even though it was a hot summer day, Lyle and Grandpa dressed in long-sleeved thick shirts, boots with their heavy trousers tucked into the tops, large straw hats with loose, thin scarves covering their faces and tucked into the buttoned-up shirts and finally, heavy leather gloves. So attired, the two were ready for battle with the wasps.

Lyle got a ladder and propped it up next to the nest. Grandpa held the ladder in one hand and a pump-type insect sprayer in the other. (The contents were likely DDT.) Lyle climbed the ladder with his weapon of choice, a large broom. Roy and I watched from the middle of the gravel driveway while Grandma watched from the safe side of the screened door in the mudroom. Lyle wacked the nest once and a lot of wasps escaped the nest and went into a frenzy. Lyle wacked the nest again and it tumbled onto the floor of the milk house. At that point, there was a swarm of hundreds of wasps. Lyle was off the ladder in a flash, swiping at the wasps with his broom and stomping on the nest with his heavy boots. Grandpa let go of the ladder and started spraying the insecticide on the nest and then spraying indiscriminately in all directions. Meanwhile, the wasps got angrier. They swarmed out of the milk house to get away from the insecticide and flew straight at Roy and me. They flew around our heads, arms, and legs, landing and stinging us over and over. We ran around waving and screaming, trying to get away from the wasps. Lyle attempted to assist by chasing us, swatting at the wasps with his broom. Grandpa was also chasing us, spraying us with his sprayer, but he soon ran out of insecticide and the chaos just kept getting worse. Everyone was running around like chickens with no heads. From behind the screen door, Grandma was yelling, "Don't run! Don't run! They won't sting if you don't run!" This seemed like the worst advice we had ever heard, so Roy and I kept running. Her next instruction was to run into the mudroom, which made much more sense. The next time my travels took me close to the screen door, I ran toward Grandma. She opened the door a sliver and yanked me inside. When Roy ran toward the door, Grandma nabbed him as well. A little crowd of wasps accompanied us inside, so Grandma brushed them off and stomped on them.

Roy and I were covered with wasp stings: torso, face, head, arms, and legs. It felt like my whole body was on fire. So while Lyle and Grandpa killed off the wasps with the broom and the reloaded DDT sprayer, Roy and I took a cool shower. Grandma made a paste of baking soda and water, and slathered the paste on every sting. We were covered head-to-toe in stings and baking soda. Maybe Grandma and Grandpa felt bad that their little grandkids were stung so badly, but I don't remember them saying anything about the wasp incident to our parents. Perhaps it was embarrassing to know they had underestimated the wrath of a swarm of wasps or perhaps they just thought this was one of the prices you paid when you lived on a farm.

Roy and I continued to stay with Grandpa and Grandma Woodworth and Lyle periodically in the summers through our grade school years. After Grandpa Woodworth died in 1958, Grandma and Lyle moved to a little house in Alliance, and Uncle Merlin took over the farm. Roy and I often stayed with Grandma during our high school years, especially when the weather was bad and we couldn't make the trek home to the ranch.

The Jesses

My father's Jesse and Bauer ancestors emigrated from Europe. Samuel Jesse was born in England and immigrated to Iowa in 1854. He served two years in 10th Iowa Infantry Regiment during the Civil War. In 1887, Samuel and his five sons secured jobs as teamsters (men who managed horses) with the Union Pacific railroad company that was building tracks through Nebraska. The Jesses liked Nebraska and were lured by the Homestead Act. They returned to Iowa, sold their farms, loaded their wagons, and moved to western Nebraska in 1888.

Franz Zeller immigrated to the US from Germany in the 1840s. Upon landing in Baltimore, his last name was changed from Zeller to Bauer and he moved to Illinois. Franz served in the Illinois Calvary during the Civil War. After the war, he and his wife, Christiana Hilt Bauer, moved with their children to western Nebraska. Their daughter Anna married Frank Jesse, one of Samuel's sons, and the newlyweds homesteaded on a ranch in Sheridan County. There were no trees for a log cabin, so Frank and Anna dug into the side of a hill and hollowed out the sand. Once settled into their dugout, they began having children. Neighbors noted that every time the Jesses had another baby, they dug out another room. My dad's father, Frank Samuel, was the first-born son and the first Jesse born in Nebraska. He attended a small, one-room school through sixth grade and then began his career as a cowboy, following in his father's footsteps.

My dad's mother Elizabeth (Bess) Moss Jones, was the youngest of seven sisters who moved with their parents, L.B. and Addie Jones, from Terra Alta, West Virginia, to Alliance in 1910 when Bess was nine years old. John Leslie Bedell (L.B.) Jones attended West Virginia College in Flemington, a Seminary in Missouri and a music school in Iowa. He was a respected Methodist minister and composer who inexplicably left West Virginia to accept his call to a new Methodist Church in uncivilized Alliance, Nebraska. He only served the church a short time before he went in search of greener pastures. The family moved to Chadron, Nebraska, so the older girls could attend the normal school, a school that trained teachers. The logic was that after the girls graduated from the school, they could get teaching jobs and L. B. wouldn't have to support them. After the stint in Chadron, L.B., Addie, and Bess homesteaded in the remote sandhills north of Ellsworth, Nebraska. Bess walked several miles every day to a one-room school outside of Ellsworth where she completed eighth grade. One evening, after supper, L.B. stepped out of the house to smoke a cigarette and vanished. Addie searched but there was no sign of him—no cigarette butts, no boot prints, no missing horse, nothing. Addie contacted the sheriff, and after several days of searching, the sheriff and his deputies gave up. L.B. had just disappeared into the night. Addie never heard from him again.

After L.B. disappeared, Addie must have burned every photo she had of him because there are no photographic records of the couple, their wedding, or their family. Addie sold the homestead in 1917 and bought a little diner, the Liberty Café, in the potash boom town of Antioch, Nebraska. Over ten thousand people lived in Antioch and Addie's business was busy. Bess waited tables and helped her mother with the cooking and cleaning. It was at that café that Bess met and fell in love with a handsome young cowboy named Frank Jesse.

Bess and Frank were married in 1919. Frank bought a fairly large cattle ranch, the Case place, and the young couple moved into the tiny two-room cottage on the north end of the property. My dad, Lester, was born in 1920. Frank said that when Bess went into labor, he drove her through the Sandhills in a horse-drawn buckboard to the doctor in Antioch. It was a long, grueling trip for Bess, even though Frank did his best to avoid bumps and jolts. Two years later, their daughter Eleanor was born and after that, Lois. When Lois was small, Frank bought another ranch eighteen miles south, close to ranches owned by his Jesse relatives. Frank and Bess moved from the Case place to the new home place in horse-drawn wagons. A few years later, their youngest son, Robert, was born. Frank's sisters and brothers all had ranches fairly close to the new place. It was good to be surrounded by family but Frank's parents and all of his siblings joined a conservative Christian sect in the 1940s. They pleaded with Frank and Bess to join, but the sect was restrictive and required church involvement in all aspects of everyday life. The only music allowed was Christian music, and dancing was forbidden. Frank and Bess loved music and dancing and since Bess had been raised a Methodist, they refused to join.

Eleanor and my dad were very close because of their similar temperaments. Eleanor and my mom became friends because they were in the same grade in high school. Eleanor served in the Women's Army Corps (Wac) during World War II and she married Tom Dill, a Navy veteran. They had three children: Marilyn, a year younger than me, Thomas, and then Cynthia. Tom and Eleanor lived in Alliance their whole lives.

Lois was a few years younger than Eleanor and she also married a WW II Navy veteran, Vern Ravert. Grandpa Jesse went into partnership with Vern, just as he had done with my dad. Vern and Lois lived on the ranch just north of our house in a small two-bedroom, cinderblock house. Mom and Lois became friends because they were in-laws and because they lived close to each other. In 1952, Lois and Vern had a daughter, Debra, and several years later, they added a family room, a bedroom, and another bathroom to their house and adopted a baby boy, Randall.

Bob was the youngest of the Jesse children. He married Shirley and they had two children, Ann and Chris. Uncle Bob was the first Jesse to graduate from college, and he and Aunt Shirley moved away for work. One summer, Grandpa and Grandma Jesse took Roy and me to visit Bob and Shirley in Cheyenne, Wyoming, where they taught school. Roy and I sat in the backseat and watched the scenery go by while Grandpa spun stories of the old days. About midway through the trip, Grandma noticed that the gas gauge was getting close to empty. She told Grandpa that he should stop for gas. Grandpa said, "No. I'll just drive faster so we get to Cheyenne before we run out of gas." Roy and I giggled but Grandma was not amused and glared at Grandpa. We stopped at the next gas station.

Five of my grandmother's six sisters, moved away from Alliance and never came back. The sixth sister, Mary, married Ward Norton and they lived in California for a few years before moving back to Alliance. They amassed a fortune in farm and ranch holdings but Ward died young, leaving Aunt Mary alone with her fortune. Addie Jones lived with her daughter Mary in a large, elegant house in Alliance. Great-Grandmother was a tiny, frail woman who quietly watched her great-grandchildren play around her. She smiled sweetly when we posed next to her for family photos. She died in 1952 when I was two and a half years old. Aunt Mary didn't have children so she "adopted" Frank and Bess's children and grandchildren as her own. She always attended family get-togethers and hosted gatherings at her house. As children, my cousins and I were in awe of Aunt Mary. She drove a gold-colored Cadillac with air conditioning and she wore tailored suits, silk blouses, high-heeled pumps, and sheer stockings, and her jewelry looked expensive. In the winter months, Aunt Mary wore a calf-length mink coat. When she walked in the door wearing that mink coat, we girls rushed to her, hugged her and started petting that coat. Aunt Mary never, ever shooed us away. Not once did she tell us to get our grubby little hands off her coat. No, she smiled, took off her coat and asked us to put the coat on the bed with all the other coats. We did so, but lingered awhile to continue petting that silky, luxurious mink.

After Christmas every year, Aunt Mary went to warmer climates and returned just before Easter. Some years, she took the train to San Francisco and then a steamer to Hawaii. Other years, she took the train to Miami, Florida. She mailed postcards to my cousins and me from those exotic locations, with wonderful stories about the beach, the hotel and her adventures. I couldn't imagine such a life. When I was in high school, she gave me the huge black steamer trunk that she used to transport her possessions on her trips. The trunk didn't fit in my room so Dad stored it for me.

First Cousins

I had several cousins on the Woodworth side of the family, but some were much older than me and most of the others moved away with their parents so I never really knew them. It was different with my cousins on the Jesse side. When I was three, my Uncle Vern and Aunt Lois Ravert had baby Debra. As Debbie and I grew older, we became fast friends and during summer months were pretty much inseparable. We had sleep-overs, helped each other with chores, played with our dolls, rode horses, explored barns, outbuildings, corrals, and the ranch land surrounding our houses. We took advantage of our freedom and went on adventures.

One adventure was picking up the mail on horseback. We and the Raverts were on Hickory Route, a rural mail delivery route out of Alliance. This route offered Monday through Saturday mail delivery to mailboxes located on Highway 2, three miles south of our house. To Dad and Uncle Vern, this was preferable to the alternate, Long Lake Route. Our neighbors to the south, the Earl Bauers, didn't care about daily delivery but liked the convenience of the Long Lake Route, which offered mail delivery to a mailbox next to their house. The Long Lake mailman (only men could deliver mail) came every Monday, Wednesday, and Friday. After delivering the Bauer's mail, he drove north to the auto gate south of our house, west, through Dad's pastures, past the school house, past ranches west of the school and then back to Alliance.

Someone picked up the Hickory Route mail at the highway mailboxes nearly every day. Mom or Aunt Lois picked up everyone's mail if they went to town for groceries, doctor's appointments, or to run errands. If no one else had picked up the mail, Grandpa Jesse stopped and collected the previous day's mail when he drove past the mailboxes first thing in the morning.

When Debbie was about seven and I was about ten, we were allowed to ride our horses to the highway to get the mail. We gave ourselves several hours for the task because it was three miles one- way and there were lots of gates to get through. We saddled our horses and set off through the pasture, south of our house. We followed the road, two sandy tracks, through the hills. When we got to a fence, we had to dismount, open the barbed wire gate, lead the horses through, close the gate behind us, remount, and ride to the next fence line. We rode past the Bauer house and through their pasture toward the railroad tracks. The Hoffland ghost town and the remains of the potash plant stood next to the railroad tracks. There were a couple of crumbling cement smoke stacks and the ruins of boiler buildings and some large brick arches. We didn't venture too close because it was creepy and there were rumors that hobos often set up camp in the shelter of the wreckage. Sometimes, Debbie and I thought we heard voices and singing when we got close to Hoffland. We didn't know if it was the wind blowing through the smoke stacks, the voices of the ghosts of people buried in the abandoned cemetery, or the voices of the hobos singing and laughing. It didn't matter. It was spooky, so Debbie and I hurried our horses past Hoffland before making our way through the final gate next to the railroad tracks. We stopped and looked up and down the tracks to make sure a train wasn't coming. We quickly led the horses through the gate and crossed the tracks.

Highway 2 was immediately south of the tracks, and the mailboxes were a quarter mile west of where we crossed the tracks. We generally led our horses along the highway because if there were cars or trucks, the horses were less spooked if we guided them with our face close to the horse's face. If a train went by, we stopped walking, held the horse's reins close to the horse's mouth, stroked the horse's neck, and spoke gently into the horse's ear until the train passed. When we got to the mailboxes, we gathered the mail and reversed the whole process.

Once, Debbie and I had the great idea that we should get the mail in bare feet. We saddled the horses, left our shoes and socks in the corral next to the windmill, and set off. Everything went well while we were actually riding, but we quickly realized that there were lots of sandburs around the gates. Getting off the horse to open and close the gates turned into a painful experience, and walking the horses from the railroad track to the mailbox and back was very slow because we had to pick our way through the sandburs. I think we stepped on more than we avoided and our feet were bleeding by the time we got to the mailbox. After a painful walk back to the railroad tracks and through the gates to pastures, we made it home with swollen, bloody feet. We told Mom what we had done while we were plastering our feet with bandages. She laughed at us for not wearing shoes and told us it was a good lesson.

On another trip to the mailbox, Debbie and I encountered our friendly neighborhood Nebraska highway patrolman, driving west on Highway 2. He stopped his car beside us, rolled down the window and asked what we were doing. We told him that we were getting the mail. He looked at us suspiciously, but said OK and drove on west. We picked up the mail and were on our way east toward Hoffland when the patrolman drove by us again, going east this time. He slowed down, waved, and drove on, probably noticing that we had our hands full of bundled mail. When we told Mom, she said that the patrolman might have thought we were running away from home and that's why he checked on us. She said he had probably turned around and driven past the mailboxes again, just to make sure we still weren't on the highway.

Debbie and I spent a lot of time with Marilyn Dill who was also younger than me. Marilyn was tolerant of her country cousins and she came to the ranch to spend a night or two with Debbie or me, and Debbie and I had sleepovers with Marilyn at the Dill's house in Alliance. We shared secrets and talked about movie stars. Uncle Tom and Uncle Vern tolerated giggling girls, and told silly stories during and after supper. I suspect the stories were silly so the three of us would giggle. We helped our aunts prepare meals, and afterward, we washed dishes in a big sink, dried the dishes carefully and put them away. At bedtime we climbed into bed together so we could continue talking about movie stars and discuss what it would be like to live in Hollywood. Debbie and Marilyn were my best friends until I started high school.

One summer when we were spending the night at the Ravert house, Marilyn opened a kitchen drawer and saw a small doll-like figure about eight inches tall under the pot holders. The doll had short arms and a head with a painted face. There was a single, connected "leg" and the doll was hard because it was stuffed with sawdust. It looked like one of those voodoo dolls we had read about. Marilyn pulled the doll out of the drawer, turned to Aunt Lois and asked, "What's this?" We expected that Aunt Lois would say something crazy, like it had to do with one of Grandma's superstitions, but instead, she said, "Oh that! That's my dammit doll. When I get mad, I take the doll out of the drawer, bang it against the counter three times and yell, 'dammit, dammit, dammit!'" We howled with laughter and gave it a try. We each smashed the doll against the counter three times and shouted, "dammit, dammit, dammit." It was great fun because it was the first time any of us were allowed to utter a cussword. We all wanted one of the dolls, but Aunt Lois said, "No. It's a doll for grownups, mostly housewives who are mad at their husbands." We dutifully put the doll back in its drawer.

Besides letting her daughter and nieces use profanity, Aunt Lois was the official family beautician, which meant she cut hair and applied permanent waves when needed. My mother was a fan of permanents, so every six months or so, Mom bought a Toni brand permanent at the Rexall drug store and called Aunt Lois to make an appointment. On the afternoon of my appointment, I went to Aunt Lois's house and sat on a chair in the kitchen. While Debbie watched, Aunt Lois draped me in an old plastic table cloth and began the process. She rolled my hair onto tiny plastic rollers, doused the rollers with the permanent wave solution, set a timer and we waited. The solution burned my head, my nostrils, and my eyes. Finally, the timer went off and I walked to the sink, put my head under the faucet and Aunt Lois washed the solution off the rollers. She applied a neutralizer solution, took the rollers out of my hair and rinsed my hair in the sink. Finally, she applied a conditioner and I was finished. The permanent left me with tight, frizzy curls which I hated. My hair was hideous for weeks but Mom thought it helped tame my fine, blow-away hair.

My aunts and my mother required proper etiquette and ladylike conduct from Debbie, Marilyn, and me. We had to respect our elders, we could not point, chew with our mouths open, slurp soup, or refuse to eat food that was served. We learned how to sit properly with knees together, and Mom put books onto our heads so we would learn how to walk like a lady. The goal was to glide around the room erectly and smoothly without letting the book drop.

World War II Veterans

*It is, I believe, the greatest generation
any society has ever produced.*

—TOM BROKAW

My father and nearly every one of my uncles and my Aunt Eleanor served in World War II. My dad was drafted into the army in May of 1945. He had received a couple of deferments because he and Grandpa were in an essential industry (farming), but by 1945, there were no more deferments. He went to Denver for induction and afterward, he and his group of inductees traveled by train to Ft. Leavenworth, Kansas. The group was there a few days before going by train to Ft. Worth and then on to Camp Wolters, outside Mineral Wells where the group began regular training. During a night training exercise in August, the soldiers saw a bright flash of light on the western horizon. They later learned that the flash coincided with the timing of an A-bomb test in New Mexico. "That was something," was all Dad said about the event.

Dad was scheduled to be at Camp Wolters for six weeks so he asked Mom to come to Texas. She took the train from Alliance to Lincoln, changed trains, took the train from Lincoln to Ft. Worth, changed again, and took the final train to Mineral Wells. It was a brutal trip for Mom with two-and-a-half-year-old Ronnie, standing most of the way, because the train was overflowing with hundreds of women traveling to be with their husbands. After the grueling trip, Mom and Ronnie arrived to Dad's waiting arms. She and Ronnie lived in a rented bedroom of a lieutenant's small house and Dad came to visit on weekends. One of Mom's favorite memories of Mineral Wells was when Dad came to the house on a weekend and the three of them sat on chairs in the yard and ate cantaloupe halves filled with ice cream.

After training, Dad was granted a short leave, so he, Mom, and Ronnie took the train back to Alliance before he was shipped to Camp Upton in New York, which was a staging area for overseas deployment. Dad was assigned to the *Wainwright*, a troop transport ship, and he volunteered to be a meat cutter in the galley. As soon as the ship left the New York Harbor, it began to pitch and roll. Being below deck, Dad didn't know what was going on, but he learned from others that the ship was in the middle of a bad blizzard. Dad knew about blizzards, but being on a ship in the middle of the ocean during a blizzard was more than a little disconcerting.

Toward the end of the journey, the *Wainwright* passed through the Strait of Gibraltar into the Mediterranean. From the deck, Dad saw a Liberty Ship that had been broken in half. It was a sobering reminder of where they were going. The *Wainwright* docked in Naples, Italy and the troops took a train north to Livorno (Leghorn), close to Pisa in the Tuscany region. Dad's company went to their regular assignment, a Quartermaster Station at Tombolo. The Quartermaster Corp was responsible for dividing shipments and disbursing food, ammunition, and supplies. Dad believed that he was assigned to the Quartermaster Corp because he was good with numbers and had attended business school. He had access to supplies that other soldiers didn't and could get anything anyone wanted, including steaks.

Requisition forms had to be handwritten with six legible copies. Dad grew tired of pressing hard to get six carbon copies so he asked his sergeant if he could requisition a typewriter. With a typewriter, Dad argued that he could complete forms much faster and the copies would all be legible. The sergeant accepted Dad's reasoning and requisitioned a typewriter. Dad's prediction was correct. He worked faster than any other clerk and his forms and the copies were perfect. Dad was promoted from private to private first-class and then to T5 during his time in Italy.

In his free time, Dad and his friends went to Italian beaches and made one trip to Pisa to see the Leaning Tower. Other than that, free time was spent watching movies. Dad began to hate movies and probably didn't go to one movie after he left the army.

In 1946, the army chose to discharge soldiers who had dependents at home, so Dad boarded a ship and left Italy in August of 1946. While sailing to New York, a soldier on board died of diphtheria, so the ship was quarantined in New York Harbor. Everyone on board got a skin test before they could disembark. Dad's test was negative, so he boarded a train bound for Chicago, another to Denver, and finally a bus to Alliance. He arrived home in early September, having served only sixteen months.

Mom's older brother, Merlin, joined the Navy and was assigned as a cook aboard the hospital ship USS *Comfort*. The ship was anchored just off Okinawa on April 26, 1945, when it was struck by a Japanese suicide plane, killing sixty-three people. At the time, the ship had a nearly full load of wounded who had been evacuated from Okinawa. The kamikaze plane struck the stern and missed the hospital wards forward and aft. Merlin said that many more would have been killed if the plane had struck one of the fully loaded wards.

After the attack, the ship sailed five days to Guam for repairs. Uncle Merlin said it was the longest five days in his life because he and everyone else feared another attack. There were rumors that the Japanese had reported that the ship was "wounded" and they wanted to "get the *Comfort*." Luckily, there were no more contacts with the enemy during the five-day trip.

My Uncle Vern Ravert also served in the Navy. He was assigned to the USS *Marvin H. McIntyre*, an attack transport ship. (Marvin McIntyre was President Franklin Roosevelt's secretary, and this ship was the only one not named for a county in a US state.) The ship was commissioned in November 1944 and Uncle Vern was assigned shortly after that. He served on the *McIntyre* until the ship was decommissioned in 1946. The ship made many trips across the Pacific, landing in Hawaii quite often. While the crew members waited for the ship to leave San Diego or the Hawaiian port, they played baseball. Vern loved baseball for the rest of his life.

Dad's sister, Eleanor, volunteered for the Wac Medical Corps. She was having dinner with her family and some neighbors when the special newscast came over the radio in 1941 and she heard President Roosevelt's message about the attack at Pearl Harbor. She knew at that moment that she wanted to help somehow and volunteered for the Wac soon after my dad was drafted. The two shipped out to basic training just a few days apart.

Aunt Eleanor worked in the tuberculosis ward at the army's Fitzsimons General Hospital in Denver. At the end of the war, she and other nurse aids were given the option to be discharged or go to Japan to help the occupation and cleanup. She and most of her friends decided to be discharged, but Eleanor said that there were times when she wished she had traveled to war-torn Japan to help.

Eleanor's husband, Thomas Dill, is a bit of an enigma. He didn't talk about his service or about his experiences and the only record is one photo of him smiling in his jaunty sailor's cap. Records of his Navy service cannot be found in the Department of Defense archives.

There was a ranch family, neighbors of Grandpa and Grandma Jesse, who had three sons. One was Dad's age; one was a year younger, and one was a year older. None of those young men were drafted and none of them volunteered during WW II. They all avoided service, which was unusual. It is unlikely that all of them were physically unfit to serve because they were hardworking ranchers like my dad. They couldn't have qualified as conscientious objectors because they were Methodists like my dad. One or two of them might have received deferments like my dad, but it is unlikely that all three sons would have received more deferments than Dad. The consensus was that their father had influenced the draft board to keep his sons from military service, but no one was willing to discuss the matter beyond closed-door secretive gossip.

The Ranch

The House

The house where I grew up was wonderfully comfortable and people entered through the south-facing kitchen door. Once in the door, the steps leading down to the partial basement were in front of you and the kitchen door was one step up on the right. In the kitchen, the refrigerator was next to the door on the left and the cupboards next to the refrigerator continued around the corner and along a small nook on the north wall, where a small window added some light to the dark corner. Cupboards and counters lined the south side of the kitchen to the right of the door and were only interrupted by the kitchen sink under two large windows. The door to the dining room was on the east side of the kitchen and the rest of the east wall was occupied by a stove and oven. The door to the master bedroom was on the north side and a small kitchen table was situated next to the bedroom door. In the late 1950s, my parents remodeled the kitchen by installing new cabinets, countertops, gas cooktop, wall oven, an upright freezer, an automatic washing machine and an electric dryer.

The house's combined living and dining room was just off the kitchen and also faced south. A six-foot window seat and bay window were the focal point in the dining room. My grandmother planted a large rose bush below the bay window, and in the early summer the yellow blooms were beautiful and the aroma intoxicating. With the windows open along the window seat, the sweet fragrance of the roses wafted into the dining room. Mom snipped roses close to the bloom, carefully placed the blooms in rose bowls or in pretty tea cups, and scattered the roses around the house. In June, the whole house smelled of roses.

The living room extended east from the dining room. There was a window on the south side of the room and, at the far end of the living room, the front door with glass panel and a large picture window faced east. When standing at that picture window, I could see the lake, the meadow, and the hills beyond. The hills continued far to the east before finally touching the sky. The world was vast but warm and welcoming.

No hallways took up valuable living space and the three bedrooms were lined up along the north side of the house. A small Jack-and-Jill bathroom occupied the space between the master bedroom and a cozy second bedroom. The third bedroom was in the northeast corner. Mom and Dad were comfortable in the master bedroom, and when I was a baby, I slept in a wicker bassinette in the northwest corner of their bedroom. A crib replaced the bassinette when I got older. My brothers slept in the middle bedroom and Grandpa Jesse took the east bedroom because he spent so much time on the ranch helping Dad.

For several years, it seemed like Grandpa was always there. It was clear that Dad needed another pair of hands on the ranch, and we loved the stories that Grandpa told us about the old days. He got on Mom's nerves though. One evening my parents were quietly talking in the kitchen and we heard Mom say, "Sometimes, I wish your father would just go home." This wasn't something we should hear, so we quickly retreated to the living room. Grandpa spent weekdays with us for several years but eventually stopped because he was getting older and because more grandkids were being added the family.

Don't matter if you believe in them or not.
If they're there, they're there.
—JOAN LOWEY NIXON

At the bottom of the basement steps, heavy winter coats, winter trousers, hats, and mufflers were hung on sturdy hooks. Smaller hooks held dusters, chaps, spurs, waders, and fishing equipment. The floor was cluttered with work boots for all types of work and play. Rifles and shotguns hung on long nails on the floor joists above your head and ammunition for the firearms was tucked on the top of joists on the opposite wall.

In the adjoining room, the fuel-oil tank and fuel-oil furnace were on the left and the propane water heater sat next to the furnace. The rest of the basement was for storage—toys, summer and winter clothes, and boxes filled with Halloween, Easter, and Christmas decorations. Clothes lines were strung just below the floor joists. When it was too rainy to hang clothes outdoors to dry, we hung clothes in the basement.

In the northwest corner of the basement there was a creepy six-by-eight-foot fruit room with a dirt floor.

Shelves lined the walls and this is where we stored root vegetables, canned fruit, canned vegetables, and pickles. Rice, noodles, sugar, and flour were also stored on the shelves, but always in a metal can or a glass jar with a tight-fitting lid to deter bugs and mice. The fruit room was scary. It had a creaky door and there was one bare light bulb in the center of the room with a chain switch. You had to swing your arm back and forth overhead to locate the chain that you pulled to turn on the light. Even with the light on, the room was dimly lit. Shadows lurked in the corners of the room, behind jars and boxes and behind the door. This house, which was moved from a ghost town, might have been haunted. Who knows who might have died in the house during the glory days of Hoffland? The house probably wasn't haunted, but if it had been, the spirits would have taken up residence in that fruit room. My siblings and I hated being sent to the fruit room to fetch a can of peaches or a jar of pickles. We raced in and out, not giving the ghosts time to jump out of the shadows. Mom also disliked that little room. It was eerie and scary for her so she sent the kids whenever possible.

The house and milk house were surrounded by a weathered gray picket fence, needed to keep cattle pastured in the meadow from wandering into the yard. The gate on the north side led to the chicken houses, the clothes lines, and up the hill to the windmill. The gate on the southwest, next to the milk house, led to sheds and barns. The gate on the east side of the yard led to the hired man's house and the garden. The main gate was on the south side of the yard. A narrow, paved sidewalk led from the gate directly to the kitchen door. Nearly everyone entered the house through the kitchen, not through the front door in the living room.

Only the occasional salesman or stranger tried to use the front door on the east side of the house because it was hard to get to the front door. Visitors had to go through a barbed wire gate and then through the yard gate on the east side of the house. The path from the gate to the porch was unpaved. This entrance to the house was not welcoming, but adding two or three large and intimidating barking dogs to the mix meant that strangers stayed in their car until someone rescued them or until they just gave up and drove away.

The fenced yard was large, and the elm trees that Grandpa planted were tall and shaded the house. In the summer we played in the yard because Mom needed the peace and quiet and children needed the fresh air. By the time Ronnie was ten and Roy and I were four and three, Ronnie played with us because Mom gave him no choice. He bossed us around and told us which toys we could play with and which ones were off limits. He climbed trees in the front yard to escape his pesky siblings while Roy and I ran around the tree and tried to climb up to the branch where Ronnie sat. Some years later, Dad built us a swing just west of the house. We loved that swing and spent hours on it during warm summer months. We thought that if we tried hard enough, we could swing all the way around, over the top bar and back down. Unfortunately, or perhaps fortunately, no matter how hard we tried, we never succeeded.

Grandma planted a long row of asparagus just inside the fence on the west side of the yard. Mom would mention that the asparagus shoots were sprouting in the spring, but no one ever harvested the shoots. The sprouts just grew and grew into tall, lacy-looking weeds that hovered along the fence all summer.

The Garage, Milk House, and Little House

The car entrance to the detached garage was outside the picket fence. It was technically a two-car garage, but we only had one car. One-half of the garage was for the car and the other half was for storing junk (at least it looked like junk to me). While the foundation was concrete, the floor was dirt, more dust than dirt. Still, the garage kept the car out of the elements.

The milk house was just inside the gate on the southwest side of the yard. In the days when Grandpa and Grandma lived on the ranch, storage batteries for the electricity generated by the windmill were kept in the milk house. There was enough power to light the shop, the milk house and house but not enough power for appliances like a refrigerator. To keep food from spoiling, my grandparents used a holding tank in the milk house. Slowly running icy water pumped by the windmill kept milk, cream and other perishables cool in the summer and kept perishables from freezing in the winter. The Nebraska Rural Electrification Association (REA) ran power lines to ranch houses in the Sandhills in the late 1940s so the water holding tanks and the batteries lost their purpose. When Mom and Dad moved into the house, the wind generator still hovered over the milk house but it was idle. In the early '50s, my father dismantled the old wind generator and repurposed the parts.

The milk separator in the milk house was used morning and night for years because we milked cows in the morning and at night. In the early '50s, our electric washing machine was also located in the milk house. From the water hydrant just north of the milk house, Mom hauled water to the machine to wash clothes. We also used the hydrant to wash the milk separator and to fill the dogs' water dishes. We attached a hose to the spigot in the summer so we could water the lawn and play in the sprinkler.

The little house was a few yards east of the main house. My dad and grandfather employed a ranch hand or hired man, because the workload was too large for two people. The hired man and his family lived in the little house as part of their pay. Electricity, water, and propane gas were provided, but the house was Spartan. There were two rooms: a kitchen and a combined living room/bedroom. In the kitchen, a small, round oak table and three chairs were located next to the south window. A sink and short counter were on the west side along with two cupboards above and two beneath the sink. A faucet with cold running water was attached to the sink, but there was no hot water. The propane cooking stove in the kitchen was used to cook and also to heat water. Baths were taken in a tub in the tiny pantry just off the kitchen. Water was heated on the stove and poured into the tub. The toilet was an outhouse behind the house.

There was a propane heater, a double bed, a small dresser and a rocking chair in the living room. The hired man was responsible for any other furnishings, but in most cases, these men were poverty-stricken, so had no other furnishings. One of the hired men left behind a small Hartley dresser when he moved out of the house. The dresser looked like a normal dresser from the front, but the drawers were shallow because a vanity took up the space behind the drawers. When you lifted the hinged front portion of the dresser top, you could spin the dresser drawers around to the back, which moved the vanity to the front. It was the most unusual dresser/vanity I had ever seen and I asked

Dad if I could have it. Dad agreed but the dresser didn't fit in my bedroom so Dad stored it for me.

In the late 1950s, Dad, Grandpa, and Uncle Vern built a small lean-to addition next to the living room on the east side of the little house. This became a separate bedroom for the hired man. They also installed a water heater, a toilet, and a small shower in the pantry. These improvements were mandatory to attract future ranch hands.

The Garden

A weed is a plant that has mastered every survival skill except for learning how to grow in rows.

—DOUG LARSON

Our fenced garden was east of the little house. It was about 40 ft. by 150 ft. and because of the size, Grandpa plowed it each spring with a tractor and field plow before turning it over to Mom. She bought baby tomato sets and garden seeds from the Co-Op in Alliance before the garden was plowed and she was ready to plant as soon as the tractor moved out of the way. Using a hoe, she made long east–west rows for the radish, turnip, lettuce, carrot, zinnia and marigold seeds. In separate patches, Mom dug shallow holes in the sand for her tiny tomato sets, the green pole beans and cucumber seeds. Ronnie, Roy and I helped with the planting. Carrots, radishes and lettuce were the easiest because we could just sprinkle the seeds along the row and push a small bit of soil over the seeds. At the end of the row, we laced the empty paper seed packet through the square end of a small stick and pushed the stick into the ground so Mom would know which plants were emerging in each row.

There was a water hydrant on the west side of the garden so we watered the plants with a rotating sprinkler attached to a hose. On watering days, we changed the sprinkler position every couple of hours so every plant got watered. We loved it when it rained because that meant one less chore for the day.

When the plants pushed their way through the sandy soil, it was time to start weeding. This was definitely not our favorite activity because it was tedious and boring and endless. Every few days, Mom took us to the garden and we weeded our assigned rows. When I was very little, I couldn't tell the difference between a carrot and a weed, so I yelled, "Is this a weed?"

"No, those are carrots. Don't pull those. Pull the plants that are different from all the rest in the row." This made sense even to me. Since weeding was not a favorite job, Mom used the chore as punishment. If Roy and I were naughty or were fighting too much, Mom sent us to the garden to weed, where we could basically fight as much as we wanted out of earshot.

Harvesting began a month after planting because the leaf lettuce grew quickly. Onions, turnips and carrots took a little longer and the cucumbers, beans and tomatoes didn't come on until July and August. In spite of hating to weed the garden, I loved eating the produce. When pulling carrots for a meal, I washed a few in the hydrant and stuffed them into my mouth.

Chicken Houses

The henhouse was outside the fenced yard, west of the house next to the calving lot. There were windows on the south side and the roosts for the hens were lined up along the north wall. When the weather was warm, the hens and roosters ranged far and wide in the trees, scratching for seeds, grain and insects. In the winter, the chickens stayed in their house and Mom fed them grain. All year long, Mom made sure the chickens had a pan of clean water and she gave them broken oyster shells because that helped make eggshells strong.

We had more than a dozen hens and a few roosters. Each hen laid one egg per day so we had eggs for cooking and we ate eggs for breakfast every day. Beginning when Roy and I were five or six, we were charged with gathering eggs. We took a bucket from the house, headed to the henhouse and went directly to the nests where hens sat on their eggs. We pushed the hen aside and reached underneath to grab her egg. We were wary of some of the hens because they would peck at our hands when we tried to move them aside. This wasn't as worrisome as the roosters who clearly didn't like children in their territory. Sometimes, a rooster squawked, flapped his wings and stood tall on his legs. If we didn't budge, the rooster stepped toward us. We yelled, waved our arms and took a step toward the rooster. Often, he backed off but other times, the rooster didn't back off and kept squawking and flapping his wings while moving closer and closer to us. We knew the stories of roosters who flew onto children's heads and scratched out their eyes with their knife-like spurs, so Roy and I screamed and ran as fast as we could back to the house. We bolted through the kitchen door, slamming the door behind us. Mom looked at us and knew exactly what had happened. We told her about the rooster who terrorized us and Mom was sympathetic. She remembered being terrorized by roosters when she was a little girl so she excused us from egg-gathering that day.

In the spring, Mom bought fifty or more baby chicks from the feed store in Alliance. She carried the cardboard boxes filled with cheeping chicks into the pullet house, which was a few yards east of the chicken house. This house was a chicken incubator with its large, low-hanging, round light in the center of the room. Once out of their box, the little chicks huddled together under the light, climbing over one another, trying to secure the warmest spot. Roy and I loved catching the soft chicks and cuddling with them because they were so cute. Mom monitored the baby chicks a few times every day. She filled a tray with water and filled another with grain. She brushed the chicks aside, checking to make sure they were all OK. She pulled out any dead chicks and threw them behind the pullet house. These unfortunate little ones became a yummy fast-food lunch for barn cats or owls.

As the chicks aged, Mom opened the door to allow them to roam into the trees on the south side of the chicken house. When the pullets reached the right size in midsummer, it was time to slaughter. Grandma always wrung the chicken's necks, but Mom was too squeamish for that hand's-on method of dispatching the pullets. Instead, Mom chopped off the heads with an axe. Once headless, the chickens ran around like crazy—first in one direction then in another, swirling and bleeding around the trees. The grizzly scene greatly amused Roy and me and we scurried after the headless chickens, picking them up by the legs only after they had stopped flopping around.

Mom gutted the birds and dropped them one by one into a bucket of boiling (or at least very hot) water. Once cool enough, she handed a bird to a kid, whose job was to pull off the feathers. When we had done our best, Mom finished the job. The yard next to the pullet house and henhouse would be white with flying feathers. Some feathers were small, fine and soft, so Roy and I gathered them up, thinking we would use them to make something warm and cozy, but that scheme never materialized. After defeathering, Mom burned off any remaining pin feathers and rinsed the birds. We carted two or three of them into the house for a fried chicken dinner. The rest of the birds were wrapped in freezer paper, labeled, and taken into Alliance to be frozen in the meat storage locker that my parents rented. After they bought the upright Amana freezer, Mom stacked the chickens in the freezer.

The Barracks and the Barn

The barracks was outside the yard and west of the garage. My grandfather bought the barracks from the government when they closed the airfield east of Alliance at the end of WW II. Grandpa sat the building on a concrete foundation but only paved the front half. We parked the pickup truck on the pavement unless equipment or a tractor needed repair. In that case, the truck was moved out to make room. The barracks smelled of dirt, oil, gasoline, and axle grease.

The shop was on the right side of the front section. A welding machine was just inside the door, and Grandpa built a work bench across the entire right (north) side of the paved portion. There was an anvil secured to the corner of the bench, and tools of every description were on the benchtop or in cubbies under the bench. Nuts, bolts, and screws were organized in cans or jars in the cubbies or on shelves above. The workbench seemed disorganized with its chaos of tools, but Dad knew exactly where each tool was even when there were a dozen tools around, covering and overlapping it. I always tried to return the hammer or other tool to the place where I had found it, but the position wasn't always precise. Dad knew I had been using his tools and said, "Next time, put it back where you found it." He wasn't mad, just serious.

The back half of the barracks was not paved and was used for storage. Bags of oats, cattle nutritional cake pellets, mineral blocks, salt blocks and bales of straw bedding lined the walls. Sometimes Dad parked a tractor there but during haying season in the summer, Dad set up the sickle sharpener in this middle section. He had a sickle mower attached a tractor to cut the prairie grass during haying season. The mower had a multitooth blade bar that moved back and forth across the stationary bottom tooth bar. The haying crew took all of the movable blades into the hayfield every day and when one blade quit cutting smoothly, a new blade was inserted so the mowing could continue. On a good day, the hay crew went through all of the blades. Each evening someone had to sharpen the movable-tooth blades so they were ready for the next day's work. After supper, my dad or my grandpa went to the barracks and spent hours sharpening each tooth on each blade with a grinder.

Sometimes my brothers and I watched the sickle sharpening. We sat on a bag of grain or on a salt block, chewed on blades of grass or straw, and watched. It was a symphony for the ears, eyes and nose. The sound was mesmerizing. There was a metallic, rhythmic greeech, greeech noise as Dad sharpened one side of the sickle, then clunk, when he moved the bar to the next sickle. Then greeech, greeech, clunk, over and over until he finished the entire bar before removing it and inserting another. When grinding, sparks flew off the sickle into the air and the fireworks surrounded Dad. We weren't allowed to get close because we could get burned, but sometimes a spark landed on Dad. He brushed it off and kept working. (He wore heavy denim jeans, a long-sleeved work shirt, boots, his hat, and, of course, his heavy leather work gloves.). The caustic burning metal odor singed our nose hairs but we didn't care. The whole endeavor was mesmerizing and comforting. We stayed there, watching, talking and laughing until Mom called that it was time for bed. We drifted back into the house, leaving Dad to grind sickles long into the night.

Dad built a small shed on the far west side of the barracks next to the calving lot because he needed a shed for shelter when he helped cows that were having trouble calving. Beginning in February, the shed got lots of use. Dad kept the cows that were in labor or close to labor in the calving lot, and he monitored the lot on horseback day and night. When a cow was in trouble, Dad brought her into the shed and he became a midwife. Sometimes it took hours to extricate a calf and after the difficult birth, Dad walked into the house exhausted. He washed his hands, opened the freezer, grabbed his bottle of Old Crow bourbon, gulped a mouthful, and put the bottle back into the freezer.

Infrequently, a calf was born in the pasture before Dad had moved the cow into the calving lot. On his rounds through the pastures on horseback, Dad found the calf, curled up in the snow with its mom hovering close by. He picked up the calf, put the little thing over the pommel of the saddle, mounted the horse and rode home, with a mooing mom following closely behind. Dad put the calf and his mom in the calving shed so the baby could warm up before being turned loose into the calving lot.

The barn was south of the house and it was bordered on the west and south by corrals. The windmill and horse tank were on the south side of the corral. We weren't allowed to play in or near a tank. Horse tanks were set into the ground, and the water in the tank was about three feet deep while the outside of the tank was only about two feet tall. If a kid leaned over the edge, he or she could topple into the water and drown. Children were allowed to walk horses to the tank so they could drink, but that's all. If Mom couldn't find us, the first thing she did was run to the tank to see if we had drowned. The terrified look on her face when she ran into the corral and peered into the tank was enough to deter us from disobeying this rule.

The west section or room of the barn held four or five milking stanchions. There was a large wooden grain box just inside the door and it was filled with sorghum-coated grain for the cows and the horses. A half-gallon tin can lay on top of the grain, and we used this can to scoop grain into each cow's trough in front of her stanchion and to transfer grain into each of the horses' mangers. We also used this can full of grain to lure horses out of the pasture, and naturally, Roy and I nibbled on the grain because it was crunchy and sweet. We opened the grain box lid, shooed away the flies, and gobbled down handfuls of the stuff.

In the middle section of the barn there were three or four very large horse stalls with mangers in front. Two large draft horses could easily stand side by side in each stall. Saddles, horse blankets, bridles, horse harnesses and other tack hung on the south wall. The barn smelled of horses, horse manure, leather, saddle soap, and hay.

The haymow, the area where Dad stored hay for horses or milk cows, was behind the horse stalls on the north side of the barn. We used pitchforks to transfer hay from the haymow to the horses' mangers. The haymow was also the perfect hiding place for cats and kids.

Beyond the Buildings

Pastures surrounded the ranch buildings and the perimeter of the pastures were fenced with barbed wire. Barbed wire gates were positioned strategically to allow horseback riders and cattle access to the various pastures. For routes through the hills used by trucks or cars, there were trail roads with auto gates between pastures.

[Auto gates (drive-over cattle guards) are installed where a road crosses a fence line. A ten-foot long, eight-foot-wide rectangle was constructed of railroad ties and replaced a section of the fence. This "box" anchored the gate in the sand. Heavy pipe supported the span lengthwise, and shorter pipe sections, wide enough for a truck to drive over, were welded to the support beam along each edge. The center of the gate between the pipe sections was an open pit about five-feet deep. Because cattle have poor depth perception, they see the hole as a bottomless pit, and will not walk over it.]

The south pasture was, predictably, south of the ranch buildings. Horses, milk cows, and a small herd of cows and calves spent time there. Another pasture further south had a steep hill that Roy and I called Pineapple Peak because it looked a little like a pineapple. That pasture adjoined the Bauer ranch. The summer pasture was west of the south pasture and it housed a larger herd of cows and calves. The hills were a little steeper and the gullies a little more hidden. This pasture adjoined the Krause meadow.

There was a small pasture north and west of the house which adjoined Uncle Vern's ranch. Our house sat at the west end of a large meadow with tall grass and a small alkali lake. There was another pasture with steep hills east of the meadow and Dad rented a school section beyond that. School land was established in a 1785 ordinance, and the law mandated that section #16 (1 square mile) in the center of every of thirty-six square miles be used for public education. Counties owned the school sections but schools were generally not built on the school section. If a school section was adjacent to his land, a farmer or rancher rented that section from the county. The county redistributed the rental funds to the school districts in the county for school maintenance, school supplies, and teacher salaries.

As small children, Roy and I rarely ventured far from the house but Mom still had guidelines. She said that getting turned around or lost in a pasture happened but it was OK. Sometimes you could see the house from a hill, but it was important to remember that the house was farther away than it seemed. If on a horse, loosen the reins and the horse will likely start toward home. If that didn't work, we could follow a cow path because those led to a windmill and we could find our way from there. The last option was to walk in one direction until we found a fence and then follow the fence. As long as we didn't cross a fence line, the fence would eventually take us home. "Just follow the fence," she said.

Horses

The essential joy of horses is that it brings us in contact with the rare elements of grace, beauty, spirit and fire.

—SHARON RALLS

In the 1950s, Dad and Grandpa kept eight to ten draft horses. Dad adored his work horses and his bond with the horses was almost magical. When Dad walked into the barn with work horses standing in their stalls, he first made some noise by slamming the barn door and then he spoke to the horses in a strong, firm voice to announce his presence. Dad talked to the horses like he talked to people. He asked how the horses felt and if they were ready for a "hot one." The horses turned their heads to look at Dad and replied with a bluster or snort. If Roy or I needed to walk beside a horse, we mimicked Dad, kept talking, firmly slapped the horse's hip, and then walked toward the horse's head. We were not allowed to walk between two horses even if they were tethered to the stall. Horses, like people, shifted their weight and a child could fall next to the horse or get stepped on by those gigantic feet. To pet the horses, we reached high to pet a shoulder or climbed into the manger and petted their noses. The barn was a wonderful place with huge horses blustering, stomping their feet, and swishing their tails to clear away the buzzing flies.

Dad had Belgians and Percherons. The Belgians were a chestnut color and weighed about a ton. They stood sixteen to seventeen hands at the shoulder or just under six feet. The Percherons were also a chestnut color but were slightly smaller at five feet tall. The horses' huge heads towered over Dad's head. They were Dad's (and our) much-loved giants. Dad said he liked Belgians because they were strong, good-natured, and gentle while the Percherons were smart and a bit more adaptable to different kinds of work.

Dad stood close to each horse when he put on their harnesses. He did the task so quickly and skillfully, I imagined that he could do it with his eyes closed. After harnessing, he hitched the horses to the wagon, climbed onto the wagon, clicked his tongue, and gently rapped the traces on the horses' backs. The horses moved forward pushing the collar into their shoulders and the wagon moved forward. To stop, Dad pulled on the reins and said, "Whoa." The horses stopped and the collar no longer pushed against their shoulders.

After a day's work, Dad took off the harness, let the horses drink from the horse tank and gave them a treat of oats or grain with sorghum. He led them out of the barn and turned them loose. The horses galloped out of the corral, dropped down in a sandy spot, and rolled around in the sand. Dad said the horses did this so sand could cling to the sweat and oil on the horse's skin and protect them against biting flies. Besides, the harness was a bit confining and horses needed to scratch an itch under the harness. He also thought they just liked rolling around in the dirt.

Grandpa Jesse told us that Belgians were originally from a country called Belgium and Percherons were from France. Both breeds were taken to England in the olden days, and these mighty horses carried knights into battle. That seemed crazy so I asked why the knights didn't just ride saddle horses like us. Grandpa said that saddle horses wouldn't do because the knights and their horses wore heavy armor. A little saddle horse couldn't carry all that armor. No, it had to be a big, strong work horse.

Our horses' ancestors had exotic lives and I wondered if our horses were sad because they just did ranch work while their grandparents had carried King Arthur and the Knights of the Round Table. How different their lives would have been if they had been born long ago. They would have carried brave knights into great battles. I imagined the grandparents of the Belgians carrying knights who fought knights riding the grandparents of the Percherons.

Horses lend us the wings we lack.

—PAM BROWN

Dad and Grandpa also had saddle or riding horses. Most of the horses were quarter horses, but we also had an Arabian and a couple of Morgans, and Grandpa had a Tennessee walking horse. My Uncle Vern also had quarter horses, one Arabian and a little Shetland pony for my cousin Debbie. Dad borrowed the Shetland for Roy and me because Debbie wasn't quite big enough to ride or manage the stubborn little pony.

Grandpa Jesse said that the quarter horse was a true American horse. They had good instincts and were naturals when it came to herding cattle. They were small and quick and that made them perfect for cutting and roping. They were also hardy and could work in all kinds of weather. He told us that quarter horses could run fifty miles an hour and outrun any other horse in a quarter mile.

Morgans were also true American horses. They were sturdy, strong, and their eyes were big. When looking at them from the side, Morgans had arched backs. Grandpa liked Morgans because they were well-mannered and gentle and he had heard that Morgans were cavalry horses in the Civil War, so they were brave, too.

Grandpa's Tennessee Walking Horse was a tall, elegant mare named Blondie. She was a beautiful cream color, had a long neck and rather small ears. She was sure-footed and her gait was very smooth. When walking fast, Blondie's head seemed to nod in rhythm with her walk so I thought she was comical to watch.

One summer, Dad bought an Arabian from a horse trader. Dad said that the little horse was the best horse he ever owned because she could do everything. Grandpa told us that Arabians were from Arabia and you would know an Arabian because when looking at them from the side their back dipped a little. They also had this forehead bulge between their eyes and Uncle Vern said that meant they had big brains and were smarter than other horses. Grandpa didn't believe that, though.

Uncle Vern's Arabian was small and spirited. Once when I was visiting Debbie, we sat on a fence laughing and playing while Uncle Vern rode the Arabian in his calving lot just in front of us. Our rowdiness likely spooked the Arabian and he started bucking. Uncle Vern just sat on that horse and rode the horse until the bucking stopped. He then dismounted, led the horse around the pen for a bit, got back on, and galloped around and around and around. "You just have to show them whose boss," Uncle Vern said.

Dad had a bad-tempered horse named Spook that bucked whenever someone touched his mane or whenever the mood struck him. He was a good cow pony though, so Dad just dealt with the bucking. Dad bought another horse that leaped forward without notice—sometimes leaping the entire length of his body. Dad was not as tolerant with this behavior and sold the horse.

Finally, there was that Shetland pony, Kokomo-Joe, or Koko. He was smart and usually good-natured, but he could also be stubborn and uncooperative. Roy and I had great fun with Koko. He was like a big dog with a quirky, funny personality.

When Roy and I wanted to catch a horse, we took the bridle and a can of grain to the pasture where the horses were grazing. The grain was used to lure the horses toward us. We shook the can to let the horses know that we had grain, and when the horses came close, we grabbed hand-fuls for the horses to nibble. We gave grain to every horse, including the draft horses, but we gave extra to the horses we were targeting. While the horse was busy munching, we'd slip the bridle over his or her head and we'd have our catch.

Koko was crafty and gladly took a bite of grain before running away when the bridle came out. From a distance, he turned and looked at us tauntingly. We'd walk toward him, shaking the can. Koko walked toward us, took his bite, and then ran away again. It was a game for Koko, and while it was funny the first couple of times, our patience grew thin and we'd start walking back toward the corrals. Koko followed and finally allowed us to put on his bridle. We'd give him a snack as a reward. We had a small saddle for Koko but he was so short that we could leap onto his bare back. We often rode double, trotting and galloping around the meadow until we lost our grip and toppled into the soft grass. Koko kept going for a few steps, then stopped, turned and looked at us. We got up, walked over to Koko, jumped onto his back, and away we would trot until we lost our balance again. It was great fun for Roy and me and probably fun for little Koko too.

Roy and I also rode Reno, a good-natured quarter horse gelding who tolerated children and Sally, a Morgan mare with a gentle nature. Still, if Sally didn't want to go for a ride she sucked in a lot of air when the saddle blanket touched her back which made her middle swell like a balloon. The saddle cinch was tightened around the swollen belly and the instant the rider swung into the saddle; Sally let the air out. The saddle slipped sideways and the rider fell into the dirt.

You had to get up quickly, move the saddle into the correct position and retighten the cinch before Sally decided to suck in more air. It was a predictable little game.

All of the horses had been trained to cut cattle, an important skill for a cow pony. When the horse knew which cow needed to be separated from the herd, the horse jumped left when the cow moved left, jumped right when the cow moved right, all the while slowly moving forward, pushing the cow away from the herd. The horse had to be quick and agile. Dad told us to let the horse do the work and the job of the rider was to stay in the saddle—not always an easy task. One time Roy was riding Tony, a headstrong quarter horse mix. Tony got mad and bucked Roy off. Roy said that when he opened his eyes, he could see the bottoms of all four of Tony's feet above him. It was a miracle that Tony hadn't landed on him.

I don't know the number of times Dad was bucked off his horse or had a horse-related mishap. Dad got bucked off, picked himself up, dusted himself off, grabbed the horse's reins, and climbed back into the saddle. No harm, no foul. That said, Dad also had a lot of injuries. Every few years, he landed awkwardly and broke an ankle, a leg, a rib, or an arm. He broke his ankle before Christmas one year and Mom drove the family to Christmas celebrations. Dad sat in the front passenger seat offering driving advice while Mom gripped the wheel with white knuckles and rolled her eyes.

Daily Work and Chores

Milking and Churning Butter

Don't milk the cow too hard. She will kick you.
—MASON COOLEY

Roy was responsible for the evening milking in the summer beginning when he was eight years old, just as Ronnie was responsible for milking when he was eight and just as Dad was responsible when he was eight. It was a rite of passage. I started helping Roy when I turned eight. The milk cows grazed in the south pasture so we rode horseback to retrieve them. We rode docile and agreeable horses like Sally and Reno because they tolerated noisy children with less than expert riding skills. Sometimes we raced our horses for a little while, but not for very long because racing was not permitted. It made the horses too competitive. We rode to the windmill and then west, looking in gullies and hollows for the little herd of cattle and the milk cows. It could take thirty minutes to find the cows but once located, we rounded them up and headed home. It wasn't difficult to gather the cows because they were always ready to be milked and they dutifully headed back to the windmill.

The cows followed the familiar way back, walking single file along the well-worn trail, with Roy and me behind. We sometimes got impatient and tried to hurry the cows but running a milk cow was not good because a stressed cow wouldn't give as much milk. We generally just tagged along behind, chatting about why coyotes only yapped at night, how high birds could fly, how dumb some of the cows were, or what our favorite candy was.

When we got the cows into the corral, we dismounted and locked the gate behind us. We let the horses drink from the horse tank, unsaddled them in the barn, gave them some grain, and then tended to the cows. We herded the cows into the milking barn. Each cow walked to her assigned stanchion, stepping over the shallow gutter that ran along the length of the milking barn at the tail end of the cows. The cows put their heads through the slats, we closed the slat gates in the stanchions, and poured grain into each cow's tin pan. While the cows were occupied with their grain, we each grabbed a milk bucket and a stool and walked up to the cow's right side. The "stool" was a four-by-four post, twelve to fifteen inches tall, with a short board nailed across the top. These T-shaped, one-legged stools were certainly not comfortable but they were utilitarian.

We dropped the bucket under the cow's udder and pulled the stool close to the cow's back flank so our heads were nearly or just touching the cow and we began milking—two teats at a time, alternating between the four teats until there was no more milk.

The barn cats, whose job was to manage the mouse and sparrow populations in the out buildings, hung around while we were milking. Our game was to squeeze milk from a cow's teat, directly into the open mouth of a cat. Kids and cats became very adept at the game, but we were careful not to let the cats drink all of the milk.

Quickness, balance and a good awareness of animal behavior were required while milking. When the cow raised her tail, it meant that she was about to pee or poop, so you grabbed the milk bucket and moved it as far forward toward the cow's head as you could reach. At the same time, you turned your back to the tail end of the cow, further shielding the milk from what was to come. Once the cow had finished her business, you moved the pail back to its position under the udder and resumed milking.

We milked as fast as we could, moving from cow to cow. Roy milked faster than me—bigger hands and more coordination, I suppose. Once finished we turned the cows loose into the hog lot adjacent to the barn so the cows were close for the morning milking, which Dad and Ronnie handled. We also let the horses out of the barn and into the south pasture or into the hog lot, depending on Dad's instructions. Finally, one of us shoveled the cow poop out of the gutter in the milking barn. We threw the poop into the corral, where it could just blend in with all the other poop.

We poured a little milk into a shallow pan on the barn floor, so in the end, even uncoordinated cats and kittens got a share of fresh, warm milk. Finally, we carried the buckets of milk to the milk house in the front yard. Roy assembled the milk separator and put a large can by the spout where milk streamed out and a small can by the cream spout. Roy poured milk into the separator's reservoir at the top and I turned the separator handle. The milk separator operates on the principal that milk and cream have different specific gravities. The handle starts the centrifuge just below the reservoir. Milk enters the spinning centrifuge, and the cream, being lighter, rises to the top and is forced into a small hole at the top and flows into the small can. The milk, being heavier, sinks to the bottom of the centrifuge and flows out of the large spout at the bottom. Roy kept pouring milk into the reservoir until it was gone, and I kept turning the handle until no more cream or milk came out.

After separating, we took the separator apart, rinsed it in clear water from the hydrant in the yard and returned the separator parts to the milk house to dry. We took the milk and cream into the house for Mom. She put all of the milk and cream into the refrigerator unless she needed cream for butter. In that case, we poured cream into a can that sat on the top basement step. Once that can was half-full, Roy and I churned butter.

If Mom had all the milk the family could use, we poured the excess into the hog trough and our pigs got a treat that day. I don't believe we ever gave the pigs cream because Mom used extra cream for sweetened whipped cream to pile onto cakes, pies, or ice cream.

Most of the time, the cows ate sweet sandhills grass, so the milk and cream tasted sweet. If the cows got into a patch of skunk weed, though, the milk had a sharp, nasty, wild flavor and a pungent odor. Most of this foul milk ended up in the pig trough.

If you're afraid to use butter, use cream.

—JULIA CHILD

We made butter from the cream that was stored in the can on the basement step. Mom poured the sour cream into a gallon glass butter churn and Roy and I took turns cranking the handle of the churn until the milk curdled and separated into chunky pale curds and a watery white liquid. Mom poured the mixture through a colander on top of a large pan. The butter curds stayed in the colander and the buttermilk drained into the pan. She poured some of the buttermilk into a small glass pitcher and put it into the refrigerator. The rest of the buttermilk went to the hogs. Dad drank the buttermilk stored in the glass pitcher, but Mom never did. I tried the buttermilk once or twice, but didn't like it because it was sour and small buttery clumps floated in the watery "milk."

As for the butter bits in the colander, Mom squished them together into a ball and kneaded it, forcing out any remaining buttermilk liquid. She formed the butter into a solid block, added salt to taste, kneaded some more, wrapped the butter in waxed paper and placed it in the refrigerator to chill. We used butter in cookies, cakes, frostings, popovers, and cream puffs. We smeared it on bread, toast, biscuits, crackers, cooked vegetables, noodles, rice, potatoes, and everything else that could use a good slather of butter.

Preserving Produce

By late summer, the early garden vegetables like carrots, onions and lettuce had been eaten raw. We ate cucumbers, tomatoes and green beans as soon as we could pick enough for a meal, but all the rest had to be pickled, canned, or frozen before the first early frost killed our garden plants and spoiled the vegetables.

Before we had the upright Amana freezer Mom canned nearly everything and it was a day-long process. Roy and I snapped beans but we didn't like the job because it was boring.

It was easy, though, and if I was snapping beans, I didn't have to dust the furniture. We sat on the front step with a pile of beans between us, snapped off the ends, broke each bean into two or three pieces, and threw the beans into a huge metal mixing bowl. When we had snapped the batch or "mess" of beans, Mom washed off the sand, blanched them quickly in boiling salted water and packed the beans into clean jars. She added about a teaspoon of salt to each quart, poured boiling water over the beans, placed red rubber rings on the jars, loosely screwed on the lids, and sterilized them in a pressure cooker. When the beans were done, Mom took them out of the cooker and let them cool before tightening the lids. We carried the cooled jars to the fruit room in the basement where we lined them up on the shelves. Beans were placed together on a shelf, fruit was placed together, jams placed together and so on. When grouped together, it was easy to find them later because no one wanted to spend more time with the ghosts than absolutely necessary.

Mom canned peas one time because everyone was tired of eating fresh peas. She followed her canning rules, but the peas turned bad and she threw them out. The same thing happened with tomatoes—she canned them once, they turned bad and she threw them out. She never canned peas or tomatoes again. She made pickles from the excess cucumbers a few times, but she said that making pickles was more trouble than it was worth. Instead, she bought dill pickles by the gallon and stored the jars in the fruit room.

In the summer and fall, Mom bought bushels of peaches, pears, and apples. We ate as much as we could fresh, and Mom made fruit cobblers, crumbles, and pies. She canned the rest, adding hot syrup to the fruit that had been packed into the jars before sterilizing the jars. Any bruised or over-ripe fruit was made into jam by boiling the fruit slowly with sugar and pectin and then pouring it into sterile pint jars. She covered the jam with melted paraffin after it was cool before putting on the put rubber rings and lids.

Every spring, after Grandpa plowed our garden, he plowed a corn field south of Uncle Vern's house. He planted about two acres of field corn that would be fed to the hogs or made into silage and another acre of sweet corn for the family. In August when the sweet corn was ripe, Ronnie, Roy and I picked corn for meals. One of the boys drove the pickup truck to the field and we walked into the tall rows of corn. We selected the ripest ears by punching a fingernail through the green husk into a bright yellow kernel. If the kernel's juice was milky white, that ear was ready to pick. We tested each ear before prying it off the corn stalk. When we had enough corn for our meal, we drove home and husked the corn from the bed of the pickup. The husks went to the hogs and the sweet yellow corn went into the kitchen for Mom. She boiled the ears in a large pot of salted water before it was piled onto a platter with plenty of butter on the side.

In mid-August, Mom set aside one entire day for putting up corn. The evening before, Dad and the boys took the pickup to the corn field and loaded the truck bed with corn. Everyone helped husk the corn and the ears were placed in tubs and cardboard boxes until the next morning. On "corn day" we washed the corn in the water hydrant and then carted it into the house, where Mom blanched it in boiling water. Once out of the blanching water, Mom dropped the corn onto the kitchen table that was draped with a clean sheet. Everyone including Dad had a cookie sheet and a sharp knife. We each grabbed a cob and sliced the kernels into our pan, being careful not to slice off pieces of cob or pieces of fingers.

Corn kernels were scooped up and poured into freezer bags inside white cardboard pint freezer boxes. We squeezed as much air as possible out of the bag before tying the top with tiny rubber bands. Before we had the freezer, Dad or Mom took the corn to our freezer locker in Alliance. They also used the locker to store beef, pork, chickens and deer meat. After my parents bought the upright Amana freezer and parked it in the kitchen, Mom stacked the boxes of corn in the freezer where the corn froze into nice square shapes. We later removed bags of corn from the boxes and the squares of frozen corn remained on shelves for easy retrieval.

One of the only times I saw my mother truly mad was the pickup-full-of-corn incident. She said that she was so mad she could spit. I had never heard her say such a thing before, so I knew she was angry. Here's the story:

Mom asked Ronnie to take the pickup and get some corn for supper. Well, Ronnie was gone a long time, which annoyed Mom because she thought he was loitering in the cornfield. When Ronnie finally got back, he raced into the house and said, "I have a lot of corn for you!" Mom asked what he meant and Ronnie told Mom, "Come and see." Warily, Mom followed Ronnie with Roy, Sharyl, and me following behind. The pickup bed was piled high with corn. Mom turned white as a ghost, then bright red in the span of thirty seconds. She turned to Ronnie and said in a shaky voice, "I told you to get corn for supper."

"Yes, but the corn is perfect and I know you like to freeze corn," Ronnie said proudly.

Mom just stared at Ronnie, her face getting redder and redder. This was the last thing she needed. Freezing corn required planning. A day needed to be set aside, supplies needed to be gathered, the kitchen needed to be spotless, the freezer needed to be rearranged to make space. She didn't have time for this and Dad couldn't help because he was busy in the field. She was furious and practically in tears. Still, the corn couldn't be wasted and had to be put up within a day. Mom would drop everything on her agenda to take care of the corn.

Early the next morning, we husked the corn and washed it, Mom blanched it and everyone, including little Sharyl cut corn off the cobs. We bagged up the corn, tied off the bags and Mom stuffed the corn into every nook and cranny in the freezer.

Then came the massive cleanup because the sweet, sticky corn kernels were everywhere—on the table, on the kitchen chairs, on our clothes, on the floor, and tracked all over the house. Ronnie had to help with the cleanup and had to take all of the husks and the corn cobs to the pigs with no help from anyone. I don't think that Mom spoke to Ronnie for a couple of days.

Laundry and Housework

There is something refreshing about sheets and pillow slips just fresh from the line after being washed and dried in the sun and air.

—LAURA INGALLS WILDER

Rain or shine, Monday was laundry day. When I was very young, our washing machine, mangle, and laundry tubs were in the milk house. (A mangle is an apparatus with two rollers in a frame that was used to wring water out of the wet laundry.) Mom carried hot water from the kitchen and cold water from the outside water hydrant and poured the water into the washing machine. She added soap and the clothes and started the machine, letting the clothes swish about in the tub for ten to fifteen minutes before stopping the machine. She then turned on the mangle and threaded the clothes from the washer through the mangle into a large tub filled with cold water. Mom was very careful with the mangle and we children had to stay at a safe distance when Mom operated it. There were lots of stories about women and children whose arms got caught in the mangle and the arms pulled off before someone was able to shut the machine down. These were scary stories and, from all accounts, absolutely true. Mom respected the mangle and kept herself and the kids at a distance.

Once the soapy clothes were in the tub of clean, clear water, Mom turned off the mangle and poked the clothes with a long, thick wooden stick. We were allowed to poke the clothes while Mom put the next load into the washer and started the washer. We stepped back when Mom shifted the mangle and turned it on. She threaded the rinsed clothes back through the mangle into a clothes basket and turned off the mangle. Mom carried the clothes basket to the clothesline just outside the fenced yard on the west side of the house. When I was tall enough, I helped Mom hang clothes on the line, using wooden clothespins. The pins had to be very secure because we didn't want the clothes to blow off the line into the sand. If that happened, the clothes had to be rinsed again. Before hanging blue jeans, we inserted a wire jean stretcher tightly into each leg. As the blue jeans dried, they shrank on the stretcher. The result was crisp, straight creases on each leg of the jeans.

With the low humidity in western Nebraska, it only took a couple of hours for the clothes to dry. We released the clothes from the clothesline and placed them in the clothes basket, making sure nothing touched the ground. Even in the winter, we hung clothes on the line. The clothes just froze first, then dried—freeze-drying in its earliest form. If it was raining or snowing on Monday, laundry day was never postponed. We washed as always in the milk house, but carried the clothes into the basement, where we hung them on the lines strung along the floor joists. It took longer for clothes to dry in the basement, but generally only a day or two.

On laundry days, Mom's first load was lightly soiled clothes like sheets, pillowcases, or baby clothes. After the first load, Mom inspected the wash water. If it wasn't too dirty, she washed more heavily soiled clothes like Dad's work shirts in that same water. While she continued washing, she reused the water for a second load whenever possible. However, she washed baby diapers separately in hot water with bleach and never reused that water.

Laundry days were better after Mom and Dad installed the automatic washer and dryer in the kitchen. Those two conveniences saved Mom time and effort. The washer filled automatically, rinsed automatically, and spun automatically. We still hung clothes on the clothesline if it was sunny, but on rainy or snowy days, Mom used the electric dryer.

Mom ironed most of the clean clothes, so after we took the dry clothes off the clothesline, we carried the basket into the house and Mom sorted the clothes. We folded sheets, towels, underwear, diapers, kids' clothes, baby clothes, and the flattened blue jeans with the crisp creases. Mom sprinkled everything else generously with water, rolled the clothes together tightly, and wound a towel around the damp bundle. She set aside the bundle for ironing on Tuesday because Tuesday was ironing day.

After the breakfast dishes were washed and dried on Tuesday, Mom hauled out the old ironing board and a heavy electric iron. She gathered the bundle of clothes, and subdivided the items in the bundle before starting to iron. She ironed shirts, blouses, skirts, dresses, and aprons. When I was about eight years old, I was allowed to iron pillow cases and Dad's handkerchiefs, carefully folding each item into a perfect square. Once I could iron pillowcases and handkerchiefs perfectly without scorching or wrinkles, I could move on to ironing aprons, shirts, blouses, and dresses.

Housework won't kill you, but then again,
why take the chance.

—Phyllis Diller

Housework was women's (or girl's) work. Roy helped with housework a bit, but most of the time, housework landed on Mom and me. I hated dusting but so did Mom, so it was my job. Mom dampened an old rag (usually an old diaper that had been bleached and washed until it was threadbare) and handed the rag to me. Every surface was to be dusted. If a lamp or vase was on that surface, it had to be moved and dusted, the surface dusted and the lamp returned to its rightful place. Later, when furniture polish became popular, we sprayed Pledge on a surface and buffed the surface with an old diaper. I wasn't a good duster. I didn't move items to dust underneath but dusted around things or simply dusted the front edges of the furniture. In Mom's inspections, she showed me what I had missed, and told me to dust again. Even with a second try, I didn't always hit the mark, so Mom either gave up or, if company was coming, she dusted the furniture herself.

When I was very young, the floor of the combined living and dining rooms was hardwood, and Mom used a dust mop on the floors. Mopping just moved dust bunnies from the floor into the air, where they slowly drifted down onto the furniture. Later, Mom and Dad carpeted the living room portion of the room because they thought it would make the room warmer. They also bought a mechanical carpet sweeper. The contraption worked well and it did tame some of the dust bunnies.

Making beds was a bone of contention for me. Mom said that because Dad had been in the army, he expected beds to be made up the instant you climbed out in the morning. I didn't mind making my own bed, but I complained bitterly about making Ronnie's and Roy's beds. It wasn't fair that they didn't have to make their own beds, and I told Mom repeatedly just how unfair it was. Mom listened to my complaint and then said it didn't matter what I thought. Making beds was my job. The sheets and bed covers were pulled tight and tucked in, the pillow was fluffed, pajamas were folded neatly and then placed under the pillow. When Sharyl got older, we worked together to make beds, which annoyed both of us.

Cooking and Baking

If God had intended us to follow recipes,
He wouldn't have given us grandmothers.

—LINDA HENLEY

In the early days, Mom made most of our food from scratch and only used recipes for cookies and cakes. Mom prepared food the way Grandma Woodworth had prepared it, which meant everything was perfect. She made yeast bread every few days, and this included loaves, dinner rolls, and often cinnamon rolls. She started bread just after breakfast so at least some of it could be finished baking by dinner time. In the afternoon, she finished baking bread and also baked pies, cakes, and cookies.

It was a working ranch, so men worked outdoors every day and Mom worked both indoors and out every day. Because adults needed a lot of food to maintain strength and stamina and kids needed a lot of food to grow, we ate big meals three times a day.

Mom fried eggs and bacon, ham or sausage and toasted bread for breakfast. There was always orange juice and plenty of coffee. She prepared meat and potatoes for dinner in the middle of the day. Potatoes were boiled, mashed, fried or baked. Since we had hogs, chickens and cattle, the meat alternated between the three groups, but mostly we ate beef. Mom also prepared a salad or two, a vegetable or two and served bread. If she didn't have enough yeast bread or rolls for the meal, she made biscuits or corn bread. We slathered bread with butter and often added jam. There was always dessert—cakes, cookies, pies, or ice cream. After dinner at noon, all of the men took a ten-minute nap. Dad and Grandpa lay on the floor in the living room and snoozed. Everyone else had to be quiet as a mouse while the men slept. We left the dirty dishes on the table and the leftovers on the stove until the men grabbed their hats and went back to work.

In the summer if the men were in the hay field close by, Mom packed freshly baked cookies in a box, made a gallon of Kool-Aid or lemonade in a glass jar, added ice, and grabbed a bunch of aluminum drinking glasses. She loaded the kids and the treats into the back of the pickup and drove across the prairie to where the men were stacking hay. Mom parked in the shade of the hay stacker and we all piled out, waving madly at the men who were working in the field. Mom put the treats on the tailgate of the truck, the men stopped what they were doing and walked to the truck. Everyone grabbed snacks and stood around munching cookies, drinking Kool-Aid, and talking. After fifteen or twenty minutes, it was back to work for everyone, so we packed up and Mom drove us home.

Piano Lessons

*All humans are musical. Why else would
the Lord give you a beating heart?*

—Mitch Albom

Mom loved music. We had an upright piano in the living room, and some afternoons, she played and sang while Roy and I sat with her on the bench. Her dream was to have been a music teacher but since that wouldn't happen, she held out hope that one of her children would be a musician. The first step was to learn to read music and play the piano, but Ronnie chose the accordion instead. Mom and Dad bought a used instrument and he started lessons with Ruth Cole, a music teacher in Alliance. She lived in a little house in what was known as Indian Town, a section on the southeast side of town.

A year or so later Roy and I began piano lessons with Mrs. Cole. Once a week, Mom dropped Ronnie off for his lesson and thirty minutes later picked him up and dropped off Roy and me. We had back-to-back, thirty-minute lessons, so after an hour Mom returned, picked us up and we went home. Mrs. Cole was a disciplinarian and her lessons were structured and rigid. We learned notes, notations, scales, timing, posture, and fingering. Mom wanted us to practice our lessons every day, but practicing seemed like work, so we only practiced a few times a week. Mrs. Cole didn't inspire us to love music, so Mom decided that we needed a different teacher. She asked friends and neighbors and learned that the organist at the Methodist Church, Thelma Reynolds, gave piano lessons. Everyone loved her but there was a waiting list. Mom put us on the list and we continued our lessons with Mrs. Cole.

Several months later we left Mrs. Cole and started taking lessons with Mrs. Reynolds. What a difference. Mrs. Reynolds was kind and she smiled. She offered suggestions, gave us piano games to improve our fingering skills and encouraged our efforts. Music lessons were less work now and actually enjoyable. Mrs. Reynolds chose wonderful but difficult songs for us to play at our annual recitals.

Shopping with Mom

My mom is painfully sweet; she's from Nebraska.

—Kate Millett

One of Mom's jobs was shopping and this was a job she loved. Mom could shop for hours, wandering in and out of stores, looking at clothes, fabric, knick-knacks, candle holders, candles, kitchen gadgets, furniture, and whatever. If she didn't buy one thing when she wandered, it was fine.

She just enjoyed the experience of drifting through stores, looking at the latest, the greatest, or the most unique things. It was her idea of a perfect afternoon.

Mom chose a day to go to town and after dinner (noon) dishes were washed and put away, we headed off. Roy and I went along when we were young, and Sharyl and Rick joined the troupe when they joined the family.

Dad often added items to Mom's shopping list. Sometimes it was a cow or horse medicine at the veterinarian's office, sometimes a tool at the hardware store, and sometimes a specific engine part at the tractor dealer. If he needed a part, Dad tossed the broken part into the trunk and told Mom to just ask for one of those. We always bought Dad's items before we did anything else.

Next, we went downtown to pick up dry goods from the department store or items from the pharmacy. The only makeup Mom wore was lipstick and Charles of the Ritz face powder. The powder was a special formulation, specific for Mom's complexion. When she needed a refill, she went straight to the cosmetics counter at the Rexall drug store. The clerk opened a drawer full of small cards and looked for Mom's card with her face powder formula printed on the back. The clerk selected several powders from the twenty or more powders in numbered and lettered containers behind the counter. Most of the powders were shades of beige but others were blueish, grayish, pink, or off-white. The clerk weighed specific amounts of each color on a small scale and poured the measured amount into a cup. When all of the powders were in the cup, she mixed the concoction with a small wooden spoon and gently poured the product into a small, round cardboard container with a fitted lid. She placed the container and a new powder puff into a small bag and handed the bag to Mom. I vowed that when I was old enough, I would have face powder made-to-order, just like Mom.

The final stop on our shopping trip was the grocery store. There was a Co-Op store and a Jack-and-Jill store but Mom liked the Co-Op. We walked through the aisles, pushing the wheeled cart while Mom picked her groceries. When we checked out with the cashier, Mom paid by check, signing her name, Mrs. Lester S. Jesse. I asked Mom why she didn't use her actual name, but she said that wasn't allowed. Women used their husband's names.

If the men were going to be away for the entire day and not coming home for dinner, Mom packed lunches for them. This meant we would have the whole day for shopping. Mom drove to town after breakfast dishes were clean, and we began our shopping trip. We wandered around downtown, and at noon Mom took us to Theile's, a drug store with a lunch counter and a few booths in the back. We waited for a booth and sat down—Mom and the babies on one side of the booth with Roy and me on the other. I always ordered a toasted ham sandwich with potato chips and a chocolate malt. The diner had other food of course, but I never deviated from my favorite foods. These were the best ham sandwiches I ever had, and the potato chips were thickly cut, greasy and heavily salted. I drank my malt last because it had melted a bit by the end of the meal and was easy to drink through the paper straw. We often ran into Aunt Mary at Theile's. She sat on a round stool at the far end of the lunch counter, eating lunch, drinking coffee, smoking cigarettes and chatting with her friends. She was always happy to see us, but never joined us in our booth. After our lunch, we shopped at a few more stores downtown before going to the grocery store. We had to be home by mid-afternoon so Mom had time to prepare a large meal. The men had eaten only sandwiches for dinner and they would be extra hungry at supper.

CHAPTER 5

Spring and Summer

Breathless we flung us on a windy hill, laughed in the sun and kissed the lovely grass.

—Rupert Brooke

Springtime

After the snow melted and the sun began to warm the hills, everything started to grow. The grass turned bright green, wild flowers covered the south side of the hills, and the water in the lakes was bright blue. This was Mom's favorite season but it was a busy season. There was a garden to plant, spring cleaning to finish, branding meals to plan and prepare, end of school activities to attend, and what seemed like a million other tasks to complete. Dad had it no better. He had to mend fences and service windmills at home and on the Case place. May was also branding time and every rancher branded calves in May. Sometimes Dad went to two or three brandings each week. The bulls were also moved in with the cows in May so the baby calves would be born the next February.

In the early 1950s, we didn't go to church services for a few reasons. First, Dad had to work, even on Sunday.

Second, church was in Alliance, a thirty- to forty-minute drive from home. Third, my parents didn't have money for church clothes. Finally, none of the kids had been baptized, so Mom and Dad avoided church to avoid questions about baptism. When I was three, the Easter Bunny brought fancy clothes for Ronnie, Roy, and me. These were church clothes, and we were going to Easter services. The bunny also brought me a pair of red cowboy boots and I loved, loved, loved those boots. I refused to wear the pretty black, patent-leather Mary-Janes that came in the box with the dress and demanded that I be allowed to wear the boots instead. I sobbed and howled when Mom tried to remove the boots, and when it was time to leave for church, I continued to cry. Mom and Dad gave up the fight and they let me wear my beloved boots to church. When we walked into church, everyone turned to watch me walk down the main aisle, holding Mom's hand and sporting my red cowboy boots and a frilly, pale-blue dress with petticoats. Mom was mortified but she held her head high and smiled.

As I got older, we attended Easter services just about every year. After church, we went to Grandpa and Grandma Jesse's house and joined the rest of the extended family. Like us, everyone was dressed in their very best spring clothes. Aunt Mary, home from her winter travels, arrived in her Cadillac and asked the men to help her take Easter baskets out of the backseat. She gave each of the children a huge, cellophane-wrapped basket full of small toys and candies. It was a wonderful treat.

Summertime

Summer was the best time for the kids. School was out and we played outdoors every day unless it was raining. When Roy and I were six and seven, Ronnie taught us how to climb trees so we could play the Tarzan game. Ronnie was a voracious reader, read stories about Tarzan's adventures and retold the stories so we could also play correctly. Ronnie was always Tarzan and he tried to assign the role of Jane to me because I was a girl. I was reluctant and protested because Jane seemed so helpless. I sometimes gave in, making sure that my Jane did the same things that Tarzan did. Ronnie usually wanted Roy to be Tarzan's pet ape, but Roy didn't like that at all. Instead, Roy was Tarzan's sidekick even though Ronnie's stories didn't mention a sidekick. When it was time for the tree scene, we climbed our assigned tree in the yard and stalked imaginary animals with tree-branch spears. We fought, or ran away from, the imaginary lions and tigers that chased us.

Ronnie's favorite books were about cowboys. We all had sticks for horses and toy wooden guns and we raced around the yard, yelling and whooping like we assumed cowboys and Indians did back in the old days. (It was the '50s, and 'Native American' was an unknown term to us.) Ronnie often wanted me to be the Indian so he and Roy could chase me but, again, I was uncooperative. That meant we were all cowboys, chasing imaginary Indians or we were all Indians chasing imaginary cowboys. Either way, it was just running and chasing.

Summer also meant that we could get our BB guns out of the basement and go target shooting. There was a blow-out just north of the windmill on the top of a hill, a perfect place for target shooting. (A blowout is an area on the side of a hill where the wind has scoured away the grass, leaving behind a sandy depression. The erosion is common in the Sandhills, and ranchers take care to keep blowouts from growing big enough to destroy an entire hilltop.) We took our guns to the blowout because our BBs would land safely in the sand when we missed the target. We propped up tin cans on one side of the blowout, sat on the other side, and took turns shooting the cans. When we got older, we took Dad's single-shot .22 rifle for our target shooting.

Mom's rule about guns was explicit: NEVER point a gun at anyone. This rule applied to every gun including .22 rifles, BB guns, toy metal guns, wooden guns and even sticks representing guns. You only pointed a gun at something or someone you wished dead, so that meant you didn't point a gun at a person, ever. Dad's gun safety rules were practical. We learned how to safely carry a gun or rifle, how to keep it out of the sand, how to verify it was unloaded or loaded, and how to aim and squeeze the trigger. Forays of unsupervised children into the hills with weapons were a normal part of ranch life.

When we were exceptionally hot and bored, we played in the sprinkler in the yard and sometimes Mom let us take the pickup to the lake a mile or so east of the house. It was a nice, alkali lake and the cool water was a couple of feet deep. The trouble was that the lake was sometimes infested with leeches. If we waded around a bit and a leech or two attached to a leg, we pulled off the leech, abandoned our swimming expedition, and headed home.

In the spring after branding, Dad, Grandpa, Uncle Vern, Ronnie, and some of the neighbor men drove cows and calves on horseback north, across various neighbors' property to the Case place. The lucky cows and calves that went north for summer vacation ate the lush grasses in the pastures and were largely left alone. No one lived on the Case place anymore, so someone had to check the cattle and the windmills twice every week until the cattle were moved back to the home place in the fall. On Sunday afternoons in the summer, the whole family often went to the Case place to check the cattle. Mom and Dad and the younger siblings sat in the pickup cab while the older kids sat in the back on the truck bed floor. After driving west to Alliance, Dad went north to the sixteen-mile corner, where he turned east. We entered the Case place through a gate and Dad drove past the little house where he and Mom had lived in the late 1940s. Then he drove through the hills, locating the little groups of grazing cattle. He counted the cattle while studying each animal to make sure all was well. If his count was short, he drove through the hills until he found the missing cows and calves. If a cow or calf seemed sick, he drove back on Monday to treat the animal.

We went to every windmill to make sure it was pumping water and that every water tank was full. Then the roller coaster ride began. He drove the pickup fast up small slopes and we would get a little airborne when the pickup came back to earth with a BUMP on the other side. We screamed and laughed in delight. In other places, he drove up a steep hill to the point where the front of the pickup was pointing skyward and Dad and Mom couldn't see the slope on the other side. It had the appearance of a drop-off. Mom would say, "Oh, Lord," and hold on for dear life while my dad continued moving forward, not into a drop-off, but onto fairly steep downward slope. Dad laughed, the kids cheered and Mom frowned. Dad knew every hill, every gully, every hollow, every blowout and every drop-off. After the cattle and all of the windmills were checked and the roller coaster rides were over for the day, Dad drove home.

The Polio Epidemic

Mom and Dad didn't take us into Alliance during the summer months in the early '50s. My brothers and I didn't know it, but every summer, the polio epidemic returned and raged through towns and cities in the Midwest and South. Polio, or infantile paralysis, infected children. Lucky children only had mild flu symptoms but unlucky children became very ill and were hospitalized. Some spent time in an iron lung that helped the child breathe. Many children were paralyzed or died. There was no known cause of the outbreaks, but some news reports said that the disease was caused by flies or mosquitoes. With the first reported case in a town, men sprayed DDT around homes, on vacant lots, and in parks. The worst epidemic was in the summer of 1952 when there were sixty thousand cases in the US and more than three thousand deaths. That summer, parents kept their children inside their houses, public swimming pools and parks were closed and movie theaters shut down. Kathy, the neighbor girl who lived on a ranch a mile and a half south of us caught polio that year. She spent some time in an iron lung before she recovered. How a little child living on a ranch in the Sandhills could contract the disease was a puzzle, but it was enough for my parents to be cautious or just plain paranoid. We stayed home and didn't even get to visit relatives.

In 1953, Dr. Jonas Salk completed a successful test of a polio vaccine and the vaccine came into standard use, even in western Nebraska. Children who lived in town got their shot at school, but my parents had to take us to the family doctor's clinic to get our immunization.

Fishing Trips

The best time to go fishing is when you can.
—ED ZERN

The men in the Jesse family bought fishing licenses every year but kids didn't need a license until they turned sixteen. Generally, none of the women got a license. On many Sundays during the summer, the extended family went fishing. We went to Fry Lake outside of Hyannis, to Lake Minatare south of Alliance, to the Box Butte dam north of Alliance, or to other small, freshwater lakes scattered throughout the Nebraska panhandle.

On Saturday before the fishing trip, Mom made cookies or brownies because those treats traveled well. On Sunday, she got up at three o'clock in the morning so she could fry chicken and let it cool in the refrigerator before we left for the day. She also made salads, sandwiches, and Kool-Aid or lemonade. She packed everything that needed to be cool in our metal cooler layered with chunks of ice. She packed old plates, forks, napkins, swimsuits for the children, and frayed terrycloth towels into boxes. We also gathered old blankets and sheets and camp stools and loaded everything into the trunk of the car. In the meantime, Dad collected fishing rods, rod holders, and tackle boxes; all of which he put into the car trunk. We then set off to the fishing spot, where we met up with the Raverts and the Dills.

We retrieved the fishing gear and put the poles by the lakefront. All the men had lures in their tackle boxes, but someone also brought either minnows, earthworms, or long, red night crawlers. Hooks were baited, lines were cast, and camp stools set up next to the poles. The men set up two lines because their license allowed two. When the men caught a fish, they put it on a stringer line in the shallows of the lake, then kept catching fish until they had caught their limit. Children also tried to catch fish using small bamboo poles with a short line and a hook. We baited our hooks and held the pole patiently for five or ten minutes before we abandoned our poles so we could put on our swimsuits and play in the water.

While the men were setting up their fishing spots, the women created a shady area by hanging old blankets between two cars. They put the corners of a blanket in the windows of the cars and rolled up the windows to stretch the blanket as a makeshift sun-shade. They spread old blankets on the ground and if there was a slight breeze, it was cool and comfortable for the small children and babies who played with their toys in the shady area.

Around noon, the women laid out the picnic lunch. Everyone filled their plates and we sat on blankets or on camp stools to eat. After lunch, it was back to fishing for the men and back to cleaning up lunch for the women. Children had to wait an hour before they were allowed back into the lake for splashing. These fishing lakes were out in the middle of nowhere, so there were no toilets or outhouses. If nature called, we walked over a hill, out of sight to do our business in the grass. "Don't sit on a cactus," Aunt Lois invariably yelled.

By late afternoon, everyone was hungry again, so we ate a quick supper and packed up. The men pulled the fish off the stringer lines and put them into ice-filled coolers. We gathered everything else, loaded it into cars, and headed home. Sometimes everyone came to our house or to Uncle Vern's to dress the fish. A table was set up outside and all of the fish were scaled, gutted, and washed, then divided among the fishermen. Tomorrow we would have fish for dinner.

Ronnie always brought his transistor radio and turned the dial until he found a station broadcasting a baseball game. Usually, the only game he could get was a Yankees game so I became a huge Yankees fan. The first man I ever loved (after my dad) was Mickey Mantle. I thought he was the best baseball player ever.

Unless it was pouring rain, the Jesse family went fishing on Memorial Day, but, instead of baseball, we listened to the Indianapolis 500 on Ronnie's radio. The race commentators were brilliant. They kept us interested in an event where the only action involved cars going around and around in a circle. The sounds of the race kept us engaged in the action. When a pack of cars got close to the commentators' booth, the sound was deafening, and when the cars went by, the sound was lower but there was still a constant din. Crashes were the best part and the broadcasters described the collisions in glorious detail. We could practically see the mangled car and the crew extricating the driver from the flames. With no crashes, the races were very boring.

It wasn't unusual for a game warden to drive by our little fishing community and check everyone's license. The Warden counted poles and fish on the stringer lines. No one was willing to risk getting caught without a license or with too many fish because fines were steep and licenses might be forfeited for the rest of the season. There were times when, after a day of fishing, no one had caught a single fish. There were other times when some of the men caught over their limit, but others had not. They divided up the fish, so no one was over the limit. A few times, all of the men caught over their limit, so the plan was to tell the game warden that the overages were caught by the children, who didn't need a license.

One Sunday, the fishing was spectacular. Throw in a line, catch a fish. Throw in a line, catch a fish. Even the kids were catching fish with their little bamboo poles. The men caught way over their limit and the kids also caught their limit. As we packed to go home, there was a conference by the stringer lines. What were we going to do? If we got caught, everyone would lose their license and have to pay a fine. Finally, Uncle Tom came up with a clever scheme. The men counted the total fish and subtracted the total limit for each man and child. The remainder was the number of fish that needed to be hidden. Uncle Tom tied a burlap sack holding the extra fish to the undercarriage of his car so the fish could be smuggled out of the lake area. We packed the remaining fish into coolers and headed out in a parade of cars. Once out of the area, we stopped our cars on a side road. Uncle Tom retrieved the fish tied under the car, put them in his ice chest and we all drove away. My family—a gang of criminals.

Vacations and Outings

There was no fishing on Independence Day. On this special day, Mom packed a lunch and we drove to Crawford for the rodeo. Dad bought tickets at the entrance gate and he parked in the dusty parking lot. We ate lunch quickly because we didn't want to miss one minute of the rodeo events. There was bareback riding, saddle bronc riding, calf roping, and steer wrestling. Barrels were set up in the ring and several girls and young women raced their horses around the barrels. When all of those events were over, it was time for the main event. The crew rolled two battered barrels into the ring, and the announcer introduced two or three rodeo clowns. The clowns performed some antics and magic tricks before the announcer introduced the finale—bull riding. We watched as cowboys either rode the bucking brahma bull until the eight-second bell rang or until he fell off, landing in the dirt. Once the cowboy was on the ground, the clowns swooped in to divert the bull's attention away from the cowboy. The crowd cheered while the clowns harassed and played with the angry bulls. Finally, the rodeo was over and the winners of each event were announced. We stayed for the fireworks before heading home.

Actual vacations were not common for us. Mom told me about taking a family vacation to Yellowstone Park when I was a year old. Dad drove, Mom held me on her lap in the front seat and the boys sat in the backseat watching the park go by through their open windows. Mom didn't have many diapers, so she rinsed out a wet diaper, hung it on the car's radio antenna and as Dad drove through the park, the diaper fluttered and dried in the breeze.

Dad and Mom took us on a family fishing trip to Angostura Dam in South Dakota one year. Dad rented a small cabin close to the water, and when we arrived, we ran excitedly into the cabin, checked it out, and then ran to the little beach. When Mom walked into the cabin, she wasn't excited at all. It was infested with mice, so Mom spent the rest of the day cleaning and disinfecting with bleach before we could unpack. It wasn't much of a vacation for Mom. She ended up cooking and cleaning for three days just like she would be doing at home.

4-H

Roy and Ronnie joined the Marple Wranglers 4-H club in the spring of 1956 when Roy was eight and Ronnie was thirteen. The club leader was Dad's good friend, Ken Messersmith. Ken and his wife Verna had several kids who were going to be in the club along with some other Messersmith kids and some Bauer kids. Ronnie and Roy easily fit into the group.

I'm sure that Dad and Mom saw 4-H as a good way to socialize their isolated children. It would be good for the boys to interact with other children and learn how to get along with others. This was a safe environment because Dad and Mom knew all of the parents, having gone to high school with nearly all of them. The club was organized in Box Butte County because it was convenient for all of the parents.

The club met once a month, and the meetings were mostly business with each child demonstrating an aspect of his or her project. After the meetings there was food and often a pickup softball game. In the beginning, the only project available to members was raising and showing a calf. Roy was young so his project was raising and showing a Hereford stocker-feeder calf. Ronnie was older so his project was raising and showing a Hereford yearling or baby beef calf. We only had Hereford cattle because Dad and Grandpa liked them. As a breed, Herefords were good-natured and gentle, not at all like the aggressive, belligerent Angus cattle some people had.

I watched as Ronnie and Roy picked out their calves for their projects, tamed the calves, fed them, trained them, and groomed them. They wrote in their workbooks, completed charts, and tracked the calf's progress. My brothers took these new tasks seriously and I was very, very jealous. I wanted to join the club and be a grown-up 4-H member. I begged Mom to let me join, but she told me no. The 4-H rules were strict. You had to be eight to join and I was seven. There could be no exceptions. I had to wait.

In the spring of 1957, I was allowed to join the club and I was excited to be a part of the group. Roy and I would both have stocker-feeder calves and Ronnie would have a yearling. Ronnie chose his calf from Dad's stock of yearling steers. Roy and I picked calves that were a few months old. After the May branding, Dad loaded Roy and me into his pickup and we drove into the pasture to select our calves. Dad took us to various bunches of cows and calves, stopping and pointing out the calves that had the best Hereford coloring—red body with white belly, face, legs, and tail tip. There had to be symmetrical coloring over the entire calf, with no random red where white should be and no random white where red should be. The calf had to have a short, wide body, a thick, short neck, a straight back and straight legs. Besides the look of the calf, Dad guided us toward calves whose mothers had a gentle temperament, which likely meant the calf would have a good temperament. Dad didn't want us dealing with a bad-tempered mom and her feisty calf.

Once we had picked our calves, Dad helped us the first few times we brought the cows and their calves into the corral. We saddled our horses and rode out to the pasture to find the cows. Dad cut the two cows from the herd and we drove the cows back to the corral with the calves dutifully following behind. Once in the corral, we moved the calves into a separate corral and turned the cows back into the pasture. The cows didn't leave because their babies were still in the corral.

We gradually gained the calf's trust because we were kind and always gave them grain sweetened with sorghum. Once we could get close to the calf, we started petting the calf and eventually could put a halter over his head. We tied the haltered calves in a stall for an hour or so every day for a few days until the calf got used to the halter. After that, we taught him to lead. To ensure the calf didn't run away Roy helped me with my calf and I helped Roy with his. After the calf was trained to lead on his halter, we trained him to stand in the standard show pose with his head up and alert and his legs straight and evenly spaced.

We spent so much time with our calves that they became more like pets than range animals. We named our calves just like we named our dogs. I was enamored with boxers and boxing at the time, so I named many of my calves after famous boxers. One year, my calf's name was Sonny (for Sonny Liston), another year, it was Floyd (for Floyd Patterson), another time Cassius (Cassius Clay) and Ingmar (Ingmar Johansson).

As the dates of the county fair approached, we began to prepare our animals for show. We practiced bathing our little friends with soapy water that had bluing as an additive. The bluing made the face, legs and belly bright white. After a thorough wash and rinse, we towel-dried the hair and curled it, using a little Brylcreem to hold the curl and make the calf's coat glossy. We back-combed the calf's tail to make it fluffy, and we waxed and buffed the toenails until they shined. We practiced the grooming steps and the showing steps over and over until the fair began. We entered our animals in a class that judged animals based on how well they met beef cattle criteria and also the showmanship class that judged the showman on his or her ability to manage and show the animal.

On fair day, we got up early, loaded our calves and supplies into the truck and Dad drove us to the fairgrounds in Hemingford, a small town about ten miles north of Alliance. Mom came later with Sharyl and Rick, snacks, drinks and most importantly, our 4-H clothes. The trip to Hemingford took over an hour and once there, we waited in a long line of pickup trucks to unload. After we led our calves off the truck, Dad moved the truck and parked it while we led our calves into the barn to find our assigned stalls. We tied our calves to the stalls and used pitch forks to put down nice comfortable straw beds for the animals. Next, we went to the outdoor faucet and filled the water pans with cool water and placed the water pans and pans of grain near the calves' heads. We filled out identification cards with our names, the class of animal, the name of the animal and the 4-H club name. We hung the cards on wire, strung across the top of each stall. When we earned ribbons, we hung the ribbon on the wire next to the name card.

We washed our animals at the washing station and led them back to the barn, where we curled their hair, buffed the hooves, and back-combed the tail. By the time the animals looked their best, Mom had arrived with our fair clothes. We changed into our new blue jeans and new 4-H shirts in the not-very-clean public toilets and donned our official 4-H caps. With all preparations complete, children and animals were ready for the 4-H show.

The fair was held in late August just before school started, so the weather was generally hot. There were a few years when fall started early and the temperatures were in the high 40s or low 50s. We wore jackets and our poor animals shivered uncontrollably after their bath. A few years, we had a combination of forty-degree weather and rain. Those were the worst fairs ever. Kids, animals, parents and siblings all shivered in the cold rain. Everyone was miserable and we were very glad when we could go home to a warm, dry house.

Roy and I mostly got blue ribbons in the stocker-feeder class and Ronnie did the same in the baby beef class. A few times our calves earned us a purple, but it seemed like purple ribbons were more likely to go to a 4-H member with a more prestigious surname. Roy and Ronnie often got blue or purple ribbons in showmanship, but I got red. I wasn't that invested in being a showman, and besides, I was easily distracted by activities around me. Mom said I was always more interested in the carnival setup than in showing my calf.

Between events, we sat on the straw in the stall with our calves. We were proud to be 4-H members and rather liked showing off to the town people who walked by our stall. We were confident. We thought that town people were jealous of us because we had calves and they didn't. We had ribbons and they didn't. We didn't know how much our confidence would be tested when we left our sheltered country life and started high school.

On the last day of the fair, there was a stock sale. The 4-H children led their steers, heifers, hogs, and sheep around the ring and people bid on the animal. The prices were always much higher than the market price because the buyers knew that the funds went to the children, often into the child's college fund. Ronnie sold his baby beef steers at this sale, so he left the fair without his animals but with a nice check to put into the bank.

Roy and I couldn't sell our stocker-feeder calves at the fair, so we held them another couple of months, feeding them grain until there was a public stock sale at the sale barn in Rushville. We loaded our calves into the pickup and Dad drove to Rushville, where we unloaded our calves into a corral with other 4-H calves. Dressed in our 4-H clothes, we groomed the animals, and one by one, led our calves around the ring in the crowded, smoky sale barn. The auctioneer announced our name, our club's name and the calf's name. He briefly described the calf and the bidding began. Around and around, we led our calf as long as the bidding was active. At last, the auctioneer announced the buyer and we left the ring. One year, my calf sold for thirty-six fifty or $0.365 per pound. The steer weighed 510 pounds, so I cleared $186 that year. Some years the sale price was more and some years less. Some years, our steers weighed more, other years they weighed less. The amount of the check was ours to keep and it went into our college fund. Later, we started showing two calves each instead of one, which doubled our earnings.

After a few years, the 4-H leaders decided to offer cooking and sewing projects. I didn't see why this was important because I had been helping my mother for as long as I could remember, but when the other girls signed up for the additional projects I did too. I made cookies, cakes, and bread for my cooking projects, carefully following the recipes listed in the 4H manual. I entered my baking in the county fair competition and earned blue ribbons.

My first sewing effort was to sew an apron and a pot holder, so Mom and I selected a pattern, blue gingham fabric, and matching blue thread. With Mom's help, I followed the pattern directions and using her cabinet sewing machine, sewed the best apron I could. At the first 4-H meeting, the leader asked questions about the sewing manual. Of course, I hadn't even opened the sewing manual because Mom knew how to sew and had showed me how to do everything. The leader asked me to describe how to tie a knot in the thread after I threaded my needle. I said that I first wound the end of the thread around my finger several times, then gently pushed the needle point between my finger and the wound thread. I would do this four to five times and then pull out my finger, pull the thread tight and there would be a knot at the end of the thread. The leader said that was one way to do it, but she said we should look at the 4-H manual. The first thing you do is wrap the end of the thread around your finger several times and then rub your thumb over the thread several times. Pull the thread off your finger and like magic, a knot is formed.

I was mortified. I hadn't read the manual and everyone knew it. I was embarrassed for me but also secretly embarrassed for Mom because she didn't know everything. Lesson learned. From then on, Mom and I actually read the manual and together we learned. There were so many shortcuts and tricks. Over the years, I picked more difficult sewing projects including skirts, blouses and dresses. Some of the girls sewed dressy suits and formal dresses with sequins and lace, but I didn't bother. I had nowhere to wear such clothing.

CHAPTER 6

Winter

Winter must be cold for those with no warm memories.
—DEBORAH KERR

Sledding and Tobogganing

It always seemed like there were several feet of snow on the ground in the winter and that the drifts were higher than Dad's head. Mom dressed us in layers of clothes, snowsuits, coats, hats, mittens, and boots and sent us out into the cold. "Stay outside and let the stink blow off," Mom told us as she pushed us out the door. We trudged around, had snowball fights, and made snowmen and snow angels. When the drifts were high, we could walk onto the roof of the henhouse. We climbed over the pitched roof and jumped off the other side into soft snow banks. Over and over, we ran to the north side of the henhouse, walked onto the roof, and jumped off the roof on the south side. It was a contest to see who could jump the farthest. The racket might have upset the poor chickens in the henhouse, but then again, chickens aren't very bright. They were warm and toasty in their house, so they probably ignored the loud thumping and clattering.

When we got thirsty, we broke long icicles off the henhouse roof and ate the ice. Mom was mortified when she found out that we were eating icicles. She told us that birds sat on roofs and pooped so when the snow melted and formed an icicle, it had poop in it. "You're eating bird poop! Stop doing that!" So we carefully scrutinized each icicle and if the ice was clear, we figured it was good enough to eat. Our mother was just being silly.

With the first good snowfall, we pulled our sled up the little hill behind the house. If we slid straight east from the windmill, we could avoid the trees on the right and the machinery on the left. The light fluffy snow in western Nebraska wasn't good for sledding until there had been several freeze/thaw cycles and the top crust became icy.

One Christmas, Santa left us a toboggan. There was no label, so we thought it was for all the kids, but clearly it was for Dad too. The best times were when Dad loaded the kids and the toboggan into the back of the pickup and he drove to the bottom of the largest hill in the south pasture. Everyone jumped out of the truck with the toboggan in tow and we tramped through the snow to the top of the hill. "Who wants to be in the front?" Dad asked. Usually, Ronnie wanted to be in front. He sat down first, then I sat down, with my legs straddling Ronnie, then Roy sat down, with his legs straddling me. Dad gave a push and quickly jumped on behind Roy.

While not good for sledding, new, fluffy snow was great for tobogganing. The toboggan flew down the hill, bouncing as it hit every rut. Sometimes it was so rough that everyone fell off halfway down, tumbling into the soft snow. The toboggan kept sliding until it reached the bottom so we chased after it. Ronnie or Dad grabbed the rope handle and we climbed back up the hill. Up and down, up and down we went. After hours of fun, we were cold, wet, and exhausted, so we piled into the pickup and Dad drove home.

We ran into the warm kitchen where hot chocolate was on the stove and freshly baked cookies were waiting on the counter. Off came the boots and wet clothes and we raced to our rooms to put on warm, dry clothes. Mom put the boots upside down on the basement steps and hung the wet clothes on the basement clothesline. She poured hot cocoa for everyone and we sat at the kitchen table, describing the tobogganing adventures.

A few times Mom actually took an afternoon off and went tobogganing with us. We made our parents ride alone on the toboggan once or twice, and Ronnie pushed them as hard as he could so they would go fast. After they started on their way, we ran or toppled down the hill after them. With Mom along for the fun, there were no freshly baked cookies waiting for us when we got home, but Mom still made hot cocoa so we could warm up.

Every so often, Dad towed the toboggan full of kids into the meadow behind his horse. He held the toboggan rope and pulled the toboggan rather slowly through the snow. It wasn't a fast trip but sliding on the snow was still sliding. Climbing up hills dragging a toboggan wasn't required for this game. Dad picked us up by the house and dropped us off in the same place. It was the lazy way to toboggan, Dad said.

Feeding Cattle

Winter meant that Dad was feeding the cattle using the hay wagon pulled by a four-horse or six-horse hitch. Dad positioned the cables; the horses pulled a load of hay onto the wagon and they set off to feed the herds. Several times every winter after he had loaded the hay onto the wagon, Dad walked into the kitchen to gather the kids for an outing. Mom had dressed us in our warm winter gear and we ran out of the house and jumped onto the wagon. Dad climbed onto the front of the wagon and grabbed the reins. We created in a little nest of hay just behind Dad and we snuggled into that cozy place. Once we were set, Dad guided the horses toward the herd of cattle in the meadow. He tied off the reins and moved to the side of the wagon with his pitchfork. At Dad's command, "Hup," the horses walked along slowly in a straight line and Dad pitched piles of hay onto the ground for the cattle. The wagon moved forward until Dad yelled, "Gee," if he wanted the horses to turn left, "Haw," if he wanted the horses to turn right or "Whoa," if he wanted them to stop. We sat in our warm and cozy nest, giggling and teasing each other with bits of hay until the wagon was empty and even our hay nest was on the ground. Dad drove the horses back home and Ronnie, Roy and I either followed Dad to the barn to watch him unhitch the horses, or, if we were freezing, we ran back to the warmth of the house.

Christmas

May you never be too grown up to
search the skies on Christmas eve.

—UNKNOWN

In mid-December of each year, Aunt Mary hosted a Christmas dinner for the Jesses—my grandparents, my aunts and uncles, and all of my cousins. We dressed in our best clothes and drove to the Drake Hotel, the finest hotel in Alliance. We entered the private party room in the basement by going through a small door off the street or by walking down the stairs from the hotel lobby. The room was bright and beautifully decorated with garlands roped around pictures on the wall, candles on a fireplace and a big Christmas tree in the corner. There was a single long table covered with a white linen tablecloth and at each place setting, a white linen napkin, silverware, crystal goblet, and white china plate. When everyone had arrived, the families sat along the sides of the table with a beaming Aunt Mary at the head of the table. Mom helped us order from the menu and we settled in for a fabulous night on the town. Dad, Uncle Vern, and Uncle Tom were served alcoholic drinks in short glasses. Dad only had one or two drinks but Uncle Vern and Uncle Tom always had a few more. One year, my two uncles were tipsy enough to slide down the banister instead of walking down the steps. Everyone turned to watch the spectacle and laughed as they stumbled to their seats. Aunt Mary was generous to host an elegant dinner each year for more than twenty people. This was her Christmas gift to her family and these were grand occasions that I loved.

Throughout December, there were Christmas preparations every week. Mom baked many kinds of Christmas cookies with our help. We ate the cookie dough until Mom told us to stop before we got sick. Mom packed cooled cookies from each batch into containers and stashed them in the freezer. Mom made batches of fudge and divinity candy, but she always had trouble with divinity. She said that no matter what she did, the first batch of divinity was bad—either too soft or too hard or too grainy. The second and third batches were perfect—smooth, creamy, sweet, and delicious.

There were gifts to buy for siblings, for parents, for grandparents, and for cousins whose names we had drawn. On the specified Saturday night in December, we piled into the car and headed to downtown Alliance. Dad took us to buy Mom's gift and Mom took us to buy Dad's.

Mom bought Grandma Jesse and Aunt Mary one pair of stockings each at Rhoades, an upscale women's clothing store. The sales women knew exactly which stockings Grandma wore and which ones Aunt Mary wore, so Mom bought those. "It's something they will like and something they will use," Mom said.

We children got a little money with instructions to buy gifts for our siblings. We headed to the dime store and cruised through the long aisles of trinkets, toys and games until we found the ideal gift. We took the gifts home for wrapping and hiding.

For a few years, Dad cut down a small cedar tree from the windbreak north of the house for our Christmas tree. He shook it hard to dislodge any vermin that might be hiding in the branches before bringing it into the house and placing it in a small tub of wet sand. One year, the tree was too tall, so Dad chopped off the top. With that little haircut, the tree just grazed the ceiling. After that year, all of the cedar trees were too tall so we bought our tree in Alliance. Once the tree was set, Dad strung lights on it and we decorated it with chains of colorful construction-paper loops, strings of popcorn, paper ornaments, some glass bulbs, and a few purchased Christmas baubles. The tree was beautiful and filled the house with a crisp, clean evergreen odor. We carefully placed our wrapped gifts under the tree and waited.

Beginning in mid-December, the local radio station, KCOW, played *The Cinnamon Bear* a serial radio play for children. We loved the play and hovered by the radio listening to the escapades of a small, stuffed bear and his friends. We knew the story by heart, but it didn't matter. We couldn't miss a single episode. While we were occupied by *The Cinnamon Bear*, Mom could complete some of her special preparations.

Mom and Dad made popcorn balls about a week before the school's Christmas program. They popped batch after batch of popcorn in a large kettle and dumped each batch into a huge bowl. When finished with that task, Mom started the syrup. It was a mixture of sugar, corn syrup, water and vinegar, boiled until it reached the soft-crack stage. Mom took the candy off the stove and mixed in butter, baking soda, and food coloring. When it was thoroughly mixed, she poured the molten candy over the popcorn while Dad mixed until every kernel was coated. Mom and Dad then buttered their hands, grabbed portions of the popcorn mixture and formed popcorn balls. They placed the formed balls on waxed paper to set up, then wrapped each ball in a square of waxed paper, twisting the top to seal.

One year, Dad volunteered to pour the candy mixture over the popcorn while Mom stirred. All went well at first but then Dad accidentally poured the three-hundred-degree candy directly onto Mom's hand. She screamed, Dad yelled and we ran into the kitchen to see what was going on. The skin was already peeling off Mom's bright red hand and she was crying. She opened the refrigerator, pulled out the pitcher of milk, and plunged her hand into the ice-cold milk. This seemed to help the pain a little. While Mom supervised with her hand in the milk, Ronnie stirred the popcorn while Dad, very carefully, poured the candy into the bowl. With Mom out of commission, all of the kids helped form the popcorn balls. Dad cleaned up the mess and then put ointment on Mom's hand and bandaged it. He helped around the house whenever he could after that and bandaged Mom's hand every morning and night. Dad never poured the candy mixture over the popcorn again.

On the last day of school before the Christmas break, the children in the one-room school presented a Christmas program. Everyone in the school district was invited, along with grandparents, aunts, uncles, and cousins. Each family brought folding chairs and arranged them everywhere except on a small "stage" area which was about four feet wide and hidden behind sheets strung along a wire. It was crowded and very warm, so a few of the windows were opened a crack. The teacher welcomed guests and the program began. There were short plays and a reenactment of the manger scene, complete with dialogue. One lucky kid got to recite, "The Night Before Christmas," and the program concluded with singing Christmas songs.

After the program, everyone ate candy, popcorn balls and cookies, and drank punch. We gave the teacher her Christmas gift and she gave each child a small token. Finally, the adults helped tidy up the school, removed the chairs they had brought, swept the floor and placed the desks back in their places. After that work was done, we climbed into cars and went home. We were now officially on Christmas vacation.

On Christmas Eve, Dad started work early. He loaded a double load of hay onto the wagon and set off to feed the cattle the two-fold amount. This meant that Dad didn't have to feed cattle on Christmas Day, so after milking on Christmas morning, he would have the day off to spend with us. His work on December 24 took hours and hours but he still milked a little early because we went to the Woodworth's for Christmas Eve dinner.

Christmas Eve with the Woodworth clan was at Grandpa and Grandma's house or at Uncle Merlin's. There was wonderful food including ham and turkey, potatoes, vegetables, salads, and, of course, cakes, pies, cookies, and candy. There were no alcoholic beverages at the celebration because Grandpa and Grandma did not approve of liquor. One Christmas, though, Uncle Merlin spiked the eggnog. I was standing with Dad by the eggnog bowl when Merlin poured in a half bottle of liquor. I stood there wide-eyed because I thought this was very bad. Merlin looked at me, winked and said, "Adults only." I looked at Dad and he just smiled, so I smiled back. Merlin stirred the eggnog, grabbed a cup, filled it, and handed the cup to Grandma Woodworth. "Here Mom," he said. Merlin looked at Dad and winked again. I said nothing, but I stared at Grandma. She took a small sip of the eggnog, then a larger sip and said to Merlin, "This is the best eggnog I have ever had!"

"Thanks Mom," Merlin beamed. He turned and walked quickly into the kitchen. Dad followed and so did I. There was Merlin laughing. Dad grinned at Merlin and shook his head. I didn't quite understand why they thought this trick was funny.

It was nice to spend time with the Woodworths but Roy and I watched the clock. We wanted to go home and go to bed because Santa was coming and wouldn't stop at our house if we weren't asleep in our beds. We nagged Mom about going home and finally we got into the car and drove home. We hung our stockings on the backs of chairs, set out cookies and milk for Santa, pulled on our pajamas, and went to bed.

The next morning, we woke up early but Mom and Dad were already working. Mom had cinnamon rolls ready to go into the oven and Dad was outside milking the cows. We peered at the Christmas tree and at the new gifts that were scattered around. Our stockings were bulging so we knew that there was something in our stockings, too. We couldn't go near the tree or any gifts until Dad came into the house, so we scraped the icy frost off the dining room windows with our fingernails so we could watch for him. At last, there he was with the milk pails. He disappeared into the milk house to separate the milk and cream, and a few minutes later he came out with the separator parts. He rinsed the parts in the hydrant, shook off the excess water, and took them back into the milk house. Then, at last, he was walking up the sidewalk with the milk and cream. He opened the door to screams. "Daddy, Daddy! Santa came! Come look, quick!"

"Yes, yes." Dad laughed, as he handed the milk and cream to our smiling mother. He took off his coat, rubber boots, hat, and gloves and walked to the bathroom to wash up while we jumped around. At last, Dad walked into the living room, so we could too. Dad sat on the piano bench, Mom sat on a dining room chair, and the rest of us sat on the floor next to the tree. Now, the fun could begin.

Ronnie crawled under the tree, retrieved gifts, and delivered the gifts to the rightful owners. All of the gifts had to be delivered before we could begin opening them. Then it was pandemonium. Wrapping paper and ribbon flew. Children ran around showing off a new toy or doll. We got new clothes, new socks, new coats, or new pajamas. Everything was wonderful. Mom and Dad sat smiling as they watched their delighted children and finally opened their own gifts while we sat close and watched anxiously as they opened each box. After the gifts were opened, we looked in our stockings. There would be candy canes, chocolates, an orange and a small gift. For me, the gift was often a necklace or a bracelet to be worn to Christmas dinner a few hours later.

We ate our cinnamon rolls and our oranges. Dad had rolls and oranges but also bacon and eggs and coffee. Mom cleaned up the mess of wrapping paper—picking out the paper with no tears—and folded the paper carefully for use again next year. She also retrieved all of the ribbon and bows for reuse another time.

Mom cleaned the kitchen and prepared the food she would take to the Jesse Christmas dinner. When it was time to go, we changed into our best Christmas clothes, loaded Mom's food into the trunk of the car, and set off for family time with the Jesses. Holidays with the Jesse clan rotated locations. One family hosted Easter, another hosted Thanksgiving, and another hosted Christmas. During the fall of each year, the ladies of the family sorted out who would host each holiday. Christmas was the best holiday for the kids, but Mom was always glad to get her hosting turn over for a few years because the Christmas hostess had to prepare a lot of food and had to have a tidy house when everyone showed up. This was a challenging task when there were a bunch of kids who had opened new gifts, played with new toys, and generally made a disaster of the house. Mom dutifully took her turn, though, and gladly turned it over to others for the next few years.

Around noon on Christmas Day, each family arrived at the assigned Christmas dinner house. The hostess provided the meat, potatoes and a side dish or two and coordinated with the other women on other dishes. The assignments included breads, salads, side dishes and desserts. Aunt Lois always brought oyster dressing and Mom always brought a rice salad with marshmallows, canned pineapple, and walnuts, dressed with copious amounts of sweetened whipped cream. Each family also brought folding tables and folding chairs, and the tables were set up everywhere in the living room, dining room, family room, and kitchen. There had to be a place for each man, woman, and child to sit. Sometimes the men placed several tables end to end, making one long table. This was fine as long as there were not thirteen places at the table. Grandma Jesse was very superstitious. There was the usual avoidance of black cats crossing your path or walking under ladders, but she was especially adamant about sitting thirteen people at a table. If there were exactly thirteen at the table it meant that a loved one would die within the next year. Grandma would be frantic if someone accidentally set the table for thirteen. She grabbed the thirteenth place setting and squeezed it onto another table or simply squeezed in a fourteenth setting for a small child.

[I was skeptical about my grandmother's thirteen-at-a-table superstition until 2018. At a family lunch in December of 2017, I found myself seated with twelve others. I was anxious and there was a gnawing in my stomach. I shrugged it off, telling myself that just because my grandmother was superstitious about thirteen at a table, it didn't mean that superstitions were real. The next month, my brother-in-law Frank died, and three months later, my mother-in-law Helen died. In my head, I could be rational and tell myself that the events were unrelated and coincidental, but in my heart, I believed Grandma Jesse's superstition and will never, ever sit at a table with twelve others.]

Before dinner was served, it was time for libations. Grandpa Jesse brought a jug or two of Mogen David wine, a sweet, thick red wine that tasted like cough syrup but it didn't matter. Everyone, including the children, got a glass of wine. The adults had a regular wine glass but the kids got an ounce or two in a shot glass. We children sat at our assigned table and sipped our wine. It tasted terrible but we didn't admit that to anyone. If we complained about the taste, we might not get wine next year.

After wine, many of the grownups moved on to beer or bourbon. The men sat in the living room, waiting for dinner to be served. They smoked cigarettes until the air was hazy, they drank their drinks, told stories, and laughed.

The women were busy in the kitchen, making final dinner preparations, and more often than not, Uncle Tom brought glasses of beer into the kitchen for the ladies. For Mom, that meant red beer, a mixture of one-half beer and tomato juice. Uncle Tom lingered in the kitchen, flirting with his wife and his two sisters-in-law. He called Mom Ginger to needle her since he knew she didn't like being called Ginger.

Finally, the ladies lined up the food on the counters, on the stovetop, and on the table in the kitchen. They prepared plates for the small children, and when the little ones were seated, the men went through the buffet line, then the older children, and finally the women. You could go through the line often but you had to eat everything on your plate before you could get more or go back for dessert. Cakes, pies, cookies, and candy were lined up along with a huge bowl of whipped cream. Aunt Eleanor loved whipped cream, and if any was left, she finished it off with a large serving spoon.

After dinner, tables were cleared and the men broke out the playing cards. Again, cigarette smoke filled the air, the men laughed and they told stories. Young children played with their toys while the older girls and the women put away leftovers, washed and dried dishes, and cleaned up the kitchen. After that, the card games were put on hold and everyone opened gifts.

The aunts, uncles, and cousins had exchanged names so everyone got one gift in the exchange. However, each family bought Grandpa and Grandma and Aunt Mary gifts. Grandpa and Grandma bought each of the grandchildren gifts, generally something useful like a sweater or socks or mittens, plus a lot of candy. After gift opening, the men went back to the card games and the women sat in the living room and talked. When it was time for supper, the women laid out the food and people lined up to fill their plates. After supper was cleared, the women packaged leftovers and put them on the cold front porch for storage until people went home.

CHAPTER 7

Neighbors, Telephones, and Saturday Nights

Good fences make good neighbors.
—Robert Frost

The Hired Man and the Spies

Our closest neighbor was the hired man who lived next door in the little house. Chuck Salzbaugh worked for Dad for several years so Roy and I became comfortable around Chuck, his wife Doris, and their baby boy. When Roy and I were bored with summer games, we knocked on the Salzbaugh's door, asking to visit the baby and then chattered on about silly, meaningless topics. Mrs. S. likely had work to do but didn't want to be too short with the boss's kids, so she was patient with us. Once, while we sat outside on their front step with the baby, we watched cows lick a salt block just beyond the fence. Feeling smug, we told Mrs. S. that we loved salt because it was good for you. Mrs. S. said that if that was the case, we should just go lick that salt block. "Oh, no! There are germs all over the block. Cow tongues and slobber are germy. It wouldn't be good for us," we argued. Mrs. S. was insistent and told us that the germs would be gone if we let the salt block dry. If the cow slobber was dry, the cow germs would be gone, and it would be safe. She probably had no idea we were so gullible, but we agreed with her logic. We left our perch on the steps and ran to the salt block, shooing away the cows standing next to it. Roy and I then stood by the block, shielding it from the cows. The block didn't dry as fast as we wanted, so we fanned it with our hands, touching it periodically to see if it was dry. At last, it was only a little tacky to the touch so we decided it was dry enough. We knelt next to the block and licked away until we started to feel queasy. Mrs. S. watched us for a while and then took the baby inside.

Later that summer, Roy and I decided that we needed to keep track of the Salzbaughs. Their behavior was, after all, a little suspicious and we thought they might be communist spies. The best vantage point for spying would be from above, so we began to build a treehouse in a tall tree behind our house. We didn't choose the tree closest to the hired man's house, but one tree to the left. We still had a good vantage point for spying, but the first tree would shield us from Mrs. S. She wouldn't even know we were there.

We gathered old wood from Dad's woodpile, hammers, and nails, and set about constructing a tree house, a.k.a. platform, eight to ten feet above the ground. First, we nailed short boards to the tree trunk as a makeshift ladder. We put a few boards across two sturdy limbs and nailed them down for our floor and then nailed up vertical and horizontal boards as a railing and to camouflage the platform. For more camouflage, we broke off small leafy branches and wove them around the boards.

It took us about two weeks to build our house because we had to work around our chores, around meals, and around our other required activities, like playing cowboy or harassing Mrs. S. We were very proud of our treehouse and were sure no one knew it was there. Never mind that there had been a lot of hammering, laughter, and general ruckus in and around the tree.

We took cans of water and paper bags full of cookies or popcorn to our treehouse and sat there, watching Mrs. Salzbaugh. Whenever she did anything outside, we were quiet as mice and peered out to see what Mrs. S. was doing. She went to the outhouse, washed clothes, and hung them on her clothesline. She played with the baby and carried on with her chores with two annoying little brats watching her every move. It must have been tiresome, but if we were in our treehouse, that meant we weren't knocking on her front door making ludicrous statements.

Sadly, we didn't observe any suspicious actions or any communist activity (whatever that was). After a few weeks of observation, the spies got bored and moved on to other activities. After that we only used the treehouse to hide from Mom.

More Neighbors

The next closest neighbors were Uncle Vern and Aunt Lois, who lived a half mile north. Since Lois was Dad's sister, we were close to these neighbors both geographically and personally. Mom and Lois were close, but Mom was an incredibly private person and didn't share secrets or intimate personal information, even with Lois. Their daughter Debbie and I were fast friends. Dad and Uncle

Vern traded work. In the winter, they helped each other with feeding if one of them had broken bones or was out of town. In the spring, they helped each other move cattle from pasture to pasture, mend fences and windmills, and brand calves. In the summer, they helped each other with haying, and in the fall, they helped each other move cattle or load calves for sale. As families, we went to the same holiday and birthday celebrations, the same fishing trips, and the same Sunday dinners.

Earl and Lillian Bauer were our neighbors a mile and a half south. Earl Bauer's father was Great Grandma Anna Jesse's brother, so we were distantly related. The couple had three children. Marvin and Betty were older than us but the youngest, Kathy, was Roy's age. Earl was hardworking; Lillian was reserved and kind. We didn't interact with the Bauer's much outside of school-related activities, but Dad and Earl helped each other and traded work as needed.

Another neighbor had a ranch a number of miles east of our place. We didn't interact much with the family but Dad shared work periodically and our families were friendly. Every year, the couple hosted a revival-type gathering at their ranch and they invited us to share a midday meal with the group of one hundred people. Dad thought he was obligated to accept the invitation, so we always went to the affair. Long tables were set up in a shed, and we were served steak and potatoes, vegetables and salads, and desserts. After the meal, the wife took us on a grand tour of the setup. Men slept on cots in the barn, women slept on cots in a machine shed, children slept in the hay loft where there were rows of small beds and cradles. Several women were responsible for watching the children, other women were responsible for cooking, and others for cleanup. Men went to revival lectures and sermons but it seemed like they didn't do any work. After the tour, we went into the ranch house with the wife. She kept parakeets and her living room was filled with bird cages. She took the birds out of their cages and let them fly around the room. They landed on her shoulders and she stroked their beautiful, brightly-colored feathers. She taught one colorful parakeet to say "Maynard." She would say, "Maynard," and the parakeet would reply, "Maynard," in a high-pitched, nasal-sounding voice, similar to the woman's voice. It was hilarious.

When the couple retired, one of their sons took over ranch operations. He married a stern woman and they had three children—two boys and a girl. The daughter moved away, but the boys stayed on the ranch and eventually wreaked havoc. One afternoon, the older son flew into a rage and violently stabbed his mother and father. Both were severely injured but survived. The son was arrested, tried, found guilty, and sentenced to many years in the state penitentiary. While the parents' wounds healed, they never recovered from the trauma of the attack and feared the day when their son would be released from prison.

A few years after the difficulties with the oldest son, there were problems with the younger. The father was in a horrific accident and broke his back. The doctors didn't believe that he would survive so the wife was terrified of life alone on the ranch. The son comforted her and said he would take care of everything. All she had to do was sign over ownership of the land, the ranch buildings, and the equipment to him. She could stay in the house and he would make sure she had everything she needed to be comfort-able. If, by some miracle, the father survived, the son told her that he would return the property to his father and mother's ownership. Papers were drawn up and the wife signed over everything, except ownership of the cattle and a small ranch and house several miles west.

Many weeks later, the man miraculously recovered and his wife took him home. With this turn of events, they thanked their son for all he had done and said they would take the ranch back. Their attorney drew up papers to return ownership to the parents but the son refused to sign the documents. He told them it was best that he owned the ranch and everything else and said that they needed to move out of the house because he was going to move in. The parents were shocked and refused to move. For a time, it was a standoff. The parents stayed in their house and tried to convince the son to sign the papers they had drawn up. The son continued to refuse and took steps to get rid of the parents once and for all. This son wasn't into the whole attempted murder thing but hatched a devious plan. He told the county sheriff that there were trespassers living in his house. He produced the papers that his mother had signed and the sheriff agreed to evict the trespassers. The son suggested that it would be best to handle the evictions separately because there would be less commotion. The son watched and waited until his father rode into the hills to check on his cattle, which would take several hours. He called the sheriff, and the sheriff arrived to evict the woman. She refused to leave so the sheriff and his deputy dragged the woman, kicking and screaming, out of the house. The father came over a hill, saw the unfolding drama, raced home to rescue his wife, but he was also arrested. The son pressed trespassing charges and asked the sheriff to hold his parents in the county jail. The couple was in one county jail for about two weeks before being transferred to another county jail for two more weeks.

While the parents were in jail, the son implemented Step 2 of his plan. He loaded his parent's cattle into semi-trucks, trucked the cattle to a stock sale and pocketed the cash from the sale, even though the cattle still belonged to the parents. Nebraska law requires brand inspection for any sale of cattle, so the sale should have been invalid since the son could not provide proof of ownership. But the law was ignored, and while the parents were locked in the county jail, their son rustled their cattle and sold them. He now had a ranch and hundreds of thousands of dollars in cash. He didn't take possession of the small ranch that his mother had not signed over, so after the couple was released from jail, they moved to that ranch and put their lives together. They never again talked openly about their two sons—the one who tried to kill them and the other who stole nearly everything.

Other neighbors lived south of Highway 2. One family included Roland, his wife Connie, and their two kids. Mom was friendly with Connie, and Mom, Sharyl, Rick and I visited Connie and her kids quite often. This was unusual because Mom didn't go to neighbors' houses to visit. She didn't trust people, was cautious and exceptionally private. Connie was boisterous and funny, the opposite of Mom, but the two clearly had a connection. They sat in the living room, drank coffee, and talked and laughed. Roland could also be funny, but he was an alcoholic. Roland had been in the army during WW II and Mom told me that he started to drink in the army and couldn't stop. He was a mean drunk, especially mean toward Connie so Mom was somewhat protective of her friend.

Roland helped Dad with branding and the two shared work. Roland was a skilled horseman but new to ranching.

He ended up depending on Dad, a lot. He called Dad at all hours and Dad would talk him through a task or would drive to Roland's to help. It got out of hand after a time since Roland was not only needy but he hated to drink alone. He persuaded Dad to join him, and there were times when Dad didn't come home until very late, leaving Mom alone and stewing. One time, Dad didn't come home until morning. Supposedly, one of Roland's cows was very sick and Roland had no idea what to do. The explanation didn't fly with Mom. She was fed up and told Dad that it was either Roland or her. To prove the point, she packed a few clothes, took the car, and drove to her parents' house. Ronnie, Roy, and I had chicken pox at the time, so it turned into a royal mess. I didn't know what was going on, but I knew that I was sick and Mom was gone. Dad did his best to treat the chicken pox. He had a bottle of calamine lotion, and with a cotton ball, dabbed calamine on each of our red bumps. He always propped the bottle on the bed while he dabbed away and unsurprisingly the bottle tipped over one evening. The pink stuff spilled onto the white chenille bedspread before Dad could right the bottle. Dad was upset. His face was red, but he didn't say a word. He wiped up the spilled lotion with a towel and continued dabbing the pink spots. Mom came home the next day and she took over chicken pox duty. I think that was the first and last time that Mom left Dad.

Dad kept his distance from Roland after that, but he did help when he could and when Mom said it was OK. Connie later divorced Roland and just disappeared with the two children. Mom never heard from her again. Not too long after the divorce, Roland left his ranch. Dad rented the land and began to manage that four thousand-acre ranch along with the home place and the Case place. For months, Dad said that he found cases and cases of beer hidden everywhere. The beer was in the barn, in the outbuildings, in auto gates, under windmill towers—everywhere. After Roland moved, he continued to call Dad every few months. Mom said that Dad was Roland's only friend.

Another small family—husband, wife and two kids— lived many miles south of Highway 2. The wife, Jenny, worked alongside her husband on the ranch—haying, calving, branding, etc. Jenny also did all of the household duties—cooking, cleaning, laundry, and child-raising. I don't know how she managed to work in the fields and pastures all day and still cook three meals a day, keep a beautiful home, and raise the children. I suppose she worked twenty hours a day. We weren't terribly close with the family, but Dad shared work with the man, just like everyone else. As I got older, I thought I wanted to help in the hay fields like Jenny, but Mom refused. "It isn't good for girls to work alongside men in the fields. Work like that makes girls too rough," she told me.

The couple's son was a bully, and when he took over ranch operations, he began to bully his parents. There was trouble with the parents' marriage and Jenny moved to an apartment in Alliance. The husband, who remained on the ranch, complained that his son was trying to kill him. He called the sheriff, but the sheriff couldn't help. Finally, the husband moved to eastern Nebraska. With her estranged husband gone, Jenny moved back into her old house on the ranch. She renovated the house and then trouble began. The power lines to her house were severed, her phone line was cut and windows were broken. Someone lurked around the house after dark, tapping on the windows. For a while Jenny was annoyed and a little frightened but she didn't fear for her life. She refused to leave her home. Soon things got worse. Small fires were set close to the house. Her car tires had nails driven into them and the brake fluid was drained. Someone tampered with the gas line from the propane tank into the house, and if it hadn't been for safety measures installed by the propane dealer, the house would have filled with propane and Jenny would have died. Jenny tried to hold on, but her son kept threatening her—telling his mother that someday he would kill her. In the end, she gave up and moved away. She drove back to Alliance once to visit my parents, but she still feared her son and believed his spies would see her car. She was sure that he would sneak into Mom and Dad's house during the night and kill everyone. Dad moved his car out of the garage and put Jenny's car inside. He told Jenny that no one would guess that she was visiting, and she could stay as long as she wanted. Still, Jenny couldn't shake her paranoia and drove home after just a few days. She never visited my parents again and my parents weren't able visit her. Jenny died a few years later, still terrified of her son.

Party Lines

Everyone in our neighborhood had a telephone hanging on an outside wall. It looked like the telephones in old movies. It was a wooden box about eight inches deep, twenty inches tall and eight inches wide. The earpiece hung on the left and was corded into the phone box. The crank was on the right. A person would speak into the mouthpiece that protruded from the front and could be swiveled up or down, and a small shelf under the mouthpiece was used for writing notes. The telephone was battery operated, and twisted pairs of wires connected the phone to the telephone line outside the house. We were on a party line which meant that all of the phones on our line were connected. There were eight to ten families on our line but I only remember three numbers. Our number was 15F22. Uncle Vern's was 15F12, and the neighbors to the east had 15F02.

The number 15 meant that ours was the fifteenth party line on the Alliance Central Phone Exchange. F meant it was a farm line. (If you lived in Alliance, you had a C in your number.) The final two numbers represented the number of long rings and the number of short rings required to alert that particular household of in incoming call. Our number ended in 2 2 and that meant that the operator rang two long rings, then two short rings. If you wanted to call someone on your line, you just cranked the phone for the correct number of rings. Every customer on the line heard all rings. You just picked up the receiver when you heard your specific ring, or if you were snoopy, you picked up and listened to your neighbor's phone calls.

If you needed to call someone not on the party line, you had to call Central. The ring to alert Central was one long ring. The central operator in Alliance answered, you told the operator the number you wanted to call and the operator pressed a button on the switchboard to manually ring the number desired. She connected you when someone answered but if no one answered, the operator told you there was no answer and disconnected. You tried the call again later.

The emergency ring for the party line was one long and one short. The central operator made this ring a priority and answered immediately. It was the 911 of the 1940s, '50s, and early '60s. The emergency ring was only used in true emergencies, like an urgent call to the doctor or a call to report a range fire. If the phone line was engaged, you interrupted the conversation and told the people that you had an emergency. They hung up, you rang one long and one short and everyone on the party line picked up their receivers to learn what was going on. There would be a click every time someone picked up and with so many people on the line, sound volume and quality was very poor. It was hard to hear the operator and sometimes you had to yell into the speaker.

Phone lines were attached to short poles (probably twelve to fourteen feet tall) and generally followed fence lines. The lines ran from those poles to a location on the outside of each home. Wire was then connected to the wall phone. There were two wires; one wire was for the incoming sound and the other wire was for outgoing sound. When the phones didn't work, it was up to the people connected to the line to determine the problem. Someone either drove a four-wheeldrive truck or rode a horse along the line to see where the line was down on the ground or where it was broken altogether. Lines went down in strong winds or if cattle pushed the pole over far enough for the line to touch the ground. Dad and other ranchers were able to repair the lines in most cases.

In the summer, lightning often struck the phone line, knocking out the phones. If the lightning strike was close to our house, blue flames spewed out of the mouthpiece with a loud crack, and if the door between the kitchen and dining room was open, the flames hit the door and scorched it a little. We obviously stayed clear of the phone whenever there was a thunder storm.

One summer Earl Bauer drove to our place because his phone was out and he wanted to know if ours was out too. Our phone was fine, so that meant the problem was isolated between the main line and the Bauer house. Dad and Earl drove back to Earl's and looked at the lines. They saw that lightning had hit the barn where the phone wires were attached before the wires continued on to the house. There were scorch marks on the barn and the burned wire. Earl said he was lucky that the barn hadn't caught on fire.

Party lines were great for facilitating gossip. A bored ranch wife picked up the receiver whenever the phone rang for any household. She held her hand over the mouthpiece and listened. You knew when someone picked up the phone when you were in a conversation because there was a click that told you someone had picked up. If there was another click quickly, it meant that the person had hung up. If there was no second click, the eavesdropper was bored and curious to see what was happening in the neighborhood.

Saturday Nights

Through the 1950s and 1960s, Saturday nights in downtown Alliance were social events. My parents did a little shopping, engaged in small talk with neighbors, and discussed news events. We cleaned up, put on good clothes, ate a quick supper, and drove to town. Merchants in Alliance depended on trade from farmers and ranchers so they kept late hours on Saturday, closing at eight o'clock in the evening. Dad usually found a place to park along Fourth or Fifth Street and we piled out of the car. Mom or Dad gave us a dime or quarter allowance, and Ronnie, Roy and I ran off on our own. The first stop was the dime store to look at the trinkets and toys. The next stop was the candy store, where we bought cinnamon bears, candy cigarettes, or bubble gum cigars. We took our newly purchased treasures to the car to play with our trinkets and "smoke" candy cigarettes. Meanwhile, Mom and Dad shopped. There were three department stores: Penney's, Murphy's and Montgomery Ward. There were women's clothing stores, including Rhodes and Sweet Briar. The high-end men's store was The Famous. There were also western clothing stores, candy stores, dime stores, drug stores with soda fountains, a movie theater, a photographer, car dealerships, banks, and the Drake Hotel. There was a large shoe store with an x-ray machine that was used to check the fit of a shoe on a child's foot. I always wanted to buy shoes at this store, but Mom and Dad were uncomfortable with the advertisement: "We'll X-Ray Your Child's Feet for Free." Mom and Dad never bought shoes for us in that store so I never got a foot x-ray.

There were a few stores south of Third Street on Box Butte, but mostly bars lined the avenue on both sides all the way to First Street, where the train depot was situated. The Alliance Hotel, a three-story hotel directly across First Street from the train depot was popular among travelers. There were always people coming and going from the depot to the hotel. Mom said the hotel wasn't as nice as the Drake Hotel, but it was apparently OK.

One evening, Mom saw a bright red winter coat in a shop window. She tried on the coat. It was a perfect fit and in her favorite color. She put it on hold and went to find Dad. She told him about the coat and asked if she could buy it. Dad asked the price and when Mom told him, he told her no because they couldn't afford it. She could buy it after they sold the calves. "But I love it," Mom replied. "It's so beautiful. They won't have that coat later this fall." Dad still refused and Mom cried all the way home. As she predicted, the coat was gone by the time they sold the calves.

Mom and Dad often shopped quickly so they could talk to neighbors. On every corner, a group of adults with small children in tow gathered to talk. The Cold War was raging in the 1950s, so some of the corner conversations were about the state of US/Soviet Russia relations. Paranoid citizens were fearful of nuclear war, and in 1955, President Eisenhower told citizens that they should keep a seven-day supply of food and water—just in case. He also suggested that fallout shelters were a good investment. Neighbors told my parents that some Alliance residents were building fallout shelters in their basements. I asked Dad about building a fallout shelter, but he said a shelter would be too expensive to build and besides, he didn't think that a shelter would do much good anyway.

CHAPTER 8

Elementary School

Sheridan County Nebraska, District # 124

No one can look back on school days and say with truth that they were altogether unhappy.

—George Orwell

Kindergarten—September 1954–May 1955

My first school was a one-room schoolhouse in Aunt Maime's meadow. Grandpa Jesse's sister Maime married a man named Kraus and they lived on a homestead west of us. Maime's son and his family moved onto the homestead several years after Dad and Mom moved to the home place in 1949. The schoolhouse was built on Aunt Maime's place because the location was more or less in the center of Sheridan County's School District # 124.

It was about three miles from our house to school. We drove west, through the south pasture, up a cut between two hills, through the summer range, and finally through the last auto gate, where we entered the Kraus place. The schoolhouse was about a half mile west of the auto gate in the meadow. Either Mom drove us or the teacher picked us up on her way to school.

The schoolhouse was small, about twenty feet by twenty feet and the yard was surrounded on all sides by a barbed wire fence to keep the Kraus's cattle out of the schoolyard. A lean-to building attached to the south side of the schoolhouse had a door facing east and a wooden counter on the west. A window on the south side of the lean-to was flanked by coat hooks at different heights for children's coats and hats. The door into the schoolroom was on the north side of the lean-to.

There was no running water, but a water bucket and a small, tin washing basin was on the wooden counter in the lean-to. Every morning, the teacher selected one or two kids to bring in water from the water pump in the schoolyard. The kid(s) emptied water left from the previous day and pumped fresh water into the bucket. The children carried the water into the lean-to and lifted the bucket onto the counter next to the basin. We used a tin water dipper to pour water from the bucket into a drinking glass or into the water basin for washing.

Inside the schoolroom, there were windows along the east and west walls and sunlight streamed into the small room all day. A propane heater in the center of the room warmed the room in the winter. A piano was in the south-west corner and the teacher's desk and chair were backed up close to the north wall. There were two small chairs in front of the teacher's desk, and the children's desks were lined up in two rows facing the teacher. The teacher had a blackboard on the wall behind her and there were blackboards on the walls between the windows on the east and west sides of the room. A closet holding text books, workbooks, paper, pencils, crayons, and other school supplies was located next to the door in the southeast corner. The teacher purchased all of the school supplies and she was reimbursed by the school board.

Outside the schoolhouse on the west side, we played on a tall metal slide, two swings, and a see-saw or teeter-totter. The outdoor toilet (outhouse) was a bit north of the playground. In the winter we didn't drink too much water because we didn't want to put on our coats and run to the outhouse because it was just too cold. We didn't drink much water in the spring or fall either because with warmer weather, the outhouse reeked. A small corral north of the outhouse was used for years when kids rode horses to school but by the time Ronnie started school in 1949, children no longer rode horses to school. The corral was dismantled in the mid-1950s.

During the summer of 1954 the REA (Rural Electrification Association) linemen completed construction of the electric power line to the school. District #124 was the last school in the state of Nebraska to be electrified, so the event was front-page news in the *Alliance Times Herald*. A newspaper photographer and a reporter were there on my first day of kindergarten. The reporter wrote down everything the teacher said about having electric lights in the school, and the photographer wanted a photo of the smiling country children to accompany the story. He lined us up beside the teacher but I was terrified. I cried hysterically and even Mom couldn't console me long enough for a photo. Finally, our teacher, Mrs. Kistler, said, "Just come stand next to me for the photo. I'll hold you and I promise you'll be fine." I agreed and I stood next to Mrs. Kistler at her desk while the rest of the kids dutifully stood beside us.

In 1954 there were six kids enrolled in our school. Ronnie was eleven and in fifth grade. Gina was ten and also in fifth grade. Gina lived on the west end of the school district and her dad drove her to school. Roy and our neighbor, Kathy Bauer, were seven and in second grade. Russell Kraus and I were five and in kindergarten. Russell lived in the ranch house about a half mile north of the school.

Mrs. Kistler lived in Alliance with her husband Leo and their two children. She drove her car to and from Alliance each day, but that winter the snow drifts were exceptionally deep. Earl Bauer convinced Mrs. K. to leave her car at his place and she could drive his jeep the rest of the way to the school. Earl's army surplus jeep was sturdy and reliable, even when the snow was deep. The trouble was that those old jeeps had a narrow wheel base and the auto gate south of our house had a wider than normal center hole. With the narrow wheel base on the jeep, if the driver didn't hit the auto gate straight on, a front or rear wheel dropped into the center hole. The first time Mrs. Kistler drove the jeep, she dropped a front wheel into the auto gate. Mrs. Kistler left the jeep in the auto gate and walked the half mile to our house to get help. Dad wasn't home so Mom called Earl Bauer for help. Earl drove to the auto gate and showed Mrs. Kistler how to "bounce" the jeep out of the auto gate. All she had to do was engage the jeep's four-wheel drive, which allowed the three wheels on solid ground to pull the jeep out of the hole. With that bit of knowledge, Mrs. Kistler was fearless. She dropped that jeep into the auto gate over and over and she thought it was fun to bounce it free.

Mrs. Kistler was smart, energetic, and athletic. She kept strong control over the children, but enjoyed playing with us during recess. We had one recess in the morning, one recess in the afternoon, and another recess after lunch if we ate quickly. We played on the playground equipment or, when there weren't any cattle outside the fence, we played games in the meadow. Games included tag, kick-the-can, and pump, pump pull-away. In pump, pump pull-away, children held tight to the barbed wire fence outside the school yard and the person who was "it" tried to catch a child running across the pasture toward a second fence about ten yards away. If the running child was touched by "it" before grabbing the second fence, he or she became "it." Of course, grabbing a barbed wire fence came with its own hazards and most of us suffered periodic bloody punctures courtesy of a sharp barb.

During the school day, Mrs. Kistler taught each grade's lessons, beginning with the youngest. She called each grade class to her desk for their lessons in reading, grammar, spelling, history, geography, math, and penmanship. Mrs. K. would say, "Kindergarten reading, come up." Russell and I took our reading books, sat in the chairs in front of the teacher's desk, and began reading aloud, "See Dick run, See Jane run, See Spot run." I read two pages, then Russell read two pages, then I read, then Russell and so on. When our lesson was finished, Mrs. Kistler gave us our assignment and we returned to our desks. Next, she called second grade reading so Roy and Kathy took their books to the front of the room for their lesson. Finally, it was the sixth graders turn, so Ronnie and Gina took their books to the chairs by the teacher.

We used both textbooks and workbooks for our classes. In grammar, we learned about subjects, verbs, verb conjugation, prepositions, adverbs, adjectives, pronouns, sentence structure, punctuation, etc. As soon as we could read and write, we diagrammed sentences at the blackboard. Spelling and math lessons were also conducted at the blackboard in addition to our workbooks. The teacher supplemented our books with maps and a globe for geography and history lessons. Kindergarteners learned to print upper- and lower-case letters and we printed work until third grade when we learned cursive. All lessons were completed in cursive after that.

Mrs. Kistler played the piano and nearly every day we had a music lesson. This was a group activity so all grades participated together. We sang patriotic songs, ballads or religious songs, but after Thanksgiving, we sang Christmas carols and songs.

The summer before I started school, there was an "accident" and Mom got pregnant. In March, she went to the hospital to have the baby and while Ronnie was old enough to stay at home with Dad, Roy and I were shuffled off to the Bauer's to spend a few days. Lillian Bauer drove us to school with Kathy, picking up Ronnie on the way. I shared Kathy's room and Roy shared a room with the oldest son, Marvin. All went well for a few days and then Roy and I turned into horrible, bratty, spoiled children. We didn't play nicely with Kathy and picked fights with her. We ganged-up on her a few times and Lillian had to come to Kathy's rescue. I can only imagine Earl and Lillian's relief when Mom and Dad pulled into their drive to take us home.

My little sister, Sharyl was born on Grandma Woodworth's birthday, and Sharyl must have channeled Iva because she was sweet and good-natured like Grandma. I was enamored with Sharyl because she seemed like a real live doll. I begged Mom to let Sharyl move into my little bedroom, but Sharyl slept in a bassinette in the corner of the master bedroom. Mom said that Sharyl was too little to share my room and I had to wait until someday when Sharyl was older. Sharyl was a bottle baby so Mom bought cases of canned, condensed Pet milk at the grocery store. She diluted the milk with boiled and cooled water and mixed in a little Karo syrup and some vitamins before pouring the concoction into sterilized bottles. She stored the prepared bottles in the refrigerator until feeding time. I thought it was peculiar that Mom fed Pet milk to Sharyl because I was sure that people in cities fed Pet milk to pets. Giving it to Sharyl seemed very wrong, even though she clearly liked the stuff.

Grade 1—September 1955–May 1956

There were seven kids in school this term. Ronnie and Gina were in sixth grade, Roy and Kathy were in third grade, Russell and I were in first grade and Russell's little brother Ronnie started kindergarten. Russell and I were often chosen to get water for the day because we worked well together and because this allowed the older children to start their lessons. One fall day, Russell and I walked into the lean-to and grabbed the bucket. I looked inside to see how much water was left, and much to my horror, along with a small amount of water, there was a tiny dark animal in the bottom of the bucket. My eyes widened and I looked at Russell. He looked at me and then into the bucket and promptly dropped it. We ran inside, screaming, "Mrs. Kistler, Mrs. Kistler, there's a bat in the water bucket!" Mrs. Kistler was writing on the blackboard, and said, "No, there isn't." We repeated, "Yes, there is! Yes, it's true!" Reluctantly, Mrs. K. walked around her desk and went with us into the lean-to. She grabbed the handle of the bucket, picked it up and looked inside. She yelled,

"It's a BAT," and dropped the bucket. The other students left their seats, ran into the lean-to, and peered into the bucket. Everyone turned to stare at Mrs. K.

Upon composing herself, Mrs. K. grabbed the bucket and took it to the far north side of the school yard where she heaved the water and the bat over the fence. She phoned Mom and told her that we had bats in the schoolhouse and she would like someone to come over to get rid of them. She turned to us and said that we couldn't use the bucket for water until it was thoroughly cleaned. We would have to wash our hands and fill our water glasses at the pump for the rest of the day. She said she would take the bucket home that night and clean it. While she did take the bucket home with her, the next morning, she came back with a bright, shiny new water bucket. Dad and Earl Bauer drove to the schoolhouse the next weekend and found the place where the bats were getting into the lean-to. Somehow, they got the bats out and plugged the hole. The bats never came back.

Mrs. Kistler was a proponent of enrichment opportunities, especially important for ranch children who lived isolated lives. She arranged annual field trips to several venues to help expand our horizons. She arranged a tour of the Great Western sugar beet plant in Scottsbluff and enlisted a couple of the mothers to drive. She divided the students among the cars and we headed off in a caravan to Scottsbluff. The sugar plant's tour guide took us through the entire process beginning with the sugar beets stored in enormous piles on the ground next to the factory. We watched the beets being scooped up and dumped into large vats. We saw and smelled the beet slurry and at the end of the process, we watched as the fine, white sugar was poured into bags. When the tour ended, the guide gave each of us a few white sugar cubes to eat. The trip was great fun and everyone agreed that Great Western sugar was the best.

We also went to Scottsbluff's Cawley's Potato Chip factory. We walked with the guide along the conveyor belt. We saw potatoes sliced into thick slices, rinsed, dried, and then dunked into boiling oil. After the dip into the hot oil, piles of warm chips were salted and dumped into bags. We each got a small bag of Cawley's chips at the end of the tour as a souvenir. We all agreed that Cawley's potato chips were the best.

Grade 2—September 1956–May 1957

There were still seven kids in school. All of us had advanced one year but the routine remained the same. Just like last year, Mom packed our lunches in metal lunch boxes that had colorful characters like Mickey Mouse or the Lone Ranger printed on the lid. The matching thermos was printed with the same character. Mom sent a sandwich, an apple or orange, cookies, and milk in the thermos. We often had fried egg sandwiches because we had dozens of eggs, but Mom also made left-over beef or ham sandwiches and sometimes to mix it up, bologna sandwiches. I did not like the taste, texture, and smell of bologna and told Mom to just make butter and lettuce sandwiches for me on days when she made bologna for the boys. "What?" she said, "You can't just have lettuce and bread. That's not enough. It's not good" But I was insistent. I told her that I hated bologna and wouldn't eat it if she sent it. I think Mom relented because she didn't want to waste food or maybe because I was spoiled rotten. At any rate, from then on if she sent bologna for Roy and Ronnie, she sent butter and lettuce for me.

One day that fall, Roy got sick and Mrs. Kistler told him to call Mom so she could come and pick him up. Roy wasn't tall enough to easily reach the phone hanging on the wall. He stood on a stool, reached over his head, grasped the receiver with his left hand, and then put his left hand on the mouthpiece to steady himself. Unfortunately, he accidentally put one of the fingers of his left hand into the hole in the middle of the mouthpiece. He cranked the ringer with his right hand. He meant to crank two longs and two shorts but managed one long ring and started the second long when the finger that was in the mouthpiece touched the phone's "hot" wire and he got shocked by the current. Roy dropped the receiver and tumbled to the floor. By ringing one long and one short, it was an emergency call. Everyone on the party line picked up and so did the central operator in Alliance. Mrs. Kistler jumped out of her chair, knocking it over with a clatter in the process and raced toward the phone. She leaped over Roy, picked up the receiver, and yelled into the speaker, "Sorry, sorry everyone, this was a mistake. One of the children was trying to call his mother but he slipped and called emergency by mistake. Please disregard the call." Everyone hung up but when Mrs. Kistler called Mom, she heard clicks as people picked up to find out what was happening at the school.

Mom picked up Roy, and after school Mrs. K stopped at our house to check on him. Roy was feeling better and Mrs. K. only stayed a few minutes. As she was leaving, she turned and said that a doctor in Alliance had used penicillin to cure a child with scarlet fever. She said it was fantastic because she knew that some kids had died of the disease. Mom told Mrs. K. that she and her brothers and sisters had scarlet fever when they were young and the whole family had been quarantined. Mom thanked Mrs. K. for sharing the news. As soon as Mrs. K was gone, Mom called Grandma Woodworth to tell her about the cure for scarlet fever.

In the early winter, we were working on our lessons and heard a scratching noise under the floorboards of the school. Something or someone was digging under the school and it was scary. Mrs. K. said we should go outside as a group to investigate. We walked around the school, and stopped on the west side. There was a huge hole under the schoolhouse. Mrs. K. peered into the hole, and yelled, "Get back! Get back! I think it's a badger hole! Run inside." We ran because we knew that badgers were nasty, bad-tempered, dangerous animals that would attack if provoked (or not provoked). Mrs. K. called Mom to report the badger and we stayed inside for all recesses that day. The next day, Dad and Earl Bauer trapped and killed the badger, filled in the hole, and left us to our studies.

We went on field trips to the sugar beet factory and the potato chip factory again, but this year we were also going to take a plane ride. Mrs. Kistler's husband, Leo, was a pilot and he owned a piper cub plane. There were three seats in the small plane, one for the pilot and two for passengers. One Saturday, all of the children and all of the parents went to the airfield south of Alliance for airplane rides. Two by two, a child and a parent climbed into the plane and Leo took off for a quick turn around the airport before landing next to the hanger. Finally, it was my turn to get on board with Dad. I was perfectly calm watching others go up and come down, but now, when it was my turn, I had a panic attack. I was sitting in the plane next to Dad, all buckled in when the attack hit. I began gasping for air and crying uncontrollably, louder and louder until Leo gave up. Mrs. K. volunteered to sit next to me, thinking that this would work since it worked well when we had our pictures taken on my first day of school. But, alas, I was having none of it. I just kept bawling. Mom and Dad were mortified because I was such a brat, but there wasn't anything they could do. They relented and I didn't have to fly away in that plane.

Mrs. Kistler also arranged for us to travel to Chadron State College to attend a play that the college students produced. Moms and Dads accompanied us and we went to a production of the musical, *Brigadoon,* which I loved. The story was about American tourists who stumbled upon Brigadoon, a mysterious Scottish village that appeared one day every one hundred years. I was enamored and decided that folklore, magic, mystery, and true love were grand and thought that the legend of Brigadoon was probably true.

Since the play went so well, Mrs. Kistler decided to take us to a movie matinee one Friday afternoon. She got permission from the parents to take us to *A Summer Place.* Unbeknownst to Mrs. K., this film had serious adult themes and content. We went to the movie, ate our popcorn and watched the story unfold. I was oblivious to the plot themes, just happy to be out of school on a field trip. Over the weekend, Mrs. K. called every parent and apologized for taking the children to an inappropriate movie. On Monday, Mrs. K. stopped on her way to school. I heard her tell Mom that she had no idea that the movie would be so racy. She said she was mortified and she was practically in tears. Mom was sympathetic but Mrs. K didn't sponsor another movie field trip.

Over Christmas break that term, I overheard Dad complaining to Mom. "Kistler isn't teaching science to the kids.

That's not good." Mom said that she didn't think Ruth liked science. I didn't hear any more of the conversation.

One advantage of a one-room school is that younger students hear the older student's lessons and learn lessons above their grade level. Older students hear the younger students' lessons so their learning is reinforced. The older students also help the younger ones which benefits everyone. The other advantage is that with one teacher for six or seven children, it's like having a private tutor. The downside to having one teacher for several years in a row was that if the teacher has a weak subject, every child in the school becomes weak in that subject. Dad was right. Our weakness was science. There were no biology, chemistry, astronomy, or geology lessons. Our only science-related lesson was when Mrs. K. brought in some mercury in a glass jar. She showed us the mercury and explained that it was a liquid metal. She opened the jar and poured a little into our outreached palms. We played with it in our hands and then poured it into cups and swirled it around and up the sides of the cup. Some escaped onto the wooden floor and it was nearly impossible to wrangle the mercury back into the jar. We retrieved most of it but some slipped through the boards. In spite of having no science lessons for several years, Ronnie and Gina passed their comprehensive eighth grade exams that spring. They were promoted to ninth grade and would transfer to high school in Alliance in the fall.

My great-grandmother Anna Jesse lived in a large house on Tenth Street in Alliance, and our family visited her on some Sunday afternoons. Her house smelled funny, sort of musty and old, but we were polite when she served coffee to Mom and Dad and cookies to the children. She asked us questions about school or about the ranch and Mom and

Dad tried to keep the conversation going. I was fascinated (or jealous) of Great-Grandmother's long, straight hair since mine was always short and permanent-wave frizzy. I sat on the floor in front of her while she brushed her waist-length gray hair until it shined and then twisted and turned it until the hair was pinned into a tight bun on the nape of her neck. I was amazed that she could create a perfect bun by herself with no assistance and no mirror. While I didn't know her very well, I was sad when she died that April.

That spring, Mom had another baby. Ever since Sharyl was born, Mom and Dad worried about her because they feared she would grow up a lonely child. Ronnie, Roy, and I were in school so Sharyl would be all by herself until she started school. In spite of all the valid arguments against having a fifth child, they just couldn't let Sharyl grow up like an only child and made plans to give her a sibling when she was two. In May of 1957, just after the school term ended, Roy and I ran into the house to find Mom lying on her bed. We guessed Mom was sick, but Dad told us that Mom was going to have a baby and would be gone for a few days. Ronnie was old enough to stay at home with Dad, but Roy, Sharyl and I would stay with Grandma and Grandpa Woodworth until Mom came home. I sat on the edge of the bed and cried. "I don't want to stay with Grandma and Grandpa. I want to stay home with Ronnie." Mom told me that I was too young to stay home. Besides, it was up to me to help Grandma take care of Sharyl since Sharyl was so little. I was to be brave and strong and be the good helper for Grandma. Roy was going to be brave and be a good helper for Grandpa. A week later, Mom, Dad and Ronnie stopped by the Woodworth's, picked up the three of us, and we headed home with baby Rick.

Rick took up residence in the bassinette in the corner of the master bedroom and Sharyl moved into my room. She still had many of Grandma Woodworth's qualities. Grandma had white hair and Sharyl had a mop of white-blond hair. Grandma had an infectious smile, the corners of her eyes crinkled and her blue eyes shined. Sharyl had this permanent smile glued onto her little round face. She was happy and rarely cried. I loved sharing my room with Sharyl—for about three days. After that, she was annoying. She was curious and touched my stuff. She could be whiny and aggravating and, once again, she touched my stuff. I was frustrated and impatient with my little sister. I was not a good big sister.

While Sharyl had always been a happy baby, channeling her inner Grandma Woodworth, it was different with Rick, who didn't seem to channel anyone I knew. The moment Mom carried Rick into the house, he was impatient and demanding. He cried loudly all the time, no matter what Mom did to soothe him. I couldn't contain myself and asked Mom what in the world was wrong with him. Mom said he had colic and he would get better when he got older. We had to be patient. Mom didn't specify how old Rick would be when he quit crying. She was probably just as frustrated as everyone else because there just didn't seem to be an end in sight. I figured that Rick would still be wailing when he started school.

In midsummer, the local theater had a showing of *The Wizard of Oz* and my mother and my aunts thought it would be good to send all of the older cousins to the movie on a Saturday afternoon. We bought our tickets and popcorn and went to the balcony to watch the show. The movie was exciting at first and I understood Dorothy. She lived on a farm with her family and I could only imagine how scary it must have been to be transported from her snug home in Kansas to a completely foreign place. Then the wicked witch appeared and she terrified me. I was so traumatized that I left my seat to escape to the landing outside the balcony. After a while, I felt brave and returned to my seat but it wasn't long before the witch reappeared. I ran away again and sat on the steps sobbing until Roy and my cousins appeared when the movie ended. It was a long time before I was brave enough to go back to the movies.

As Mom predicted, Rick grew out of his annoying howling by late summer and I was grateful that Rick was turning into a normal baby. In the fall, I went off to school with my brothers, leaving Sharyl and Rick and Mom to manage on their own.

Grade 3—September 1957–May 1958

Russell and Ronnie Kraus moved with their family to Denver over the summer and with Ronnie and Gina in high school, our school enrollment was tiny. There were now three students at District #124: Kathy, Roy, and me. The school board hadn't renewed Mrs. Kistler's contract but found a newly minted teacher, a fresh graduate of Chadron State Teacher's College. Miss Lois Carson was sweet, smart, and full of great ideas. I imagine that during her interview there were serious questions about a science curriculum.

Miss Carson was single and had no family commitments. She negotiated with the school board and they agreed to provide a house and utilities in addition to the regular salary. The board moved a small, two-room mobile home (trailer) to the schoolyard. The REA workers connected the power and the propane company connected the gas line. The board moved the phone that had been at the Kraus's house to the trailer and hooked the phone to the party line. Miss C. drove to school on Sunday night and stayed in the little trailer the rest of the week, driving to Alliance on Fridays after school was dismissed.

The fall semester went well and we liked Miss Carson. In turn, she seemed to like her three little charges. In December, things outside our school walls went a little sideways. A man named Charles Starkweather abducted a fourteen-year-old Lincoln girl and murdered her whole family. After that he then began killing others randomly as they happened to cross his path. Every newspaper in Nebraska covered the horrible events, and news reporters on the radio discussed the events in gory detail. From the beginning of the killing spree, news outlets called the abducted girl, Caril Fugate, Charlie's girlfriend. County sheriffs, state patrolmen and city policemen seemed to always be a step behind Charlie as he patrolled eastern Nebraska, killing people in his wake.

After a week or so, Charlie and Caril headed west on Highway 2 toward Alliance, killing people along the way. It seemed like nothing could stop Starkweather, and we children were terrified that he would get off the highway and head through the hills to escape the patrolmen who were chasing him. So, there we were, three little kids and one teacher alone in the middle of the prairie, virtually miles from anyone. Miss Carson made light of the events. We were safe because the schoolhouse was far from Highway 2. We were so far back in the hills that only someone who actually knew about the school would know how to get there. Even getting to the Bauer house, which was closest to Highway 2, was unlikely because there wasn't a road, just some ruts in the sandy ground. In spite of Miss Carson's reassurances, we were scared.

At recess one morning we devised a plan. We would build a hiding place—a grass cave in the southwest corner of the schoolyard. From this vantage point we could see cars coming from the east and we could hide if it was a strange car. We gathered grass and tumbleweeds and began constructing a pile of brush that would look like weeds had blown into the corner and gotten stuck there. We piled up the tumbleweeds and grass until the cave was three feet high and about five feet wide. Then we hollowed out the center, making a space large enough to hide three children and made a "door" out of a large tumbleweed. At every recess after that, we continued to perfect our little hideout, always making sure that the pile of grass and weeds looked natural and normal. All day, every day we watched for a car coming toward us through the auto gate, across the meadow, and toward the school. On Mondays, Wednesdays, and Fridays the Long Lake Route mailman passed close to the school on his way to other homes on his route. There was a little panic when we first saw a car cross the auto gate and drive into the meadow, but relief when we saw that it was only the mailman going about his business.

After Christmas, the police arrested Charlie Starkweather and Caril Fugate so the scare was over. Still, we kept our cave in shape, in case another crazy murderer was lurking out there.

Charles Starkweather was charged with multiple murders and went to trial. At his trial, he told the jury that it was Caril who had used a shotgun to kill a teenage girl. He was found guilty of the other murders and he was executed in the electric chair for his crimes.

Caril Fugate was tried separately for first-degree murder in the death of the girl. Witnesses had seen her carrying a shotgun and Starkweather had implicated her. At her trial, Fugate admitted that she knew Charlie because one of his friends had dated her sister. She said that one evening she came home and found Charlie sitting on the couch with a gun in his hand. He told her that if she didn't do exactly as he said, he would kill her and her family. The two stayed in the house alone for a few days. Caril didn't know where her family was but after the short stay at the house, Charlie took Caril and headed out on the killing spree. Once on the road, Charlie told Caril that he had killed her family, including her two-year-old baby sister. Caril said that Charlie kept threatening to kill her if she said anything or tried to escape, so she rode in the car, terrified. She admitted holding the shotgun one time because Charlie told her she had to, but she said she never hurt anyone. She kept saying that Charlie was the only one who killed people. The jury didn't believe Caril's story and found her guilty of first-degree murder. She was sentenced to about twenty years in Nebraska's women's prison.

Newspapers were filled with details about the two trials and when Caril's verdict was handed down, newspaper editors said it was a travesty. Caril should get the death penalty for being Charlie's girlfriend and accomplice. I remember my uncles talking about the verdicts and the sentences. They were glad Charlie was going to "fry" in the electric chair for his crimes because he deserved that and more, but they thought that Caril should be executed too. There was no sympathy for the fourteen-year-old girl.

In the spring of that year, Roy and I ran into the house after school to find Mrs. Kistler sitting at the kitchen table talking to Mom. We were happy to see her, but Mom quickly sent us outside to play. Roy did as he was told but I stayed behind in the dining room eavesdropping. Mrs. K. and Mom were talking about Gina. She was thirteen and pregnant. Gina dropped out of ninth grade and Mrs. K. thought that Gina might get married. Mrs. K. was in tears. She said that Gina was smart. She had a bright future. She could be a teacher or a nurse or a bookkeeper or anything. Now that bright future was shattered. "Her life is wasted," she said. Mrs. K. told Mom that she should have held Gina back and not let her graduate from eighth grade. "Why did I let that girl graduate?" Mom said that there was no way anyone could have known. "You couldn't hold back a smart girl. That wouldn't be right. This wasn't your fault." There were more tears and more talking before Mrs. K. left. Mom was very somber the rest of the day but she never discussed her conversation.

The two events: Caril Fugate's story and Gina's pregnancy took place in the span of one year when I was particularly impressionable. Those unrelated incidents, plus my mother's views about being independent and self-reliant, were powerful influences. A girl had to be careful. The lesson I took away was that if a girl had a connection with a boy and something bad happened, the girl would be accountable for the event. She might share the blame or might take the blame. Girls were powerless but I knew I was different. I would never be powerless.

At the end of the school term, Miss Carson didn't renew her contract. She was getting married and her future husband owned a ranch near Hyannis. She couldn't drive from Hyannis every day to teach and couldn't leave her husband every week to stay in her little trailer outside the school.

That summer, the school board discussed the coming school term. There would be no students from the west end of the district, but a new student, my cousin Debbie, was going to start kindergarten in the fall. To make it more convenient for the parents and the children, the board decided to temporarily move the schoolhouse closer to the children. The current school in the Kraus meadow would be maintained in case another child moved into the west end of the district. Until then, they moved Miss Carson's trailer to a small plot in the meadow about a quarter mile southeast of our house. They tore out the walls separating the bedroom and main room to create one large room. They left the closet for supplies and the sink and faucet. They dug a well for running water, the REA ran electricity to the school, and the gas company installed a propane tank and a gas line to the small furnace. Finally, the board members moved the slide and swings, installed blackboards, the piano, the desks, and the chairs. Finally, they positioned an outhouse in the corner of the barbed wire fenced schoolyard. With the school in its new location and a new teacher under contract, everything was falling into place. Little did we know that a bad school year would begin in the fall.

That summer when Roy and I were playing in the barn, I climbed over one of the mangers into a stall and pierced my left thigh with a long, rusty nail. The wound bled profusely, and while it only hurt a little, the blood pouring down my leg scared me. I ran to the house, blood dripping, while Roy ran close behind me. In the kitchen, I sobbed while I told Mom what had happened. She grabbed a rag, soap, and water and washed the wound and my leg. She held the wound open and spilled in as much iodine as possible while I squirmed and cried. Finally, she fashioned a bandage with gauze and white medical tape. Once that was done, Mom phoned Grandma Jesse. She described what had happened and asked if Grandma thought I needed to see the doctor. Mom listened for a long time, told Grandma thank you and hung up the receiver. Mom turned to me and said that Grandma didn't think I needed to go to the doctor, but she did say that the nail hole in my leg needed to be cleaned. Grandma told Mom to dip a wooden matchstick in water, coat the match stick thoroughly with salt, and then push the salted match stick into the nail wound as far as she could. I stared at Mom horrified. The iodine had hurt but I couldn't even imagine how much more it would hurt with a salted matchstick pushed into the bloody nail hole. I screamed, "No!" and ran out of the kitchen and to the barn to hide. Roy followed close behind and we hid in the haymow until Dad came home for supper. Mom never mentioned the salted matchstick again because I'm sure she didn't relish that "cure" any more than I did. The wound healed but left behind a jagged circular scar.

Grades 4–5—September 1958–May 1959

Hey! Teacher, leave them kids alone.

—Pink Floyd, "The Wall"

Mrs. F. was our new teacher in the fall of 1958. She was older than Miss Carson, had more teaching experience, and was very willing to teach four youngsters in the Sandhills more than a dozen miles from Alliance. Mrs. F. drove from Alliance every day, Aunt Lois drove Debbie, and Earl drove Kathy. Roy and I walked the quarter mile from home to school.

We had our lessons, just as we did in the old school. Debbie was in combined kindergarten/first grade, so she had her lessons first. I was in fourth grade, so I was next. Roy and Kathy were in sixth grade and their lessons were last. In October, Mrs. F. told Mom and Dad that I was smart and staying in fourth grade was a waste of time for me. She recommended that I skip Grade 4 and move directly to Grade 5. She said that I could easily master the curriculum for both grades. My parents greeted this as wonderful news. Their oldest daughter was gifted and they were grateful to Mrs. F. for identifying my potential. They enthusiastically agreed and I was happy because my teacher thought I was smart.

As it turned out, Mrs. F. just didn't want to teach a bunch of different grades. For her, it was better to teach two separate grades. She would teach first-grade subjects to Debbie and she grouped fifth and sixth grade so she could teach Kathy, Roy, and me together. I don't think I received any fourth-grade instruction and Kathy and Roy got little sixth grade instruction. We all three got abbreviated instruction in a few subjects and we got As and Bs in everything, which made our parents very proud.

On weekends that fall I learned to drive. Driving was a requirement for every child living in the country. We might be called upon to deliver a tractor part to Dad in the field or fetch something from Uncle Vern. When Roy was eight, Ronnie and Mom taught him to drive Dad's old pickup. When I was nine Roy and Mom taught me to drive the old blue Chevy pickup truck that Ronnie drove to high school. The truck had a three-speed transmission and the starter was a button on the floor, just to the right of the accelerator. The brake pedal was in the middle and the clutch pedal was on the left side. The gear shift was attached to the floor, next to the driver's side of the bench seat. To start the truck, I turned the key to the "on" position, made sure the gear shift was in neutral and the hand brake engaged. I pressed the starter button with the toes of my right foot, the accelerator with the heel of the right foot while simultaneously pressing the clutch all the way down to the floor with my left foot. I wasn't tall, so I had to sit on the very edge of the seat to hold down all three pedals. As soon as the engine started, my right foot moved off the starter button and my left moved from the clutch to the brake. Now that the truck was running, it was time to start moving. Release the hand brake, depress the clutch pedal again, move the gear shift into first, press down on the accelerator while slowly releasing the clutch. One of two things happened. If the truck stalled and quit, it meant I had released the clutch too quickly and had to start over from the beginning. If the truck lurched forward, we chugged along in first gear until the engine started to whine. I then pressed down on the clutch pedal and shifted into second gear and then to third gear when I was going faster still. To stop, step on the brake and the clutch at the same time. If I pressed the brake without pressing the clutch, the truck lurched to a stop and stalled. That meant starting over. I practiced driving on the road in front of the house and in the meadow. I also practiced backing the truck into a tight place. Once comfortable driving, I could drive anywhere on country roads or in the pastures. I just couldn't drive on a public highway because I wasn't a licensed driver. Learning to drive was the best part of the school year.

In the spring of 1959, Mrs. F. and Roy had a run-in. Mrs. F. demanded that Roy gather the trash and take it outside to the trash barrel. Roy, being independent, didn't like Mrs. F's tone and the way Mrs. F. ordered him around. He also didn't like that he was the only one who had to take out the trash. When he refused, Mrs. F. got mad and told Roy he would be sorry if he didn't do as he was told. Well, that was a call to no action if there ever was one, so Roy defied the order. In the end, Mrs. F gathered the trash that day, but she wasn't kidding when she told him that he would be sorry. She took his report card out of her desk and changed his grades from As and Bs to Ds and Fs. "That should teach you a lesson," she said quietly.

My own run-in with Mrs. F. happened just after Roy's trash event. I'm not sure what the precipitating event was, but she called me to her desk at the front of the room. She was looking at my grades in her gradebook. She told me that probably because of my country upbringing, I wasn't smart enough to continue with fifth grade. In fact, I wasn't capable of handling the fourth- grade work that she had been giving me. She said she had no choice but to demote me and I would have to retake fourth grade next year.

I felt like I had been punched in the stomach. I couldn't breathe and began choking. Mrs. F. snarled, "Go back to your desk." I turned around and everyone was staring at me. I was embarrassed and wanted to disappear. Roy, Kathy, and Debbie just stared with wide eyes, first at me, then at the glowering teacher, then back at me. I sat down at my desk and sobbed as quietly as I could because Mrs. F. glared at me if she heard a sound. After school I ran home and crashed through the door crying. I told Mom that the teacher said I was going to be in fourth grade again next year because I wasn't smart. Mom quietly listened to my story, told me to stop crying, and told me not to worry. She said that I was not going to be in fourth grade next year. I would be in sixth grade, just as planned. I don't know what school board conversations happened after the two encounters with Mrs. F. My final report card showed As and Bs in every subject and I was promoted to sixth grade. Roy's report card showed As and Bs in every subject and he was promoted to seventh grade. The school board did not renew her contract and that was the last we ever heard from Mrs. F.

The summer of 1959, Dad and Mom took us to Denver for school shopping. Rick was two, Sharyl was four, I was ten and Roy was twelve. Ronnie, being sixteen, didn't want to go shopping so stayed with Grandpa and Grandma Jesse. Dad drove directly to the Adams Hotel, which was elegant and sophisticated. The rooms were big and carpeted and best of all, an elevator took us to our floor. We walked into the elevator, the attendant manually closed the solid door and then a heavy metal gate. The attendant pressed a button, we rode to our floor and he opened the gate and then the solid outer door to let us out. The poor elevator attendant. Roy and I rode the elevator up and down several times every day to visit the lobby but mostly to ride the elevator.

We shopped at large department stores and everyone got new clothes and new shoes. At one store, we wandered around with Mom while she browsed through every department, looking at women's clothes and shoes, linens, cookware, and the latest gadgets. We rode up and down the escalator, which was fabulous technology. On one of the trips down the escalator, Sharyl got her shoelaces caught in an escalator grate about midway between the two floors. As we went down, the escalator mechanism pulled Sharyl's laces further into the grates, and when we got to the bottom of the escalator, Sharyl's foot was being drawn into the escalator teeth. Dad remained cool (but he was probably panicking inside). He knelt next to Sharyl and tried to pull the lace free of the mechanism but failed. He pulled Sharyl's foot out of the shoe and then violently yanked on the shoe, shredding the shoelace but freeing the shoe. Other shoppers stood around, gawking at the drama, but no one helped Dad. Sharyl was scared, pale, and sobbing. Tears were flowing down Mom's cheeks while she held Rick and kneeled down to hold Sharyl. When the family calmed down and the onlookers had gone on their way, Dad and Mom grabbed our packages and we drove back to the hotel. We left for home the next day.

Grades 6–8 —September 1959–May 1962

After the disaster with Mrs. F., the school board hired Mrs. D. There were still only four students. Debbie was in second grade, Roy and Kathy were in seventh grade, and I was in sixth grade. Mrs. D's teaching methods were similar to Mrs. Kistler's. She was energetic, smart, and eager to share her knowledge. She made lessons fun even when the lessons were challenging.

We had the usual subjects: English language, phonics, spelling, history, geography, math, art, music, and even science. We hadn't had any science lessons since Miss Carson, so Mrs. D. taught remedial science before she could tackle grade-level science topics. This meant that we had group lessons in science where everyone participated. We played with magnets and iron shavings to learn about polarization, we learned about the solar system and crafted planets from modeling clay. We built a volcano, learned about different kinds of rocks, animals and plants, and we played with mercury again.

During science class one day, Mrs. D. wrote "Trini-trotoluene" on the blackboard. She said that this was the longest word in the English language but most people called the chemical "dynamite" or just abbreviated the word to TNT. She told us that the chemical was used to blow up buildings or bridges and any resulting fire was often uncontrollable. We hung on every word. It was fascinating.

Mrs. D. also believed in enrichment opportunities so we went to the sugar beet plant and the potato chip factory in Scottsbluff again. We drove far into the Sandhills to a place where the Sioux tribes had camped long ago. There, we sifted through the sand and found beads and arrowheads. We put our collection of treasures into glass baby-food jars and labeled the jars with our names. We set our jars on a shelf in the classroom until the end of the year.

Enrichment also included poetry, which was often incorporated into history lessons. We read poems about the historical event and then memorized either part or all of the poem. Mrs. D. was a fan of Henry Wadsworth Longfellow, so when studying the American Revolution, we read "Paul Revere's Ride" and memorized the first dozen lines: "Listen my children and you shall hear of the midnight ride of Paul Revere . . ." When studying the expulsion of the Acadians from Canada, we read Longfellow's *Evangeline,* and memorized portions of the epic poem: "Still stands the forest primeval; but far away in nameless graves, the lovers are sleeping." When studying the Civil War, we memorized Lincoln's *Gettysburg Address*: "Fourscore and seven years ago our fathers brought forth on this continent a new nation . . ." History became more relevant and interesting when reinforced with poetry.

In the fall of 1960, Roy and Kathy were in eighth grade, I was in seventh7th grade, Debbie was in third grade and Sharyl started school as a kindergarten/first grader. When

Mrs. D. started teaching the year before, her focus for Roy, Kathy and me was to make sure that we did well on our eighth-grade exams. She told Mom that she had no choice but to "teach to the test" so everyone would graduate. In Nebraska, every child attending a rural school had to pass a comprehensive exam at the end of the eighth grade term to graduate from elementary school and be qualified for high school. The exam was written and covered every topic in the curriculum from grades 1 through 8. The day-long exams were administered in Rushville, the county seat of Sheridan County. Roy and Kathy took their exams in the spring of 1961 and passed with flying colors.

Ronnie graduated from high school in May and the whole family celebrated his significant rite of passage. That summer we took a family vacation to the Black Hills in South Dakota. Mom and Dad thought this might be the last time we would do something together as a family of seven because Roy had graduated from eighth grade and would be high school that fall and Ronnie would begin his first year at the University of Nebraska. We stayed in a small cabin in a pine forest and ate breakfast at a picnic table just outside the door. Dad drove us to nearly every tourist site in the Black Hills: Mt. Rushmore, Sylvan Lake, Deadwood, and Reptile Gardens. We ate meals at diners and had ice cream cones in the afternoon. It was a wonderful, carefree trip.

Roy and Kathy started ninth grade at Alliance High in the fall of 1961. Roy was eligible to drive because he had a school permit, but he and Kathy rode to school with Jo. She had two children of elementary school age who attended school in Alliance since their school district had been disbanded years before. Mom drove Roy and Rick on the sandy trail road to the Bauer place where they picked up

Kathy. Mom drove on, across the Bauer meadow and across the railroad tracks to Highway 2 before heading west to the row of mailboxes. She parked by the mailboxes and waited for Jo who pulled her car in front of Mom and the two high school kids changed cars. Mom turned around and headed home while the others headed west toward Alliance.

I was now in eighth grade, and Sharyl was in second grade, but the little temporary school in our meadow was gone. A new student lived on the western edge of the school district, so during the summer, the school board moved everything out of the trailer and took it back to the old one-room school in Aunt Maime's meadow. They cleaned the weeds out of the schoolyard and moved the swings, slide, and outhouse. The gas company moved the propane tank, and the electricity was turned back on. Sharyl and I rode to school with Aunt Lois and Debbie while Mom delivered Roy and Kathy to the mailboxes.

A couple of weeks after we started school, Mom and Dad drove Ronnie to Lincoln to settle him into his dorm at the university. He wouldn't be home again until he rode the train back for Thanksgiving. Ronnie was busy and over-whelmed with his university experience and didn't have the time or patience for laundry. He boxed his dirty clothes and sent the box as freight on the passenger train from Lincoln to Alliance every few weeks. Mom picked up the box at the depot, did up the laundry, and even ironed his shirts. She folded everything neatly and returned the laundry box to Ronnie on the eastbound passenger train a few days later. While I didn't necessarily like washing and drying clothes, I couldn't imagine hating it that much and I thought Mom was spoiling Ronnie. After a semester, Ronnie recognized that he and the university weren't compatible, so he didn't enroll for another semester. He came home to help Dad with the ranch while he considered the next steps.

In the spring of 1962, I was terrified when I took my eighth-grade exams, but I passed easily. A couple of weeks later, I wore a white dress and a red carnation corsage to my eighth-grade graduation ceremony at the Rushville High School Auditorium. There were many eighth graders receiving their diplomas from the superintendent of schools. About half of us had attended a country school with one or two rooms and the rest had attended public schools in Rushville or Gordon. It was clear that some of these town kids thought the country kids were bumpkins because of the way we dressed and how timidly many of us acted. It was hard to miss the nudges, smirks, and quiet conversations.

Graduation was okay, but I don't remember being caught up in the moment. I was ready to move on to a new school just as Roy had done, but I was nervous about Alliance High School. The school seemed huge. I would have a locker and go from room to room for different subjects. There would be twenty kids in each class. I wouldn't know anyone—not one person. The thought was terrifying and I asked Mom and Dad if I could go to St. Agnes Academy in Alliance. Sure, it was a Catholic high school and we weren't Catholic, but that was okay. It was smaller and that was appealing. Unfortunately for me, Sheridan County had an agreement with Box Butte County, and kids who lived in Sheridan County could attend public schools in Box Butte County at no cost to their parents. There was no arrangement with St. Agnes, though. Dad and Mom would have to pay my tuition, and they refused. That was that, St. Agnes was out.

My next strategy was to ask Mom and Dad if I could go to the boarding high school in Curtis, Nebraska. Many of my 4-H friends were enrolling at Curtis, so I would have friends there. Besides the school was small and that was better. Also, Dad had attended Curtis one high school term so he knew it was a good school. This option was not acceptable because my parents would not pay my tuition at Curtis, and they said it was too far away for a 13-year-old. I had no other arguments or strategies. I was going to attend Alliance High School just like everyone else.

Roy and I had continued our piano lessons through the spring, but that summer we decided we didn't have time to continue, so stopped taking lessons. Mom was upset when I quit because Mrs. Reynolds told Mom that I was ready for organ lessons at the church. Mom was excited about this opportunity because she believed that playing the organ would be a wonderful part-time job for me. I wasn't interested, though, and declined the offer. Mom was disappointed but didn't pressure me. It was my decision, not hers. Even though Roy and I stopped taking lessons, we didn't stop playing the piano. Some weekends, I retrieved an old music book and played the piano for an hour or so. Roy did the same but he was a much better musician than I was. He could play unfamiliar music well, while I struggled until I became familiar with the notes.

In August, Mom drove me into Alliance so I could enroll in ninth grade. We met with the principal of the junior high school, which was for students in grades 7–9. Mom presented the completed enrollment forms, my report cards, my test scores, my eighth grade graduation certificate, and immunization record. The principal slowly reviewed each document and wrote the information on papers stapled into a folder with my name on it. After he finished, he smiled and told me that I was now an official freshman.

The principal said that I would receive an invitation to the orientation program for country kids who were starting ninth grade. He said there were quite a few country kids enrolled so I would have lots of friends. The subtext was that my only friends would be other kids from the country. He wasn't all that wrong.

CHAPTER 9

Alliance High School

Grade 9—September 1962–May 1963

This was going to be a banner year for Mom. Ronnie was enrolled at a junior college in Trinidad, Colorado, Roy and I were in high school, Sharyl was in third grade, and Rick was starting school. Mom could do her work in peace. It had to be liberating.

The summer before I started ninth grade, Mom, Sharyl, and I shopped in Alliance and in Scottsbluff for school clothes and school shoes. We also picked up fabric so I could sew a few new skirts. I now had an acceptable wardrobe. In August, my invitation for ninth grade orientation arrived in the mail. Mom and I drove to the junior high and we walked toward a reception table. The woman at the table checked my name off a handwritten list and gave me some papers with "very important information." I took the paperwork and Mom and I went into the gym, where we picked two chairs toward the back. There were a lot of other students sitting in the gym with their mothers. I recognized a few faces from 4-H clubs and a some from eighth grade graduation in Rushville. I was scared and nudged a bit closer to Mom.

The school principal, looking important in his suit and tie, walked onto the stage. He welcomed the group and told us we were about to embark on a wonderful journey and that we would look back on our high school days as the best days of our lives. He told us we would be automatically enrolled in the required courses and we could pick electives from the options that were listed in the enrollment packets. He described a typical school day, including start times, end times, drop-off and pickup locations, class duration, lunch duration and location of lockers. He said that each class was held in a different classroom, so we would move from room to room throughout the day. He made a point of telling us that this arrangement was much better than attending the one-room school many of us had attended. He laughed a little at this observation.

Classes were fifty-five minutes long and a bell would ring at the end of a class period. After three minutes, the bell rang again. We had to be in the next classroom, sitting at our desk, when the second bell rang. If we were late for class, we would receive a tardy slip, and after a certain number of tardy slips, we would get detention.

The principal concluded his remarks and the assistant principal walked to the podium to tell us the additional rules. Boys had to wear trousers and button-up shirts. Girls had to wear dresses or skirts with sweaters or blouses. The skirt had to be the appropriate length, which was measured by kneeling on the floor. If the skirt touched the floor, the skirt length was appropriate. If the skirt didn't touch the floor, it was too short. The girl would be sent home to change clothes and she would receive a tardy slip. The assistant principal also talked about attendance requirements, general tardiness, appropriate behavior, detention, expulsion, and so on. He told us that no student was allowed to be in the hallway during class time. If you needed to use the restroom during class, the teacher could issue a hall pass that was good for five minutes.

The physical education teachers talked about their classes, which were required for two years in high school. Our packets included information about uniforms and shoes. Athletic shoes were required for boys, but since athletic shoes weren't for girls, we had to buy white canvas, rubber-soled shoes like Keds.

The teachers who taught electives spoke next. The choir teacher encouraged enrollment in choir. The choir room was on the second floor of the high school, about two blocks south of the junior high. We could leave our class three minutes before the bell rang, giving us a total of six minutes to retrieve our coats from our lockers and walk to the choir room at the high school. The choir teacher would release us three minutes before the bell so we would have a total of six minutes to return to the junior high building for our next class. The band teacher encouraged enrollment in band, and he explained instrument options and the availability of music lessons. The Spanish and Latin teachers extolled the benefits of learning a language. The sponsors of various clubs described extra-curricular activities.

Finally, students and parents were released to tour the building. We were assigned alphabetically to a tour group and a teacher led each group. We walked down long halls lined with lockers. Each student had a locker number and a locker combination written in his or her packet. The guide made sure that each student in the group knew where the locker was located and made sure we could each open our locker. The guide pointed out the classroom numbers and we peered into one or two of the rooms. We walked by the restrooms, the physical education locker rooms, the band room, the library, the principal's office, and so on until we had toured the entire building. When back at the cafeteria door, the teacher told us how to buy lunch tickets.

I had been scared and intimidated before Mom and I went to orientation. Now I was terrified. I didn't want to go to high school. I thought about *The Wizard of Oz* movie and felt like I was about to be whisked away. I looked at Mom and she was calm. She was treating the whole orientation event and the whole high school thing like it was old hat, like it was no big deal. Of course, Mom had been through ninth grade orientation twice before—once with Ronnie and once with Roy, so it WAS familiar to her. I didn't tell Mom how scared I was.

After orientation, Mom and I looked at my class assignments. I was enrolled in English literature and composition, world geography, general math, general science and physical education. For my elective I chose choir. Mom thought I should consider home economics as a second elective because the cooking and sewing would be familiar to me, but I didn't want to be cooking and sewing at school. Mom didn't press the issue. She knew that home economics wasn't a priority for me, and choir would keep me interested in music.

When we were looking through the packet, Mom saw a woman she knew across the room and waved to her. It was Mrs. Hippe. She and her daughter Susan were also attending orientation. I said hello to Susan and learned that she had attended a one-room school and this was her first time at Alliance High. Susan was scared too, so I felt better knowing that I wasn't the only person who was nervous about this new adventure.

A few days later, while we were washing dishes, Mom told me not to worry about high school. She said I would be fine. "You'll make friends, make good grades, and have a good time." She also told me not to forget where I came from. "Be proud of who you are. No one is better than you and you are no better than anyone else. You need to be able to take care of yourself, don't blindly trust people and don't become too dependent on anyone. And, don't worry so much!"

When Ronnie started high school in 1956, he spent Monday through Friday with Grandpa and Grandma Jesse and came home on weekends. He caught a ride with the two older Bauer kids sometimes, but mostly he boarded with the grandparents. In the summer before he started eleventh grade, Dad bought a dark-blue 1951 Chevy pickup, and Ronnie drove this pickup back and forth his last two years of high school.

When Roy started high school, he and Kathy commuted with Jo and her two kids. I joined the carpool crew when I started ninth grade. Roy, Kathy, and I rode in the backseat with me in the middle because Jo dropped Roy and Kathy at the high school before dropping me at the junior high. After that, Jo drove to her cramped, one-bedroom apartment a couple of houses south of the elementary school. Her kids walked to school and Jo stayed in town the rest of the day. After school, she picked up everyone and drove us back to the row of mailboxes. Either Mom or Lillian Bauer picked us up there and home we went. If the weather was treacherous, Jo didn't drive back and forth. She and the kids stayed in the little apartment until the roads were clear. When this happened, Roy and I stayed in town with our grandparents.

On my first day of ninth grade Jo dropped me in front of the junior high school and drove on. I gathered myself and walked into the building. I found my locker, stowed my jacket, and went to my first period class. That first day was hectic, but with my slip of paper, I managed to find all of my classrooms. I was surprised to see that nearly everyone else was carrying a piece of paper with a list of classes and classroom numbers. I thought that I would be the only one who hadn't memorized the schedule and the room numbers. The locker assignments were arranged alphabetically, so kids in my section had names that began with H, J and K (no one had a last name that began with I.) There were several country girls with last names in this range, so it was good to be a Jesse. Susan Hippe, the girl I met at orientation, had a locker close to mine. Rosemary King was close by as was Beverly Hashman. These three were my first friends in high school. We had something in common and we banded together. Safety in numbers, I guess.

I became somewhat more comfortable after a few months. I had joined the pep club and gone to freshman football and basketball home games. When the high school had their homecoming, the junior high pep club joined the high school pep club at the football stadium. This was so much fun that I vowed to be in the pep club throughout high school. Joining the choir was also a good choice. I loved singing with a group, and the freshmen singers were welcomed by the high school singers and by the choir director.

Physical education classes met on Monday, Wednesday, and Friday and I hated every minute. It was the worst class and I would have dropped it if it hadn't been a requirement. When we arrived at PE each day, we went directly to the locker room, took off our school clothes, put them in our locker and dressed in our gym clothes and shoes. The gym clothes consisted of a white onesie with short pants and short sleeves, snapping up the front. We all wore white Keds shoes with white bobby socks. Each gym class lasted thirty minutes, and after class we returned to the locker room, took a shower, and dressed in school clothes. There were several PE units including field hockey, basketball, volleyball, gymnastics, and trampoline. After each unit, the teacher completed an evaluation for each girl, judging how well she met the requirements for that unit and if she had put in an appropriate amount of effort. I was a horrible gym student. I was as awkward, uncoordinated, and as unathletic as anyone could possibly be. Some of the girls were good at each unit and watched scornfully when I tried to do a cartwheel in gymnastics or serve a ball in volleyball. They smirked and talked about me in voices just loud enough for me to hear. I hated those girls.

I was strong and had stamina though. I could easily do jumping jacks, sit-ups, and squats. I could even do a headstand, which Mom thought was fabulous. She had me demonstrate my headstand trick for family members whenever they visited (and I was wearing trousers). I managed to get a B in PE because I was strong and I at least tried to accomplish the skills. I suspect the gym teacher took pity on me and on my complete lack of athletic ability.

*No one can make you feel inferior
without your consent.*

—ELEANOR ROOSEVELT

Students in junior high divided themselves into subtle cliques. The cliques likely started in the grade schools in Alliance because townspeople (even my Grandma Jesse) seemed very status- and class-conscious. By ninth grade, the cliques were established and quite powerful, so it was difficult for new students to break into a top tier. Country kids entering ninth grade were outsiders and the other students seemed distant and suspicious. We were treated differently and I often felt a little marginalized.

One clique or group included handsome, charismatic boys who played football and basketball and the pretty, charming girls who were cheerleaders or who dated the athletes. The students were social, outgoing, and boisterous. They studied, got good grades, and knew how to ingratiate themselves with a teacher who might cut them some slack when it came to homework assignments or test scores. The girls in the group gossiped. They could be mean, spiteful, and vicious when talking about another student and then turn on a dime and be sweet and kind to that student's face. It was disconcerting. I didn't like it.

The second group included girls and boys who were just not quite on par with the top tier—maybe not as handsome or as pretty or as outgoing. These students studied hard, made good grades, but didn't seem to have the inclination or the talent to manipulate a teacher or two.

The majority of students fit into the third group. These kids were generally approachable, friendly, and sympathetic to others. They earned fair to good grades, tried to get along with everyone in all groups, and tried to stay "under the radar." These were the "middle children" of the school family. The brainy kids were a part of this group. They took the most challenging subjects, studied hard and kept to themselves. They were friendly but not outgoing. Teachers liked these students because they were quiet and they studied. Students in the top tier were adept at using these smart students to gain an advantage in a class or with a particular teacher.

Many farm kids were in this third group. Boys joined Future Farmers of America (FFA) and they took shop classes and agricultural classes as electives. They participated in sports, in activities, and in other clubs. Country girls didn't have a built-in club like FFA, but we befriended other country girls. It wasn't long, however, before we were welcomed by girls who had grown up in Alliance but who had similar goals and temperaments.

The fourth and final group included girls and boys who were putting in time at school and just getting by. They were often surly and disrespectful toward teachers and ended up in detention, which didn't seem like a big imposition to them. Some of the boys wore white, short-sleeved T-shirts under their button-up shirts and, weather permitting after school, they removed their shirts, revealing rolled-up T-shirt sleeves with a pack of cigarettes tucked into the roll. Before and after school, the boys gathered on the corner just north of the school building, smoking and loudly talking. My mother didn't like these kids. She called them juvenile delinquents, but I rather envied them because they didn't seem to care what others said about them. They were not intimidated by anyone and were immune to the jabs and humiliations handed out by other students. This fourth group also included students who were misfits. They lacked social skills and couldn't easily interact with others. It was hard for them to even make eye contact. With head down, they walked down hallways, and they suffered through every class and every lunch. The teachers ignored them and clearly didn't have high expectations of them. I felt sorry for these students but I didn't make an effort to be friendly because I was self-centered and afraid of what others might think. It's surprising that I was not in this group because I was shy, lacked many social skills, and could have easily passed through high school with my head down. Luckily, that group of girls befriended me early on in ninth grade.

If I ever felt a little marginalized, it paled in comparison to the plight of students of color, who made up a tiny percentage of the school population. There was a fairly large community of Native Americans in Alliance but there were no Native American students attending high school while I was there. Native American children attended elementary school and maybe a couple of years in junior high before dropping out. I don't think that teachers or school administrators gave these kids a second thought.

A few students were of Mexican or Hispanic descent. Some were marginalized, but others, those who were outgoing, got good grades, or were skilled in sports seemed to be assimilated into school society. Still, there were students who used racial slurs when talking about Hispanic kids behind their backs. I mentioned this to Mom once and she said she didn't know about that. She said that Mexicans were hardworking people and the women always seemed so attractive—beautiful skin and deep dark eyes.

There were several African American families in Alliance and Larry was in my class. He was athletic and a star in football, basketball, and track and field. At times, it seemed like Larry carried the entire football team on his back so there was jealousy and related chatter among the other ninth grade athletes.

In mid-October, the Cuban Missile Crisis sent a shiver through the entire country. The US had apparently installed ballistic missiles in Turkey and Italy and the Soviets decided to install missiles in Cuba in retaliation. Our geography teacher pointed out Turkey, Italy, and Cuba on the world map but didn't discuss the events very much in class. We did discuss the crisis at lunch and after school though. President Kennedy ordered a blockade of Cuba until the Soviet weapons were removed, so radio stations made it clear that we were very close to war. I overheard some kids saying that their parents were building bomb shelters so I asked Dad again about an A-bomb shelter. His answer was the same: It was too expensive and wouldn't do any good anyway. After a month, Khrushchev gave in and withdrew the weapons from Cuba. Everything went back to normal.

In the spring, my parents decided that it was high time for their children to be baptized. They talked to the Methodist minister and made arrangements for all five of us to be baptized one Sunday during church services. This was mortifying! Many of the popular girls and boys at school attended the Methodist Church, and they would be in the congregation when I was baptized. I didn't want to be the center of attention and certainly didn't want my classmates to see me get baptized like a baby. I asked Mom if I could get out of it, and, as expected, the answer was a resounding "No." So, I was baptized with my brothers and sister one Sunday while my whole world watched.

That summer, Bell Telephone installed a new, automated phone switchboard in Alliance. Most of the operators were replaced with the automatic switch, and customers got new phones. People living in Alliance had had rotary dial phones for a few years, but rural households still had old wooden crank phones. Now, with the new switch, all phones were replaced with phones with a push-button dial. The phone company assigned new phone numbers to everyone and distributed our first phonebook. Mom made a "cheat sheet" listing frequently called numbers and taped it to the wall next to the phone. To make a call in or around Alliance, customers only needed to punch in the last four digits. We were still on our party line and the old party line rules applied. We punched in the new number for friends on the party line, and to make an emergency call, we pushed the O or Operator button, an operator answered and she transferred the call to the appropriate number. This was progress. We were entering a new, modern era.

Grade 10—September 1963–May 1964

Roy began driving to school nearly every day that fall. We left the house, giving ourselves forty to forty-five minutes to get to school. We picked up Kathy and continued south to the railroad tracks. Every morning, we made it to the tracks just as the westbound passenger train from Lincoln got to the crossing. The engineer pulled the whistle to warn us of the oncoming train, and Roy stopped the car several yards back from the tracks until the train sped past. Without fail, we got to the railroad crossing just as the train got to the crossing, and every day we stopped and waited for the train. One day, we approached the crossing and like always Roy stopped to wait for the train. This time, though, there was no whistle and no train. Roy just sat there and waited. Finally, I said as sarcastically as possible, "Are we going to school?" Roy looked at me, looked at the crossing and peered down the tracks. There was no train in sight, so he put the car in gear, drove over the railroad tracks and on to school. Mom told me once that she always worried about our crossing the railroad tracks. She said that she listened for the train whistle and relaxed when she heard the train move from east to west and out of earshot because that meant that there hadn't been an accident.

The high school building was the same three-story red brick building that my parents had attended. The exterior was worn but well-kept and the stairways and halls were wide and grand. You could practically hear the voices of the kids who had attended classes there twenty or thirty years ago echoing through the halls and I was happy to be there. I was an actual high school student attending an actual high school. I thought that I was mature.

I didn't enroll in challenging courses because I didn't think I was smart enough. It was important to keep my A and B grades and I was afraid if I took hard classes, I would get Ds or Fs and wouldn't graduate. Three math courses were required for graduation, so with ninth grade mathematics behind me, I took algebra in tenth grade. Two science courses were required, so with ninth grade general science behind me, I took biology. Four years of English were required, so of course I took English. I also took my second year of physical education, just to get it out of the way, and I took a semester of driver's education, which was required for all fifteen- and sixteen-year-old students in tenth grade. I was fourteen but took driver's education anyway. No one knew I was too young for the class and besides I had been driving at home since I was a youngster. For electives, I took choir and beginning typing. Dad said that everyone needed to know touch-typing and he thought it should be a required course. Even though it wasn't a graduation requirement, it was a "Dad Requirement." Mrs. Glarum taught most of the business services classes like typing, shorthand, and bookkeeping and everyone loved her. She was a great teacher—smart and kind and dedicated to making sure her students mastered her classes. I liked choir too. It was fun and not like a class at all because we were just singing. We prepared songs for the Christmas program, a spring program, high school baccalaureate, and high school commencement ceremonies. We went to the state music festival and received good scores. I was happy in that musical environment.

Since we had been baptized the previous year, Roy and I started attending Sunday school, participated in the church youth group, and started singing in the church choir. I think Mom was happy we were involved with the church activities. Dad was an active member of the Nebraska Stock Growers Association and he encouraged our involvement in the Junior Stock Growers. We attended meetings and met kids from high schools around the entire state of Nebraska.

If we cannot now end our differences, at least we can help make the world safe for diversity.

—JOHN F. KENNEDY

We have a report…that has confirmed that President Kennedy is dead.

—WALTER CRONKITE

After lunch on November 23, 1963, my friends and I took a quick walk in the warm sunshine. We returned to the high school and joined a group of friends who were waiting for the bell. Lenore asked if we had heard what happened. I said, "No, what?" She told us that President Kennedy had been shot. "It's a stupid rumor," someone said. "That's just not true," someone else said, but the faces around us told a different story. Everyone was solemn and there was no boisterous chatter, just conversations in low tones. Some of the girls were crying.

The bell rang and we walked to our lockers and then to the first afternoon class. The teacher was grim and said the day's lesson would be delayed so she could tell us what she knew about President Kennedy. The gist was that President Kennedy was in Dallas for the day. He and Mrs. Kennedy and some others were in a car, traveling along a parade route and assassins shot the president. A few minutes later, someone knocked on the classroom door and the school secretary whispered something to the teacher. She turned and told us that the president was dead and we could talk about the assassination if we wanted. No one wanted to talk so we sat in class silently. At the next class, it was more of the same, but one of the guys had a transistor radio in his locker and the teacher said it would be OK to get the radio so we could listen to the news. Again, there was no talking. We hung on every word the broadcaster said and we stayed in that class the rest of the day. That night, we watched coverage of the shooting on television until Mom and Dad were mentally exhausted and turned off the TV.

The assassin, Lee Harvey Oswald, was arrested on November 24 and he was then shot and killed by Jack Ruby in the Dallas Police Headquarters. A lot of people were happy that Ruby had taken matters into his own hands, but others were skeptical. There were rumors that there were several gunmen besides Oswald. Maybe Ruby was one of them and he had orders to silence Oswald. It seemed like someone was pulling strings and Ruby killed Oswald under orders. There was a great push by leaders in Washington to just move past the assassination, but the citizenry couldn't or wouldn't let it go. The Warren Commission was appointed to review all of the evidence and come to a final conclusion about possible additional gunmen and other conspiracies. After months, the Commission wrote that Lee Harvey Oswald acted alone and that Jack Ruby acted alone. There was no conspiracy.

In spite of the Warren Report, the conspiracy theories would not go away. Some people believed that the report was a cover-up. They believed that people who sat on the commission were threatened or were paid to ignore key facts. More time went by and a House Select Committee reviewed the data. They ended up agreeing with most of the Warren Report but decided that there was a probably a conspiracy since an audio recording indicated there were more shots fired than Oswald's three shots. Sometime later, they changed their minds and decided that the recording was defective and that there were only three shots after all. These conflicting outcomes only fueled the conspiracy theories.

When the weather was bad during the winter, Roy and I stayed with our grandparents. We stayed with Grandma and Grandpa Jesse if it was incredibly cold or incredibly snowy. They lived a bit closer to the high school than Grandma Woodworth, so walking didn't take us as long. Besides, Grandpa Jesse sometimes drove us to school when the weather was horrible. The downside for us was that Grandma Jesse often hosted bridge parties, complete with linen tablecloths, finger sandwiches, cakes, and coffee served in her fine china cups. We didn't like walking through the door and into a room filled with well-dressed, be-jeweled, perfumed ladies. They always greeted us warmly and Grandma asked if we wanted a snack or wanted to watch the games. We generally declined and excused ourselves because we were clearly interrupting Grandma's event. We escaped the bridge party, took our books, and walked into the guest room to start our homework.

Roy and I preferred to stay with Grandma Woodworth and Lyle. The household was more relaxed and we never walked into a room full of ladies dressed to the nines. Grandma W. didn't bother us with questions about our classes, teachers, school activities, or about our little brother and sister. In the evening, after supper, I helped Grandma with dishes and then Roy and I did our homework at the dining room table. Lyle watched the tiny black-and-white television in the living room and Grandma either worked on her crochet or read her Bible.

After supper one evening while I was drying dishes, Grandma yelled, "Oh, no, a mouse!" Sure enough, I turned just in time to see the little critter scurry under the kitchen table. I didn't like mice so let out a little scream, ran into the dining room and jumped onto a chair. Grandma grabbed her broom and began chasing the mouse, swatting and punching it with the broom, telling Roy and Lyle to move the kitchen table and chairs out of her way. It wasn't long before the mouse lay in a bloody little pool on the kitchen floor so I could safely leave my perch. Lyle scooped up the mouse with a gloved hand and tossed it into the alley behind the house. Next, he took the broom outside to clean off the blood.

When he came back inside, Roy pointed to me and started jumping around, doing a very poor imitation of me. "Oooo, I'm so scared!" Then he jumped onto a chair and yelled in a high-pitched voice, "I'm afraid of mice!" I was mad at Roy for making fun of me, but Roy and Lyle just roared with laughter. Grandma turned away from me, but I saw her smile and wink at Roy. She mopped up the mouse blood with an old rag, then grabbed a bottle of Lysol from under the sink and poured some on the spot. I was furious with Roy for making fun of me, but he was right. I was afraid of mice.

I am thankful for all of the people who said NO to me. It's because of them I'm doing it myself.

—ALBERT EINSTEIN

By second semester of tenth grade, I decided that I might want to be a nurse. Mom encouraged this career choice because as a nurse I would always be able to get a job and would be able to support myself. She thought I needed some experience though, so she suggested that I volunteer as a candy striper at St. Joseph's Hospital in Alliance during the summer. Mom heard that the hospital was always looking for volunteers to run errands, deliver mail and flowers to patients, read to patients, or just sit with patients and hold their hand. Mom believed that experience in a hospital would help me decide if nursing was a good choice. In the spring, I sent in an application. One of the Catholic sisters called to set up an appointment. I still didn't have a driver's license so Mom drove me to the hospital for my appointment. We walked inside and sat in the reception area. The sister walked out of her office and called my name, and I walked over to her. She nodded toward Mom and asked if this was my mother. Mom said yes and said that she would just sit and wait until after the interview. The sister said, "No, no. That's not necessary," and she invited Mom and me into the office. The sister asked about school, the classes I had taken, and my grades. She also asked about school activities, activities outside school, and church involvement. She asked me where exactly I lived since the address on my application was Hickory Route. When I told her that I lived on a ranch east of Alliance, she frowned and asked how I planned on getting to my job as a volunteer. I explained that I was going to stay with my grandparents who lived in town and I would walk to the hospital. The sister looked skeptical. At the end of the interview, she told me that she was sorry but there was no place for me as a candy striper. She said that, in her experience, country girls were not reliable. She wouldn't be able to count on me to be at work when I needed to be at work. Mom intervened and told the sister that I was very responsible, but the sister cut her off and told us we were excused. I wouldn't be a candy striper because I lived in the country. On the drive home, Mom said that the sister probably only hired Catholic girls but she just didn't want to say that. It was easier to just say she didn't hire country girls. I replied that maybe that was true, but in my heart, I knew it had nothing to do with our being Methodist. I knew lots of girls who were candy stripers and they were definitely not Catholic.

I was not deterred by this setback at the hands of a Catholic sister. I still wanted to be a nurse and I wanted to go to the University of Nebraska to get my nursing degree. I would go to Lincoln for one year of pre-nursing classes and then transfer to Omaha for the final three years. I would graduate with a BSN.

That spring, Ronnie graduated from college in Trinidad. We all went to graduation and Ronnie came home with us for a couple of weeks before starting his new job. He was moving far away to Seattle, Washington, because he had a good job at the Boeing plant. Dad and Mom were very proud of Ronnie for starting a new vocation and starting to make his way in the world. I was sad that he would be so far from home.

Grade 11—September 1964-May 1965

Our neighbor, Kathy, had a car of her own now, so she drove by herself to school. This left Roy and me alone on our commute. Roy had started dating Cherie in the spring of the previous year but by the fall of 1964, they were very serious. The drive to school was fine, but Roy frequently drove around town with Cherie snuggled close to him after school. This delayed our drive home, which meant I would be late starting my homework. It annoyed me so Roy and I argued. After one particularly bitter argument, Roy told Mom that I was jealous of Cherie and I wished I could have a boyfriend. That weekend, Mom told me that Roy thought I was jealous. "He's crazy. I'm not jealous," I insisted. After that conversation though, I thought about Roy's comment. Was I jealous? Even a little? I knew that I wasn't jealous of Cherie because I didn't even like her, but maybe I wished I could be dating. Sure, there were a few boys that I rather liked, but many already had girlfriends, so they didn't count. Of the remaining boys, no one interested me. I was happy with how things were going at school. Maybe Roy just assumed I wanted to be dating because he liked having a girlfriend. Who knows? I was happy with the status quo and that's all that mattered to me. I didn't need to be dating a boy to be happy.

Susan N. was the smartest student in my class. Her immediate and extended families were Japanese American and had been relocated from California to internment camps in Wyoming and Colorado during World War II. After the war, with their homes and livelihoods in California permanently gone, many families moved to Nebraska. Some opened businesses in Alliance, others purchased farmland and their children attended school in Alliance. Susan studied harder than anyone I knew and got straight As even in the most difficult classes. She served in leadership positions on school committees, councils, activities, and clubs and was the accompanist to the choir and the chamber group. Everyone was nice to her to her face, but some students were jealous of Susan and secretly (or not so secretly) hoped she would fail at something. They didn't like that she was certain to be the valedictorian of our class.

At the beginning of eleventh grade, a new minister was transferred to the Methodist Church. He brought his family with him and their oldest daughter, Mary, was in eleventh grade. Mary was smart. She got straight As and became involved in school activities. Some well-connected students knew every student's grade point average (which was a little scary). In hushed conversations before or after class, students said that Mary's GPA was two decimal points higher than Susan's. These students were elated because they didn't think a *(racial slur)* should be valedictorian of our class. If Mary could just hold on, it would be great. A white girl would be valedictorian and it would be OK if a *(racial slur)* was salutatorian.

I didn't tell anyone about the conversations because I was afraid of what others would think. I didn't even tell Mom. She was on friendly terms with some of the Japanese American merchants in town, and I thought if I told her, she would either be upset or just say, "I don't know about that." I tried my best to ignore the chatter around me.

I now had a job of sorts. Uncle Tom and Aunt Eleanor owned a little fast-food joint about three blocks from the high school. When the weather was warm, it was mass chaos outside the joint, so my aunt and uncle enlisted several high school students to help with the noon-time crunch. Roy volunteered to help when he was in tenth grade and worked lunch hours in the warm months the rest of his time in high school. I joined the Dari Isle team in eleventh grade.

The Dari Isle had two walk-up windows for ordering food but no inside seating. The menu consisted of hamburgers, hot dogs, french fries, soft drinks, soft-serve ice cream cones, ice cream sundaes, and milkshakes. Even on chilly days, the place was busy at lunch time because high school students abandoned the school cafeteria for some loud socializing and some tasty, greasy, fast food. Kids walked up to a window, ordered food, and then milled around on the sidewalk, waiting for their order. After they got their food, they continued to linger on the sidewalk while they ate.

A couple of students worked the window taking orders. Uncle Tom and Roy cooked hot dogs and fried hamburgers. They slapped the dogs and burgers onto buns and wrapped them in paper for delivery to the window. Aunt Eleanor helped at the window and filled drink and ice cream orders. My job was to fry french fries. I retrieved frozen fries from the freezer, poured the allotted amount into the fryer basket and dropped the basket into the deep fat fryer. After a few minutes I pulled the basket out of the hot oil, let the basket drain a bit, and then dumped the fries into a hopper. After a generous shaking of salt, I scooped the fries into small paper bags and lined them in a row to make it easy for the window crew to pick them up. I repeated the process over and over throughout the lunch hour.

The student workers were paid with food—basically we ate all we wanted for free. Dad said that Uncle Tom was hiring cheap labor because we only had time to gobble down a burger and some fries and guzzle down a drink before we headed back to class. If we stopped by for ice cream after school, we had to pay, just like everyone else. The whole thing annoyed Dad, but he didn't stop us from working there. For me, the worst part was that the smoke from the boiling oil permeated the entire space and when we walked back to school, we reeked of oil and french fries. Some students made fun of our "perfume" but I wasn't that offended because everyone loved eating at Dari Isle. One of the girls who worked the window had a bottle of cheap spray cologne in her purse. While we walked back to school, she sprayed herself liberally with cologne, trying to cover up the cooking fat odor. She ended up wreaking of cooking fat and cheap perfume.

I chose my eleventh grade classes carefully. I liked biology in tenth grade, but chemistry and physics looked too hard, so my science career ended with biology. I enrolled in English, world history, a second year of typing, and the beginning shorthand class. My friends and I thought shorthand would be helpful when taking notes in college, so that's why we enrolled. Besides, Mrs. Glarum taught shorthand and we loved her. I took geometry to fulfill my math requirement and had a little trouble with the concepts. My friend Bev was a geometry whiz and I called her often for help with homework. We talked through each problem, but only for ten to fifteen minutes at a time because of our party line. After fifteen minutes, I had to hang up for ten minutes before calling Bev back in case a neighbor needed to make a call. I also had to hang up if I heard a click on the line, which meant someone wanted to make a call. Sometimes I ignored the click, pretending that I hadn't heard it because I wanted to finish my homework. I was confident that no one eavesdropped on my math conversations.

I took choir again and decided to try out for the chamber choir, a group made up of a dozen students who sang special music at all of the music programs. The choir director, Mr. Scholl, encouraged every choir student to audition for the group. At tryouts, students sat on the bleachers in the choir room and the accompanist, Susan, sat at the piano in the middle of the room. Mr. Scholl stood next to the piano and called students up, one by one. He wrote the student's name on a sheet of paper, and we stood next to the piano while Susan played a single note. We sang that note and Susan played another note, then another, then another. The student also sang a few scales and a few short tunes before being excused from the room. Mr. Scholl wrote something next to each student's name before the next student was called. I was glad that the room had cleared out a bit by the time it was my turn. I was nervous because I had never done anything like this before and I certainly didn't want to embarrass myself. Still, when it was my turn, I hit every note spot-on. It was easy for me, but I also knew that other students sang well too. The next week Mr. Scholl posted the list of students who would join the chamber group. I was shocked to see my name on the list. I was happy and proud and couldn't wait to tell Mom. She was proud of me because it was music and because I was brave enough to try out.

The chamber group received high scores at the state music festival and were invited to the local radio station, KCOW, to sing on-air. It was an honor, but more importantly, we were excused from classes for a few hours. We practiced our song in the studio before going live, but several of us couldn't hear harmonies and wandered off-key because voices simply died in the sound-proof room. I knew I was flat and decided to plug my left ear with my finger and move a half step closer to my right. I was able to hear the harmonies on my right and I thought I was in tune throughout the song. Our radio concert was successful and everyone in my family said it was wonderful.

There is plenty to learn even from a bad teacher:
what not to do, how not to be.

—J.K. ROWLING

Mr. F was a well-liked world history teacher. Mixed into his lectures about history, Mr. F. talked politics. In the fall of 1964, Barry Goldwater and Lyndon Johnson were running for president and Mr. F. was a zealous supporter of Goldwater. We heard the reasons why Goldwater was the only option for president. Mr. F. told us that if the country reelected Lyndon Johnson, we would lose the Vietnam War. The dominos would fall and, one after another, countries in Asia would be overrun by the Chinese Communists. Taiwan would fall, then Japan, then Australia, then who knows what next. It would be a disaster. He railed about how only Barry Goldwater could save the world because he wasn't afraid to use nuclear weapons in Vietnam. With the nuclear option, we would win the war and push back the Chinese.

I hung on Mr. F's every word. Every night I told my parents what Mr. F. had said in class that day. I don't remember them responding one way or the other to my (Mr. F's) arguments. I also don't know how they voted in the 1964 election, but they probably voted for Goldwater because they always voted Republican. Johnson won the election, though, so Mr. F. and his students waited for the communists to take over the world.

I didn't think that Mr. F. even gave me a second thought. I was quiet, kept my low profile, and studied. I liked history, liked Mr. F., and reviewed every lesson thoroughly. When Mr. F. asked a question about the day's assignment, I actually raised my hand and answered the question. He would smile, ever so slightly, and say, "Yes, that's right." I put in a lot of effort and I got good grades on the homework and all of the exams.

Things changed in second semester. Toward the end of class one day, Mr. F. asked me to stay a minute after class. I didn't know what to expect and stood nervously in front of his desk. Mr. F. said he knew what I was doing. He knew I was cheating, but he just didn't know how I was doing it. He had purposely moved me closer to students who were doing poorly in his class. The problem was that, while students around me were writing wrong answers on exams, I was still writing correct answers. Since I was answering questions correctly, it meant I looked at the other students' papers, knew their answers were wrong, and then wrote down the correct answer. He said he would watch me and would find out how I did it. He excused me abruptly and started leafing through his papers. He didn't allow me to speak during the encounter, which was probably good because I wouldn't have known what to say. I felt like I had been kicked in the stomach—the same feeling that I had when I stood in front of Mrs. F's desk in fifth grade. I walked to my locker choking back tears, opened my locker, put my head inside, and pretended that I was looking for something. I couldn't believe it. How could Mr. F. think I was cheating? I studied. That's how I knew the correct answers. I went to lunch with my friends and stewed. I was angry and hurt but I didn't tell anyone about my encounter.

I knew that I had two choices. I could stop studying and start missing questions to please Mr. F., but that would validate his ridiculous assumption that I had been cheating. The other option was to continue studying. I chose the second option. I still answered questions in class when I was sure I knew the correct answer, and I still studied and got good grades on the homework assignments and the exams. Mr. F. never mentioned his concerns again even though he either stood right beside me during a test or sat at his desk and stared at me. I was relieved when I walked out of that classroom for the last time.

Roy and I (and Cherie) attended Sunday school every week, and the three of us participated in the church youth group and sang in the church choir. Dad was getting more and more involved in some influential organizations in Alliance and in Nebraska. He was a respected member of the Nebraska Stock Growers, so Roy and I were members of the Junior Stock Growers. Dad was a leader in the American Legion Post, so I was a member of the Ladies Auxiliary with Grandma Jesse since Mom didn't join clubs or participate in activities. Dad was a board member of the Nebraska Panhandle REA and he and Mom attended national meetings in Dallas and in Miami. Dad was able to secure board support to sponsor a Junior REA, mirroring the tenets of the Junior Stockgrowers. Roy and I were drafted as charter members of the group.

*It's hard to make out the difference
between insults and bad advice.*

—Cass McCombs

Toward the end of eleventh grade, all students were required to meet with a school guidance counselor to discuss career plans. Mom and I had an appointment with Mr. D. I didn't know what to expect because I had never met Mr. D. He had a reputation of being cold, distant and a little unkind, so I was nervous. Mom and I sat in the chairs in front of Mr. D's desk while he opened a folder with my name printed on the cover. It seemed like he leafed through the file for a long time before he looked up and smiled. He asked a few general questions about my classes, teachers, and activities. He said my grade point average put me well in the top 25 percent of my class, so my parents should be very proud. Next Mr. D. asked me what my career plans were, and I told him that I was going to the University of Nebraska to get my bachelor's in nursing. He asked why I had taken typing and shorthand. I told him that my father said everyone needed to learn how to type, and I took shorthand so I could more easily take notes in college lecture classes. Mr. D. grimaced, closed my file and looked at me. "Just know," he said, "you will not be successful in college." He said that girls, like me, who had grown up in the country without the advantages offered in larger public schools didn't have the skills needed to be successful at college. I would be better off going to a business school and then taking a position as a secretary, a bookkeeper or a file clerk He said he could give me folders from several very good business schools, including one in Lincoln if I wanted to go to Lincoln. He went on to say that if I was set on being a nurse, I should go to the nursing school in Scottsbluff and train to be an LPN (licensed practical nurse). He looked straight at me and told me I was being irresponsible. I should not waste my parent's money by going to the university and then failing. Mom said that my oldest brother had gone to the university and my brother Roy was enrolled in the fall. I just wanted to follow in their footsteps. Mr. D. said he appreciated those wishes, but college was not a good option for me.

Mom nodded and quickly said, "I understand. It was nice meeting you." We walked out, got into the car and headed home. Mom and I didn't talk all the way home, but she knew what was happening in my head. I was stubborn and once I got something in my head, there was no stopping me. She was right. I was not going to be discouraged or kept from my goal by a guidance counselor who didn't even know me. If I had ever doubted my decision to go to the university and get my bachelor's in nursing, the doubt was gone. I would show Mr. D. I was more determined than ever.

Friendship is the hardest thing to explain.
But if you haven't learned the meaning of friendship,
you haven't learned anything.

—MUHAMMAD ALI

I was lucky to have a wonderful group of friends. We enjoyed each other's company, and without this group of girls, I would never have learned the social skills needed to survive in the big, bad world. We shared our hopes and dreams and encouraged each other. None of us had a car, but sometimes one of the girls borrowed her family's car on a Friday or Saturday evening. Six or seven of us would scramble into the car and off we would go to "Cruise the Butte." Box Butte Avenue, the "Butte," was the main north–south street in Alliance and dozens of high school students drove up and down the avenue for hours on weekend nights, burning gas and listening to KOMA, our favorite radio station broadcast from Oklahoma City. We cheered and yelled at other students passing by on the opposite side. We drove south to the Burlington train depot on First Street, made a U-turn at the dead end and drove north past Tenth Street before looping around onto the southbound lanes. Up and down, up and down the Butte we drove, closely following the car in front and closely followed by the car behind.

Most of us didn't have dates to the Junior-Senior Prom, so we went as a group. Mom bought me a pretty dress and I stayed with one of my friends on prom night so we could go together. We dressed and her dad drove us to the junior high gym where we met the rest of the group. We ate dinner together and we stayed and watched the dancing for a while. We laughed at each other's jokes and made snide comments about some of the couples before we got tired and went home.

Roy graduated from high school in the spring, and I settled into my summer routine of helping Mom, loitering, and looking forward to school starting in the fall. As always, Uncle Bob and Aunt Verna and their family visited Alliance in June. Aunt Verna told Mom that she couldn't find a sitter or nanny for her three kids, and she asked Mom if I would go back to Las Vegas with them and watch the children for the summer. At the end of the summer, she would put me on a train and send me home. Mom and I talked about it and I, rather reluctantly, agreed. I rode in the car with my aunt, uncle and cousins to their home in Las Vegas. It was a huge city and the lights in downtown were as bright as day. It reminded me of the wizard's Emerald City. Aunt Verna gave me Jerry's room, making Jerry sleep on the sofa in the living room. Most evenings I would go to "my room" and write letters home or read books or cry myself to sleep because I was homesick. It wasn't so bad in the daytime because I was busy. I did laundry, cleaned house, cooked lunch for the kids, and sometimes lay in the hot Nevada sun, baking and trying to get a tan.

The kids and I had a good summer. Jerry was about my age, so we talked about school, teachers, music, college plans, and life in general. I could relate to the two younger kids because they were the same age as my young siblings. Aunt Verna was kind and very grateful for everything I did around the house. She tried very hard to keep me occupied and busy, but insisted that I have some fun as well. She let me shepherd the kids to the neighborhood swimming pool and to a little Las Vegas souvenir shop, a short walk from the house. One evening, Aunt Verna and Uncle Bob took Jerry and me to The Red Skelton show at one of the casinos. I didn't have any dressy clothes, so Aunt Verna loaned me one of her dresses and a pair of her high heels and gave me a tube of red lipstick. Jerry wore his best suit and Aunt Verna was dressed to the nines. We had a wonderful dinner and the show was funny—at least the parts of the show that I understood were funny.

While Aunt Verna was warm and welcoming, Uncle Bob was not. He was cold and distant whenever Aunt Verna wasn't around, and since he seemed to hang around the house a lot, he was cold and distant a lot. He sat on the couch and when I entered the room to dust or vacuum, he looked up with his eyes hidden behind tinted glasses. I couldn't see his eyes, but I felt the stare. When I was awestruck about something in Las Vegas, Uncle Bob scoffed and said, "Yeah, they don't have stuff like that in the boondocks." The message I got from the looks and the off-hand comments was that I was a country girl who was simple-minded and stupid. As the summer days drifted on, I began to resent Uncle Bob more and more because he just wasn't a nice man. He made me feel incompetent and small.

One day, Aunt Verna suggested I cook a pot roast for lunch. I prepared the roast just like Mom did with potatoes, carrots and onions. At lunch, I served the meat and vegetables with the beef broth on the side, just like Mom did. I thought it was a success. We sat down to eat and when Bob spooned broth onto his potatoes, he asked, "You call this gravy?" "No, I call it broth," I replied. It was a logical, straightforward reply to a question, but Bob took it the wrong way and thought I was being smart or insolent. He lowered his glasses and glared at me, which frightened me. No one spoke again throughout the meal, and I felt even more uncomfortable after that.

Aunt Verna let me call home nearly every week so I could talk to Mom. Unfortunately, these talks made me even more homesick. By the end of July, the combination of being homesick and being anxious around Uncle Bob made my stay in Las Vegas unbearable. I needed to go home and broke the news to Aunt Verna. She begged me to stay because it was still a few weeks before the kids went back to school. She even asked Mom to beg me to stay just a couple more weeks, but my mind was made up. I HAD to go home. I felt guilty that I was letting Aunt Verna down, but that feeling was overridden by the overpowering desire to get out of there. So, Aunt Verna bought me a train ticket, I packed my bags, and off I went, leaving the bright lights far behind.

Grade 12—September 1965–May 1966

Roy was away at the University of Nebraska, so I didn't have my usual ride to school. I could have gotten my driver's license because I turned sixteen in May, but I wasn't interested. I rode to school with Jo and her kids sometimes, but I mostly stayed with grandparents. Staying in town made it convenient to be involved in outside activities. I still sang in the church choir, participated in church youth group, was a Junior Stock Grower, a member of the Legion Auxiliary, and I was elected as secretary-treasurer of the Junior REA.

I thought about enrolling in advanced algebra or trigonometry, but I had struggled with geometry and these advanced math classes looked too difficult. I did enroll in Mr. Hvorka's American government class. Mr. Hvorka was a great guy, and he made a dry subject interesting. We learned how government works and Mr. H. didn't interject his politics into lessons. I don't know if he supported or opposed the president because he didn't let on. He called me Jesse most of the year, thinking it was my first name. Many of the kids laughed whenever he called me Jesse but it didn't matter. There were certainly worse names.

I took Mrs. Merdinger's English literature class. Ronnie and Roy both had classes with Mrs. Merdinger, and they both said that she was the best English teacher in the whole world. They weren't wrong. I loved the class and I loved Mrs. M. because she treated me like I was smart. She encouraged my writing and wrote complimentary notes on my papers, even if I had made some errors in my analysis of a Shakespeare play or sonnet. She told me that I would excel in English composition in college. I also enrolled in advanced shorthand with Mrs. Glarum because I thought I needed more practice before using shorthand in college lectures. Mrs. Merdinger and Mrs. Glarum were the two teachers in high school who encouraged me and made me feel like I could do anything.

The school board hired a German teacher the summer before school started, so I decided to enroll in beginning German. My foray into the German language lasted about a month. I decided German was way too difficult so I dropped the class early in October.

Larry, the sole African American in my class, was still the school's star athlete and still drew the ire of jealous classmates. Toward the end of the football season, I was sitting at my desk, waiting for the teacher to come into the classroom and begin the day's lesson. Some of the boys started talking about Larry, using racial slurs. One boy said, "Well, maybe we should just kill him." The boys and some of the girls laughed. Then, another boy said, "Let's wait until after football season." The same people laughed, more loudly this time. The teacher stepped into the room and everyone quickly turned toward the teacher's desk and stopped laughing. The conversation worried me. I wished I had been late to class that day and hadn't heard the comments. I considered saying something to the teacher, but decided against it. I sat there, staring straight ahead pretending that I hadn't heard what I heard because I was afraid to get involved. I never told anyone, not even Mom. I knew she would say something like, "Well, I don't know about that." Or, "Just don't worry about it."

In December I completed my enrollment forms for admission to the University of Nebraska. There was a long admissions application that Dad and I signed. I enclosed my immunization records, my application for student housing, and Dad's check. I wrote that my major was nursing and I was enrolling in pre-nursing courses. I requested that the counselor's office forward my transcripts through grade 11 directly to the university admissions office, and that they forward my final transcript to the university that summer. I received my formal acceptance to the university in the spring.

In January, everyone in my class who planned to attend the university took the Regent's Exam. For me, it was a formality. I was taking the exam to qualify for a Regent's Scholarship, but I knew that I wouldn't qualify. Still, I held out hope. It would be so great to say I was a Regent Scholar and get my tuition paid. When the scores came back, I didn't qualify. I was disappointed, but not surprised. I suspect that my parents were even more disappointed because they would continue to have two kids in college: Roy was enrolled at the University of Nebraska College of Agriculture and I was soon to be enrolled in the university's pre-nursing degree program. Still, Mom and Dad didn't say they were disappointed that I didn't get the scholarship. Mom told me that she was glad I took the exam. At least I had tried to earn a scholarship.

I didn't take the ACT or SAT exams. First, I hated taking tests; second, I knew I wouldn't score high enough to earn a scholarship; and third, there was no real need to take the exams. I was a Nebraska resident and I would graduate from an accredited high school so I could attend any public college or university in the state. Once enrolled, all I had to do was maintain a 2.0 GPA to stay in school and I knew I could keep a C average.

A few of my friends didn't want to attend college because they were ready to start working and start a career. My good friend Susan got a job in the county clerk's office in Alliance immediately after graduation and soon became the clerk of the District Court for Western Nebraska. Other friends wanted to go to college but didn't want to go far from home. Some, including Larry, enrolled at colleges in Wyoming, some enrolled at Kearney State College and others at Chadron State College.

The remaining handful of us were enrolling at the University of Nebraska. Cherie enrolled because she wanted to be close to Roy (much to Mom's dismay). Sharon was enrolled because she wanted to be away from home. I enrolled because I wanted to follow my older brothers and because, like Sharon, I wanted to become my own person, far from Alliance. My friends who were enrolling at the university were choosing older dorms in Selleck Quadrangle right in the middle of campus. While the Quad was near the Union and Love Library, Roy told me that the rooms in those old dorms were small, dark, and not very clean. He told me that I wanted to be at Sandoz Hall, a new dorm that was due to open that fall. The rooms would be bigger and have huge windows. I would have to walk farther to class, but it was worth the walk to live in bright, spacious quarters. He was right, of course. He knew that I needed as much light as I could get to be happy. Squeezing into a small dark space would not work for me (or for my roommate). I filled out the form, selecting Sandoz, and since none of my high school friends were selecting Sandoz, I filled out a roommate selection form. The housing office would pick a compatible roommate for me.

I was still in the choir and the chamber choir and always sang the alto part. By second semester, though, I had expanded my range and began singing mezzo-soprano. For the spring concert that year, Mr. Scholl selected me to sing a short mezzo-soprano solo as part of a choral selection. I was excited to be singing this part, even though it was not a long solo. I told Mom how happy I was about the honor, and I sang my solo in the living room for the family. I was staying with Grandpa and Grandma Jesse that week, and when I woke up the morning of the concert, the weather was bad with snow and wind. The weather deteriorated during the day into nearly blizzard conditions. After school, I walked back to my grandparent's house. Dad and Mom were to drive in later to attend the concert. At supper time, Mom called and said that she and Dad would not be able to drive in to Alliance because they were snowed in at home and Highway 2 was impassable. I was devastated. I started to cry and begged Mom to come. I wanted her to hear my solo. Mom was sympathetic but said they just couldn't come. I knew she was crying too because I heard it in her voice, but no matter what I said, she was steadfast and told me that they couldn't come. She said that she had already talked to Grandpa and Grandma and they would take me to the concert and stay to hear my solo. Mom said she was sorry, but all I could do was cry.

I got ready for the concert and Grandma and Grandpa dressed in Sunday clothes. We drove through the snow to the concert at the junior high gym. We walked in and agreed where we would meet after the concert. On my way to the staging area, I grabbed a program because I wanted to see my name in the program as a soloist. I was shocked to see, not my name, but the name of another girl. I was upset.

How could Mr. Scholl do this to me? I could sing this solo! I walked up to Mr. Scholl and showed him the program. "I thought I was singing the solo." He told me that of course I was singing the solo and he looked at the program. "Oh no," he said. "This is a mistake. I am so sorry, Leah. It was just a mistake. I thought I put your name in the program." Just a mistake? It wasn't just a mistake to me. I was going to sing a solo for the first and probably the last time in my life and I wasn't going to get the credit. I was furious but I sang my solo and Grandpa and Grandma said it was wonderful and that I had a beautiful singing voice. They said that they were proud of me. They were kind to me on a day that I thought was the worst day of my life.

In twelfth grade, a crazy, unexpected thing happened with the valedictorian drama that had begun the previous year. Mary's father, the Methodist minister, was caught in the church office with a church member in a rather compromising position. The minister and his family were gone the next day—transferred to some tiny Methodist Church in some tiny town in eastern Nebraska. Mary was gone and much to the dismay of some students, Susan would be our valedictorian.

During the year, with Roy studying at the University of Nebraska, Roy's girlfriend, Cherie, made every attempt to get closer and closer to me. Mom said that Cherie was getting close to me so she could wheedle her way into the family's good graces. When I stayed at Grandma Woodworth's house, Cherie often stayed at Grandma's too, trying to be as helpful and ingratiating as possible.

In the spring, the new pastor told the youth group that he wanted everyone to attend a youth conference in Lincoln. Mom and Dad agreed to let me go and Mom was happy that I would get a chance to see Roy. She was less happy that Cherie was also going and would do her best to renew her relationship with Roy. About fifteen kids and six adult chaperones boarded the eastbound Burlington passenger train on a Thursday morning. We arrived in Lincoln that evening and went as a group to a hotel in downtown Lincoln. There were two or three girls per room on one floor and two or three boys per room on another floor. The chaperones were assigned two per room on each floor. On Friday, we attended the youth conference, but had free time on Friday night. Roy, Cherie, Roy's roommate Chip, and his girlfriend Vernetta had a date on Friday night. I was going to spend the night in the hotel with the rest of the youth group. Then things changed. Cherie told me that Roy had arranged a blind date for me, so I was going out too. I didn't know it, but Roy had a family photo in his dorm room and several boys told Roy that they wanted to be set up on a date with me if I ever came to Lincoln. On that particular Friday night, only one boy was available. His name was Dennis Lambert.

Roy, Chip, Vernetta, and Dennis picked up Cherie and me at the hotel. Chip and Vernetta rode in the front seat, the rest of us were crammed into the backseat with the boys next to the doors. We drove to King's and ate burgers and french fries and drank cokes. After supper, Chip drove into the country and parked on a deserted road. Chip and Vernetta and Roy and Cherie began making out heavily, leaving Dennis and me to sit there uncomfortably. It was too cold outside to escape the car so we sat in the backseat, talked and tried to ignore the other four people in the car. We talked about families, high school, the university and career plans. We exchanged addresses and agreed it would be nice to get letters from each other. I told Dennis that I would be back later in the spring because my parents needed to pick up Roy after the semester ended. Dennis suggested that we get together again, and I agreed. Finally, after an eternity, Chip started the car and he drove back to Lincoln and to the hotel. We got out of the car and Roy and Cherie shared a long, passionate kiss while Dennis and I stood there. We agreed again to write and agreed again that, if possible, we would get together the next time I was in Lincoln. That evening I told Cherie that I liked Dennis. He was so much different from any other boy I knew. After another day of the youth conference meetings and meals, our church group caught the westbound Burlington train home to Alliance.

When the weather turned warm, I finally got serious about driving. With my learner's permit in my purse, I drove to town with Mom and honed my skills in parking, changing lanes, stopping at stop lights, and making right turns and left turns using the correct hand signals. Mom's driving advice was to always be careful and anytime between October and April, throw a blanket, a coat, hat and gloves into the car. You never knew when you would get stranded and a warm coat could save your life.

Dad drove to Alliance with me one time and he made me nervous. I stared at the hood of the car in my attempt to keep the car straight on the highway, but I wasn't successful, and the car weaved a bit. Dad told me not to look at things close by but to look far down the road to where I was going. With that piece of advice, I kept the car going straight, with no weaving into the oncoming lane. Dad also told me to not be tempted to watch the right side of the road because the car will always go where you are looking. If you look at the side of the road for a while, you will land in the ditch. Dad's final driving rule was to always keep the top half of the gas tank full because you never knew what might happen.

I was finally ready to get my license in early May. I drove to town with Mom and we went to the courthouse for the written and driving tests. I had studied, so the written test was easy, but I was scared to get into the car with the state patrolman for the driving test. I just didn't want to come back a second time if I failed. I followed the patrolman's instructions carefully, and when I parked back in front of the courthouse, Mom was waiting on the sidewalk. The patrolman got out of the car and told Mom that I did just fine. I was so relieved. I was a licensed driver but I still didn't drive to school.

Stacy K. asked me to prom that year. His mother was my first teacher at District #124, so Stacy and I had been friends since kindergarten. He was a nice boy, friendly and kind. Mom was thrilled because she and Dad knew Stacy's parents and besides, I was finally going on a date. Stacy and I were going to double-date with Sharon and Craig. Mom and I bought a pretty dress and made some attempts to create a prom-like hairstyle. On the day of the prom, Mom drove me and my dress to Sharon's house. Sharon and I dressed in our finery and created fashionable updos. Stacy and Craig picked us up and we drove to the junior high. The gym was decorated with crepe paper streamers, flags, garlands, balloons and cardboard ornaments. It was magical, like stepping into some fairyland. We ate dinner, drank punch, and attempted to dance. Later, Stacy and Craig drove Sharon and me back to the ranch and dropped us at the gate. It had been a very nice evening—nothing to write home about, but nice.

High School Graduation

*For better or worse, the formative years of schooling contain some of life's greatest moments.
Don't let it pass you by.*

—George Orwell

Immediately after the spring concert, the choir began practicing new music for the baccalaureate service and for the graduation ceremony. The band was busy with their new music and the student speakers wrote speeches. The high school yearbook was distributed and we spent time looking at every page and checking out the photos of our classmates. We hauled the book from class to class, and most of us managed to get many teachers' and dozens of classmates' autographs.

I celebrated my seventeenth birthday, and the next week the seniors were sent to the junior high so we could practice for the baccalaureate and graduation ceremonies. We lined up in our assigned order, we walked into the gym and sat down in our assigned chairs. The principal stood on the stage and told us the sequence of events for baccalaureate and graduation. He explained how the choir members should leave their chairs in an orderly fashion, join the choir, and then return to the assigned chairs after the song. We practiced walking to the risers, standing in our assigned position on the risers, and then returning to our seats.

Next, he explained how diplomas would be distributed. After the explanation, we walked in order to the stage, up the steps on the right side, across the stage, stopping in the middle pretending to get our diploma, and then to the left side of the stage, down the steps and back to our chairs. Finally, we practiced marching out of the gym to the lobby, where were we would meet our parents. It was all very exciting.

Mom ironed my graduation gown and hung it carefully in a doorway. Baccalaureate was on a Sunday and went off without a hitch. Graduation was the following Wednesday so Mom ironed the gown again. We arrived early for the ceremony and I ran to the staging area, holding my gown above my head so the bottom wouldn't get dirty. I found my group of friends. We put our gowns on over our clothes and put on our caps, securing them to our heads with bobby pins. About ten minutes before the ceremony, we lined up in the lobby of the gym. The band played "Pomp and Circumstance" and we walked into the gym to our chairs and sat down. An hour later, it was over. We marched out of the gym clutching our diplomas and milling around, waiting for our families.

After hugs, kisses, congratulations, and photos, we took off our robes and caps and threw them into a bin. We walked out of the junior high as high school graduates. For four years, graduation was the goal. Everything we did was with that goal in mind. We thought graduation would be the best day of our lives, but, just like that, it was over. I figured I might not see some of these kids ever again.

Dennis wrote to me just about every day after the youth conference in Lincoln and I wrote back. In our May letters, we agreed to go on another date when Dad, Mom, and I picked up Roy. A few days after graduation we drove to Lincoln. Once Dad, Mom and I were settled into the hotel in downtown Lincoln, I called Dennis. I gave him the name and address of the hotel and he said he would leave in a few minutes. I dressed in my date clothes and waited for

Dennis at the front door of the hotel. He had borrowed a car from a friend, but was delayed leaving the dorm. He got a speeding ticket and a second ticket because he didn't have a Nebraska driver's license. While he had a valid Missouri license, Nebraska law required that anyone living in the state longer than thirty days had to get a Nebraska license. He was furious because he had gotten two tickets and because he was late picking me up.

The date consisted of burgers and fries and a drive-in movie, *The Pink Panther*, starring Peter Sellers. It was a funny movie, but I missed much of the plot. Dennis and I spent most of the time talking, and Dennis taught me how to kiss. No surprise, but after that date, I was even more enamored with Dennis. We agreed to write each other over the summer and made plans to meet again after we had moved into our dormitory rooms.

CHAPTER 10

The University of Nebraska

Promise me you'll always remember:
You're braver than you believe, stronger than
you seem, and smarter than you think.
—A.A. Milne

Year 1

Preparations and Moving In

In June, Dad and I attended two days of new student orientation at the university. We stayed on separate floors at the Marie Sandoz residence hall, the dorm that I had chosen. Just as Roy described, the dorm was new and the rooms were beautiful. Orientation was exciting. New students were assigned to groups depending on their college major. Since I was pre-nursing, I was assigned to the Arts and Sciences group. Dad and I went to orientation lectures, took a walking tour of campus, ate our meals in a dormitory's cafeteria, and received a packet with campus maps and other college information. The student guides were energetic, outgoing, and positive. They made sure the incoming students and their parents were engaged in the process. On the last day,

Dad bought my season ticket to football games and we drove home. If I had any doubts about attending the university before those two days, those doubts were gone. I loved every minute of orientation and I knew that the university was my future. The effect of this orientation was so much different from the effect of high school orientation four years earlier. I wasn't terrified this time.

I spent the remainder of the summer doing the usual chores at home, listening to KOMA in the evenings, and reading and rereading letters from Dennis. I thought I was in love and couldn't wait to see him again. I frittered away afternoons sunbathing north of the house in a sunny patch between the tall trees. I slathered myself in baby oil mixed with a little iodine. The concoction was supposed to make you tan faster and darker but it didn't really work. It was certainly oily, though, and sand stuck to my skin. I day-dreamed and looked forward to my new life at the university.

Mom, Sharyl, who was going into seventh grade, and I shopped in Alliance and Scottsbluff for everything I would need from early September until Thanksgiving when I could come home. I needed clothes for warm September days, rainy and chilly October days and cold November days. Because of the dress code, I didn't buy any slacks because slacks weren't allowed. I did buy a new pair of jeans that I could wear in my room. The rest of the time I had to wear skirts or dresses of the appropriate, below the knee, length. I wasn't fond of dresses so we bought skirts, blouses and sweaters. When I had my wardrobe, Mom and I boxed blankets, bedspreads, towels, and toiletries. We boxed clothes, socks and shoes, a hair dryer, a radio, an alarm clock, an iron, my typewriter, paper, pens, pencils, notebooks, envelopes, and about fifty postage stamps. Mom and Roy were also packing. Besides clothes and toiletries, they were packing things needed to set up an apartment because Roy was moving to an apartment close to the Ag Campus. I wouldn't see him often because Ag Campus was several miles east of main campus.

In early August, I received final university documents. I had my room assignment at Sandoz Hall, my roommate assignment, my class schedule, and the date for move-in. Everything was arranged and I was getting nervous.

Finally, move-in week arrived. Mom, Dad, and I drove to Lincoln in our very large, full-sized Dodge sedan packed to the brim with suitcases and boxes for Roy and me. Roy drove separately in a small, white Dodge Dart that Dad bought from a mailman that summer. After the nine-hour drive, we went directly to Roy's apartment. Roy unloaded his car, and Dad, Mom, and I unloaded Roy's belongings from their car. Mom helped Roy unpack and set up the kitchen. We all went to supper before we took Roy back to his apartment. Mom, Dad, and I went to a motel for the night, and early the next morning, Dad drove to Sandoz Hall. The dorm was located on the far east side of the main campus on the corner of Seventeenth and Vine Streets. It housed about 500 women and was next to Abel Hall, which housed about 900 men. Between Abel and Sandoz, there was a canteen and an indoor swimming pool for the residents. The cafeteria was on the second floor of Abel. The bonus for me was that Dennis lived in Abel Hall. I was going to be a short walk away from my new boyfriend.

Dad parked close to the door, which was miraculous given that there were hundreds of girls moving in at the same time. I stood in line at the front desk with my room assignment form. When it was my turn, I gave the woman my forms. In return, she gave me a dorm handbook that out-lined the rules, a separate paper with my mailbox number, the combination to the mailbox lock, my meal card, and a key to my room. I signed a form, agreeing to pay for a replacement if I lost the key.

I was assigned to room 511 on the fifth floor. It was a standard double, about fourteen feet by twelve feet. The furniture consisted of two twin beds, one on each side of the room, twin desks next to the beds, and closets and stand-up vanities with mirrors opposite the windows. There was a huge west-facing picture window with smaller roll-out casement windows on each side of the big window. Mom said that this was good. I would get the west sun all year and if I needed some air, I could open the small window on my side of the room. We could see the main campus from my window and Mom liked the broad view. We gazed out the window and Dorothy from *The Wizard of Oz* flashed through my brain. In that instant, I was Dorothy, far from home and scared. At least there were no witches. Besides, it was time to move in my belongings. Mom, Dad, and I grabbed boxes and suitcases from the car and carried them to the bank of elevators. It was a long wait for an elevator, but better than walking up five flights of stairs. We made trip after trip, waiting patiently for the elevator each time. As we carted boxes to my room, some people turned and looked at us. I decided that it was because my dad was the only dad wearing cowboy boots and a Stetson. Other dads wore trousers, dress shoes, and dress shirts, but *my* dad was the handsome dad wearing a western shirt, boots, and a Stetson. My mom was pretty and small, but she wasn't like the other moms, watching while their husbands carried heavy boxes to their daughter's room. No, my mom was not a delicate flower. I was a little proud that she was strong and matched Dad and me on every trip from the car to the fifth floor.

When we only had two boxes left, Mom stayed in my room to start unpacking. Dad and I took the stairs down to pick up the last of my stuff, and we walked up the stairs instead of taking the elevator because it was faster. After all of the boxes and bags were in my room, Mom and I unpacked everything and put things away in what we thought were logical places. Last, we put sheets, a blanket, and a red bedspread on my bed. Mom had crafted a white swan out of a coat hanger, white netting, and tulle. It actually looked like a swan from a distance. Mom put the swan in the middle of my freshly made bed. With that final touch, my room was perfect.

The next task was to buy books. I grabbed my class schedule, locked the door, and Dad, Mom and I drove to the Nebraska Book Store. With the help of a clerk, I located the books required for each class along with an assortment of pens, paper, notebooks, three-ring binders, a Nebraska shirt to wear to football games and a Nebraska pendant to hang on my bulletin board. Mom also bought a Nebraska shirt, but there were no purchases for my dad. He was perfectly happy with his western shirts and his Stetson. Dad drove back to the dorm, Mom and I grabbed the bags and we took the stairs so we could deposit my purchases.

After that, it was back to Roy's apartment to pick him up for supper—the last meal with our parents for three months. After supper, Dad and Mom dropped Roy off at his apartment and they dropped me at Sandoz Hall. Mom promised to write me a letter every week and I promised to write home. Mom made sure I had my checkbook to buy the sundries and incidentals. I could cash a check at the Union when I needed cash.

Mom told me to call home using a pay phone in the lounge if there was an emergency. I would deposit a dime, give the operator my name, and tell her that I wanted to make a collect call. Long-distance collect calls were expensive, so I agreed to call only if it was a true emergency, never because I was just homesick. Mom told me to remember where I came from, remember to be independent, don't be too trusting, and don't worry too much. I hugged Mom and Dad tightly. Mom and I were both crying by the time we said goodbye. I ran up the stairs to my room to meet my roommate and to spend my first night completely on my own. Dad and Mom spent the night at the hotel and headed home early the next morning.

**SEMESTER #1—
SEPTEMBER 1966-JANUARY 1967**

*A university is just a group of buildings
gathered around a library.*

—SHELBY FOOTE

The questionnaire I completed for roommate selection was long and detailed, so I assumed that my roommate would be someone who shared some of my interests. But no, my new roommate Kathy and I had nothing in common. She was from Bellevue, Nebraska, a town just outside Omaha and had graduated from a large, suburban high school. Kathy was an only child, spoiled by her parents, and had not participated in any high school clubs or activities. She seemed a bit rigid and gruff. Still, she was the only person I knew in the entire dorm of 500 people, so, like it or not, I was stuck with her. We talked about the upcoming semester and tried to make the best of the situation. I'm sure Kathy was as disappointed with her new roommate as I was with mine.

We ran out of things to talk about so decided to investigate our surroundings before getting something to eat. Rooms lined the outside walls and there was a lounge in the middle of the floor on the north end. There were four phone booths, one at each corner of the floor, and next to them, four tiny study rooms. The bathroom was in the middle of the floor on the south end and there was little privacy. At least the toilets had doors, but the showers had flimsy shower curtains that billowed and waved when the water was turned on. Pedestal sinks lined a center wall and one long mirror covered the entire length. There was barely room next to each sink or on the narrow shelf above the sink for a bar of soap, toothbrush, and toothpaste, let alone a towel. During our tour of our floor, I started to panic. I was Dorothy—lost in a strange land.

Kathy and I took our meal tickets and followed the crowd of girls to the cafeteria The cafeteria was noisy with clanking dishes and the loud chatter of several hundred boys and girls. We grabbed trays and started through the line. There were lots of options, but I felt sick and took a bowl of Jell-O and some milk. Kathy, on the other hand, ate a huge meal. We went to bed early because we didn't have anything else to do.

The next day was the day before classes started. We went to breakfast and I took orange juice and toast, but I could only manage a few bites of toast. Kathy was hungry. She ate bacon, eggs and toast and washed it down with a big glass of milk. She didn't like the noise in the cafeteria, though, so she ate quickly just to get out of there. It was fine with me because I wasn't eating anyway. Back in our room we picked up a campus map and our class schedules and set out to find our class buildings and classrooms. We went through Kathy's schedule first, found all of her classrooms and then we did the same for me. We judged how long it would take to walk from the dorm to the first class so we would know what time to leave. After we were comfortable with the location of classes, we went to the student union to see what it was like. We also went to Love Library to see where we could study between classes if we didn't want to walk back to the dorm. The stacks seemed like the ideal place. We walked back to Sandoz in time for lunch. Kathy was hungry and loaded her tray with food. I was still feeling queasy, so picked up Jell-O and soup. After lunch, Kathy and I headed back to our room and there was a lot of activity on the floor. Girls were standing in the hallway, talking and laughing. We met the girls who lived to the right and left of our room and talked to them for a while. The Resident Adviser (RA) for the floor walked by our open door. She introduced herself and reminded us that there was a floor meeting that night at seven in the fifth-floor lounge. She said there would be periodic floor meetings and these were all mandatory. At the meeting tonight we would review the dorm rules that we received in our welcome packets.

After a light supper of Jell-O and soup, Kathy and I arrived early for the meeting. The lounge was already crowded. All of the chairs and sofas were occupied with girls who seemed to know each other, so we stood against the wall. The RA introduced herself. She was a junior and had lived in one of the older dormitories the previous two years. She said that she was very happy to be living in this brand-new dormitory and she told us that we were very lucky to have been assigned to Sandoz. She asked us to introduce ourselves by saying our name, year, major and hometown. The group of girls who seemed to know each other were all members of the same sorority, Phi Mu. They were living in the dorm because they didn't have a sorority house. One girl, Christine, lived just down the hall from us in one of the larger corner rooms. Christine had more of a presence than the RA. She was tall, pretty, had very short blond hair and blue eyes. When she spoke, everyone turned in her direction and actually paid attention. It was clear that she was a leader. "I'll bet she was a cheerleader in high school," I thought.

After introductions, the RA reviewed the dorm rules. This was an all-girl dorm and available for full-time students only. Every girl had to be enrolled in at least twelve credit hours. Boys or men were only allowed on the floor during open house hours. If a man (even a dad) was going to be on the floor any other time, he had to yell, "Man on the floor," when he stepped off the elevator. The RA reminded us about the dress code—only dresses or skirts were permitted in the first-floor lounge, canteen, cafeteria or anywhere else on campus. Pants were only allowed if we were on a resident floor or in the basement laundry.

Curfew was the next topic. There was a large co-ed lounge on the first floor with one television set, couches, tables, and chairs. From Sunday through Thursday, men were allowed in the lounge from eight in the morning until ten thirty at night. At ten thirty, men had to leave and the outside doors were locked. While residents could get out in case of an emergency, no one could get in. On Fridays and Saturdays, men were allowed in the lounge until one o'clock and the dorm doors were not locked until then. The RA stressed the importance of returning and being through the outside doors before they were locked at curfew. If a girl was even one minute late, she would not be able to get back inside until the doors were unlocked the next morning at eight o'clock. The exception to the curfew rules was for freshman women. Our Sunday to Thursday curfew was nine o'clock at night instead of ten thirty. She told us that there would be random bed checks to make sure we were in our rooms after curfew. Girls who were absent at bed checks received demerits and their curfews would become stricter.

After the discussion about curfew, the RA took a lot of time to stress the rules about alcohol and men. Neither was allowed in a dorm room. If the RA found liquor in your room, you could be expelled. If the RA found a man in your room, you would definitely be expelled, and if you got pregnant, you would definitely be expelled.

Next, it was on to more mundane topics. We could pick up clean sheets every week on our floor's assigned day at the laundry service counter in the basement of Abel Hall. If you forgot to exchange your dirty sheets for clean ones on your assigned day, you had to wait a week to make the exchange. I loved the smell of clean sheets, so I vowed to never miss the exchange. There was a coin-operated, self-service laundry in the basement of Sandoz and it never closed. We could to do our laundry anytime, day or night. Surprisingly, the laundry was never crowded. Many girls went home every weekend, taking their laundry with them. This left the dorm laundry for the rest of us who were stuck on campus.

The RA described the buzzer system. There was a small metal plate on the wall in each room. The buzzer was enclosed under the plate and there was a small light bulb and a red button at the bottom of the plate. Each girl in a room was assigned a certain number of buzzes for a phone call and another number of buzzes for a visitor. If there was one buzz, it meant that I had a phone call. I pushed the button and walked to one of the four telephones in the hall. I picked up the receiver, told the operator my name and room number, and the operator connected me to the caller. If I had a visitor at the front desk, there were two buzzes. Again, I pushed the button but ran downstairs to the lobby to meet my visitor. If I didn't answer the buzzer because I was out of the room, the light on the buzzer blinked until I pushed the button. I would then call the desk to see if the caller left me a message. Girls were allowed to have a private phone in their room but they had to pay for the phone line and the phone. I didn't even ask my parents about getting a private phone. The buzzer system was fine with me. After the meeting, Kathy and I wandered back to our room to prepare for the first day of classes. Several of our neighbors were in the hall discussing the curfew. They said not to worry about the curfew because you could always get into the dorm. The switchboards were open late, so you simply called a friend to come downstairs to let you in. Your friend walked through the dark, vacant lounge on the first floor to a small exit door on the east side of the building. She opened the door and let you inside. Then, you both ran up the stairs as quietly as possible. I didn't think I would ever need this information, but tucked it away, just in case.

After what seemed to be a very long summer of writing letters, Dennis and I started dating soon after I arrived at the university. Since Dennis lived in Abel Hall, he only had a short walk to Sandoz to have me buzzed. We didn't go anywhere during the week because we were both busy studying. We went on dates on weekends, and sometimes he borrowed a car and we went to a movie. Most of the time we walked to the Union or met in the canteen and had a coke or an ice cream cone. I was enamored with Dennis. He seemed perfect.

I didn't see Roy much because he was busy with his studies and very busy making time with Cherie. He did pick Dennis and me up a few times on Sunday afternoon to take us to his apartment on the Ag Campus. He picked up Cherie first so they could have some time alone before adding Dennis and me to the mix. Roy lived across the street from Valentino's Italian Restaurant so we always got Valentino's pizza for Sunday supper.

Mom came to Lincoln in late October for a visit and she met Dennis. Mom liked him and told me later that she was sure he was "the one" for me. I was skeptical, but she was insistent and I did like him. A week or so later, Dennis told me that he was dating another girl back in Kansas City and we broke up. This was a blow. I just didn't get it. I was naive about dating behavior, but it was obvious to me that dating two girls at the same time was wrong. I also couldn't understand how he could like someone else better than me. We broke up just before Thanksgiving and I was heartbroken. I told Mom that she was wrong about Dennis. He definitely was *not* "the one." Mom replied, "Maybe." I saw Dennis periodically in the cafeteria after that, but avoided him.

That first semester, I was enrolled in the pre-nursing curriculum: English composition, algebra, sociology, biology and Introduction to Nursing. As my favorite high school teacher Mrs. Merdinger predicted, I did well in English. I found writing essays almost fun. Sociology was interesting and algebra and biology were challenging. The pre-nursing class included overviews of pharmacology, anatomy, physiology, psychology, etc. The instructor kept going back to her main theme that nursing was a calling. Several nurses came to the class to talk about their work in pediatrics or obstetrics or surgery. They reinforced the idea that nursing was a calling. After six weeks, I realized that nursing probably was a calling, but it wasn't my calling. After Thanksgiving, I changed my major to Undeclared.

Dad had purchased a season ticket for me so I could attend Cornhusker football home games. I attended every game and fell in love with Nebraska football. Bob Devaney was the coach and he was Nebraska royalty—maybe the God of Nebraska. The weather was quite warm the first two or three games, got a little chilly in midseason, and then downright cold just before Thanksgiving. Students were packed into the student sections, so even when it was cold, the energy and mass of bodies kept us a little warm. Following tradition, I bought a red, helium-filled balloon on the way to every game. With the first Husker touchdown, we let our balloons drift away. Masses of red balloons flying into the blue sky was an incredible sight. For homecoming, I also bought a white mum corsage with a red ribbon because that was what female alums and students wore.

Soon after first semester began, I joined Kappa Phi, billed as a Christian Sisterhood, but most of the members belonged to the Methodist Church. The group met at the Wesley Foundation on Sixteenth Street, a quick walk from Sandoz Hall on Seventeenth and Vine. Several of my Methodist friends from high school had also joined Kappa Phi, so I went to meetings mostly to catch up with them. It didn't take too long for my friends (and me) to become disenchanted. The group wasn't relevant once we gained confidence in our new lives at the university and didn't need that lifeline. One by one, we quit going to meetings.

My roommate Kathy and I were friendly, but she was a bit distant and judgmental. Her dad picked her up every Friday after her last class, and she didn't return until seven in the evening or after on Sunday. After Dennis and I broke up, I had nothing to do on weekends, so I gravitated toward other girls on the dorm floor who didn't go home on weekends. Susan was from Bayard, about thirty miles from Alliance, Kathy P. was from Bridgeport, also in the Nebraska panhandle, Dee was from a tiny town in mid-Nebraska, and Jane was from a tiny town in Kansas. We got along famously—it was a group very similar to my tight-knit group of friends in high school. For weeks, my stomach was upset all the time and I existed on toast and Jell-O. Unlike my new friends who were gaining weight on the dorm diet, I lost weight—some feat, since I only weighed 110 pounds when I graduated from high school.

The semester clicked by. Roy and Cherie were heavily involved, so my trips to Ag Campus for pizza on Sunday became infrequent. Finally, Thanksgiving came and Roy drove Cherie and me home to Alliance for the five-day break. I took all of my warm-weather clothes home to make room for heavy sweaters and winter clothes. On the Friday after Thanksgiving, Roy and Cherie announced that they were getting married on December 29, just a month away. Mom was quiet, hands in lap. I knew she was sad (or maybe mad), but she did an admirable job of pretending to be happy for the couple. Roy, Cherie, and I drove back to Lincoln on Sunday. Cherie sat next to Roy and I sat next to Cherie. They spent most of the trip talking about wedding plans. Once in Lincoln, Roy dropped me and my boxes of winter clothes at Sandoz, and then the happy couple went for a drive before Roy dropped Cherie at Raymond Hall.

There were four weeks of classes left, then the two-week Christmas break, and finally one week of classes in January before final exams. I studied a lot in December and didn't see too much of Roy or Cherie until we headed home for Christmas. Again, Roy and Cherie sat next to each other in the front seat and I sat next to Cherie. Wedding plans were in full swing by the time we got home. Mom was busy sewing my dark green velvet bridesmaid dress and a matching one for Sharyl. Between Christmas plans and wedding plans, Mom was busy and stressed.

At the beginning of winter break, Mom told me that she and Dad talked to Cherie and Roy at Thanksgiving and made them promise that Roy would continue his studies and graduate. Roy and Cherie agreed. They were both enrolled at the university for the spring semester, and they planned to continue their studies. If necessary, after the spring semester, Cherie would quit school, get a job and put Roy through school. After he graduated, she would go back to school to get her degree. Mom said that she was glad they had a plan, but she confided that she didn't trust Cherie. I asked what she planned to do and Mom said that she would do nothing. "I'll make the best of it," Mom said. "I just hope that Cherie will keep her promise."

The wedding was lovely and the Methodist Church was festive with greenery, poinsettias, and a huge Christmas tree in the corner. Cherie's dress was white velvet, perfect for a holiday wedding. The couple was happy and eager to start their life together. Just a few days later, the three of us were back in the car and heading to Lincoln for the final weeks of the first semester. Roy and Cherie moved into a little apartment close to Ag Campus and I returned to Sandoz.

Semester # 2—January-May 1967

Today is a great day to reconstruct your future.
Starting over beats staying put any day.

—Unknown

Second semester started and in mid-February Mom wrote that Aunt Mary had died. I knew Aunt Mary's health had been failing but this was unexpected and I was sad. I loved Aunt Mary. She was smart, self-assured, and elegant, and I wished I could be like her. I was disappointed that I missed the funeral but I wouldn't have been able to go anyway because I didn't have a way to get home and back.

I was enrolled in a beginning zoology class because I had liked biology. The instructor was John Janovy, a newly minted PhD from Oklahoma. He was handsome and girls in class mooned over him. They made appointments to meet him during office hours just so they could talk to him. I agreed that he was good looking, but I didn't see a need to meet with him. I didn't have time to moon over a professor.

While my undeclared major would work for another semester, I knew that I needed to pick a major. I began researching all of the colleges and their graduation requirements. Acceptable majors for girls were nursing, teaching, nutrition, or food sciences. A degree in nursing was already out and a degree in education was out because it required two semesters of physical education. Given my PE experience in high school, there was no way I would suffer through another two semesters. I wasn't interested in nutrition or food science because those majors sounded boring. I also wasn't interested in business, although Dad told me that business was a good option. I eliminated engineering, agriculture, journalism, and architecture. I did give pharmacy a lot of consideration, but that degree would take another five years, which was much too long. Finally, I decided to continue my enrollment in the College of Arts and Sciences because I could take all sorts of classes and they would all apply toward graduation. Since I liked the zoology course I was taking, I decided to major in zoology. The downside was that I had to take one semester of physics, two semesters of a foreign language, and several semesters of chemistry. I had avoided challenging classes and most science classes throughout high school, so why I chose to major in science was a little mystifying. I wanted to do something different, to step out of my box and reinvent myself. I also had something to prove to Mr. D., my high school counselor. Even though I had dropped German in high school, I decided to take German as my foreign language because someone told me that many science papers were written in German. I enrolled in the fall semester: zoology, chemistry, German, sociology, and English.

I also applied for the work-study program which was offered to students with limited financial means. The application was detailed and lengthy and Dad had to provide copies of his taxes and other documents. Students in the program worked for minimum wage ($1.50/hour) for twelve hours per week, got a check, and were allowed to use the money any way they wanted. If selected for the program, I figured I would work in an administrative office somewhere. I also applied to live at Sandoz Hall my second year, but picked Susan as my roommate. Kathy, was too rigid for me. Susan and I were much more compatible.

I started dating again, and I had lots of offers since there were more boys than girls in all of my classes—a reflection of the fact that there were twice as many boys as girls enrolled at the university. Boys often sat next to me in lectures and asked for my notes. I took notes in shorthand as per my high school plan, but when boys started asking for my notes, I needed to transcribe them first. I hadn't planned on this extra step, so it was clear that I needed to start taking notes in cursive rather than in shorthand, just to save time and effort.

First dates were either a review of class notes or "coke dates" at the Union or at the canteen between Sandoz and Abel. Second dates were generally movies or burgers and fries at King's, the local drive-in restaurant. When asked, I always gave a boy the Sandoz phone number and my room number. Sometimes he never called, but it was OK. I didn't really care.

To whom should I complain? Who would believe me?

—William Shakespeare,
"Measure for Measure"

I went on several coke dates in the canteen with Don, who I assumed lived at Abel Hall. He told me that he was a junior, had taken the classes that I was taking, and he knew my instructors. He had grown up on a farm; he was nice and funny and we talked for a couple of hours before going back to our respective dorms. After cokes one evening, he asked if I wanted to go for a ride. He had parked behind Sandoz, even though students weren't allowed to park there. He drove this Pontiac GTO, one of the first muscle cars, and it was a very cool car. We drove around Lincoln for 30 or 40 minutes before he dropped me back at Sandoz. We made out a little before I went back to my room. I didn't hear from Don again for several weeks, but then he called me one Friday evening. He said that he knew about a fraternity party in a barn east of Lincoln and he asked if I would like to go. "Sure," I said. I had nothing to do and I was not opposed to crashing a frat party. He drove up behind Sandoz and I ran out and climbed into his car. We drove east on Vine Street until we were out of town and Don turned onto a little side road adjacent to a field. He stopped the car and told me that there wasn't a party, but he just wanted to be with me. He climbed over the stick shift and started to paw at my clothes. I was shocked. This was unbelievable. I tried to get out of the car, but couldn't find the door handle in the dark, so I fought him for what seemed to be an eternity. He was a big guy, probably outweighing me by a hundred pounds. Finally, I think my elbow or my fist caught him in the eye. He cursed at me, backed away, started the car, and drove back to Lincoln. We said nothing on the way back. When we got back to Sandoz, I sneaked a look as I opened the car door. Don's right eye was starting to swell, which scared me. I thought I might be in trouble and I hated that I had been too trusting. Mom would be so disappointed.

I tore up the steps and burst through the back door of the dorm. There were several couples hanging around and it felt like everyone turned and stared at me. I probably looked like I had been through a war. My hair was a mess, my makeup was smeared, my clothes were in disarray, and my blouse torn. I wasn't going to wait for an elevator, so I ran through the lobby to the stairway door, yanked it open, and charged up the five flights. I raced to my room, opened the door, and slammed it shut. I stood by the door, panting a little. On this rare weekend, Kathy was in Lincoln. She was sitting at her desk, studying when I burst into the room. She looked up at me and asked what had happened. I was mortified and said, "Nothing." Kathy asked again and again, telling me that I looked horrible. I finally told her I had had a fight with my date. She asked if I was hurt, and I told her no. Kathy said I should tell the RA because this was wrong. I disagreed because I didn't want anyone to know how stupid I was. Besides, I knew that reporting a fight like this was very bad. I had heard about girls who had been attacked or even raped and who had been foolish enough to report the attack. No one ever believed the girl. Campus police always did the same thing. They asked the girl what she was wearing, and no matter what she answered, they would say that the outfit was too suggestive. "Dressed like that? What did you think would happen when you got into that car?" They would say that it was the girl's behavior that made the boy act the way he did. "Everyone knows that boys will be boys." I was scared and ashamed and didn't want anyone to know about the mess I got myself into. I remembered third grade when Caril Fugate and our neighbor Gina got blamed for something beyond their control. I was not going down that path. It was best to pretend it didn't happen. I just hoped Don didn't turn me in for punching him and giving him a black eye.

Don't spin your wheels and stress. Take a deep breath, center yourself and make a plan.
—DOUGLAS ADAMS, "THE HITCHHIKERS GUIDE TO THE GALAXY"

After the incident with Don, I didn't go on dates other than the occasional coke date the rest of the semester. I certainly didn't get into anyone's car. I focused on my classes and had some fun with my friends at Sandoz. One friend, Kathy P., often stayed out past curfew. She would call and ask me to come downstairs to let her in. I walked through the lounge to the small door on the east side of the building, opened the door and let Kathy inside. We ran up the stairs as quietly as possible, even though Kathy was often quite drunk and quite loud. I knew she would do the same for me.

I hadn't seen much of Roy and Cherie since the wedding, and that spring they announced they were pregnant. They would both finish the semester but then Cherie would quit school. Roy was enrolled in the fall semester, but it was not clear if Cherie could or would find work after the baby was born so Roy could continue his studies.

After final exams, Dad and Mom drove to Lincoln to pick me up. We loaded the car with all of my stuff and we headed home. I would spend the summer helping Mom with gardening, cooking, and cleaning and, of course, sunbathing.

Mom confided how upset she was about Roy and Cherie. She told me that she knew at the wedding that Cherie was pregnant, and she was skeptical about Cherie's motives. She thought that Cherie got pregnant to trap Roy and she never planned to help Roy get his degree. I could hear the disappointment in her voice but there was nothing I could do or say to make her feel better. I don't know if Mom shared her thoughts with anyone else, but I doubt it. It seemed like I was her sounding board. In August, Cherie and Roy had their baby, a beautiful little girl with dark hair and dark eyes. Mom drove me to Scottsbluff after Cherie was released from the hospital so I could help her with her new life. I cooked and cleaned while Cherie got to know the baby and developed a schedule. After a week or so, I went home to begin packing.

I received a letter that summer saying that I had been accepted into the work-study program. Mom, Dad and I were happy. The letter said that because I was a zoology major, I was assigned to work in Dr. John Janovy's research laboratory in Bessey Hall. I was to report to Dr. Janovy the first week of classes. I was uneasy about this assignment. I had assumed that I would file papers or sit at some desk in an administrative office and answer the phone. This was intimidating. While handsome, Janovy seemed distant and unapproachable. I confided to Mom that I was worried about working in a lab. I don't know anything about a lab. What will I be doing? Mom told me that I could do it. I was smart and my new boss wouldn't expect me to know everything. "You worry too much," Mom said. "It will be OK. You'll be fine."

As Mom expected, Roy decided not to return to the university that fall. I think it broke Mom's heart, but she knew he had obligations and responsibilities. He had a bride and a beautiful little daughter to take care of.

For the first time ever, I was going to be completely on my own with no family support. I think Mom worried about me but I was ready to be on my own. Mom confessed that she had been a little sad when she and Dad left me at school the previous fall. She knew she was going to miss me terribly, but she was also jealous of my new adventure. Even as a young girl her dream was to go to college and become a music teacher. But it wasn't to be. Her parents couldn't afford college and besides, she fell in love with Dad when they were in high school. When she and Dad left me at the university that first time, her old dream came back. She envied that I was setting off into the world, shaping my own path and had choices that she never had. She remembered her old dream, the one that didn't come true, and she cried. Mom's eyes teared up when she told me her story and

I couldn't help it when my eyes filled with tears too. Mom turned away quickly and started peeling potatoes for supper.

Year 2

SEMESTER #1—SEPTEMBER 1967–JANUARY 1968

Keep it simple and focus on what matters.
Don't let yourself be overwhelmed.

—CONFUCIUS

In August, Dad, Mom, and I loaded the car and headed to Lincoln. It was a repeat of the previous year. We unloaded the car, we unpacked and put things away in my room, we drove to the Nebraska Book Store to buy books and trinkets, and finally we went to supper at a restaurant. Afterward, I went back to Sandoz Hall and Mom and Dad left for Alliance the next morning.

My roommate Susan had already moved in and I was amazed to see a small refrigerator under her desk. Susan said she had diabetes and the refrigerator was for the insulin, but there was plenty of room for my snacks and cokes if I wanted. After we had settled into the room, Susan and I strolled down the hallway. We stopped and talked to friends who were back for their second year. Kathy P. was in a room just a few doors down and Dee was in a room on the opposite end of the floor. It was good to see friends after a long summer, and I knew it was going to be a great year. Kathy, my roommate from my freshman year, was in my old room but this year she didn't have a roommate. I guess she didn't want to deal with the drama that came with sharing a room. Susan and I bought our season tickets to football games at the same time so we could sit together. This was much better than sitting in the student section alone.

The semester started. English and sociology would be a skate, and with them my goal was to get As but be willing to accept Bs. Zoology and chemistry were going to challenge my brain cells and my goal was to get Bs but be willing to accept Cs. The sciences each had three hours of lecture and three or four hours of hands-on laboratory instruction each week. The lectures were presented by PhD professors but the labs were led by graduate students. The labs would likely be laid-back, informal, and often fun.

The most stressful part about the first week was meeting Dr. Janovy. I dressed in my best skirt and sweater and went to his office for my appointment. His desk was cluttered with notebooks, loose papers, and books. It was a mess and I couldn't imagine how he could conduct his life in that bedlam. I decided that he was just moving in for the new semester. He was gracious at that first meeting. He asked me to tell him about myself: where I lived, what my dad did, where I went to high school, and what I liked about the university. He asked if I had ever worked with animals and I told him that I grew up on a cattle ranch in the Sandhills. We had cattle, horses, pigs, chickens, pet dogs, and pet cats.

"That's fine," Janovy said. "We use rabbit blood for our research since our cultures need blood to survive. I doubt that you'll do anything with the rabbits, though."

Dr. Janovy told me that his grant was for parasitology research, specifically a human parasite named Leishmania. He worked with several Leishmania species, all highly infectious and potentially deadly in humans. He said the work was dangerous, but as long as I followed his proce-dures, I would be safe. He said that I would work in the lab for twelve hours each week, according to the work-study rules, and he had to sign my time card before I submitted the card to the student aid office. Since my work schedule couldn't interfere with my classes, we established my work schedule. He said that he would tell me what needed to be done each week and all I had to do was complete those tasks. If I finished the assigned work in less than twelve hours, the graduate students would give me additional jobs. He asked if I could do the work and of course I said yes.

"Great! Let's go to the lab." He led the way into a corner lab on the first floor of Bessey Hall. We went through the door and he introduced me to his graduate students, who were all working toward their PhDs in Zoology. The front room of the lab had two desks flanking a large window. The desks were covered with books, loose paper and notebooks, coffee cups, coke cans, and candy bar wrappers. There was a large slate workbench along one wall with a couple of Bunsen Burners and several squirt bottles labeled ETOH sitting on the benchtop. Above the bench, hanging on pegs, were beakers, Erlenmeyer flasks, jugs, and bottles. There was a refrigerator-type appliance with a glass front packed with racks of tubes and small glass vessels filled with what looked like old, dark blood. Dr. Janovy said it was the incubator and the tubes held the cultures. Next to the bench, a doorway led to a second room that was filled with complicated-looking equipment and another workbench. A large cabinet against the wall was filled with glassware that was both clean and sterile. There was also a large, black slate sink piled full of dirty dishes.

Dr. Janovy said that my first job every time I came to work would be to wash the glassware in and beside the sink. He said that washing glassware was sort of like washing dishes at home except that there were additional steps to make sure the glass was exceptionally clean and free of soap residue. Everything had to be triple rinsed with distilled water, dried, and then sterilized in the auto-clave. Clean, sterile glassware was important to everyone in the lab because everything they did required it. If there was no clean glassware, no one could do their work. He told me that one of the grad students would show me the whole process. I would also be responsible for keeping the benchtops clean, but before I cleaned anything, I had to check with the grad students to make sure they didn't need anything on the bench. So that's how the job began. I would be cleaning the benchtops and washing dishes. This was great. I knew how to do these things.

I spent the remainder of my four hours that first after-noon with one of the graduate students. I learned how to wash dishes, rinse dishes, place the dishes on pegs to dry and finally how to prepare the glassware for sterilization. I wasn't allowed to autoclave glassware because everyone thought this job was too dangerous for an undergrad. I did help carry glassware to and from the autoclave and I put the sterile glassware away in the cabinet.

The graduate students told me that 70 percent ethyl alcohol (ETOH) was the best all-purpose disinfectant. When working with cultures, they sprayed alcohol on the benchtop, wiped it off with a paper towel and allowed the benchtop to air dry thoroughly before lighting the Bunsen burner and starting work. After they completed an experiment, they squirted ETOH into each tube and let the tube sit overnight. This killed the Leishmania, making the glassware safe for me to handle.

In October, I took a few ounces of alcohol back to the dorm. I was going to pierce my ears, and since ethyl alcohol was such a good disinfectant, I would first bathe my ears in alcohol. I didn't tell Mom that I was going to pierce my ears because she would disapprove. As a youngster, I had begged to have my ears pierced because I thought it would make me pretty, but Mom refused. "Gypsies have pierced ears," she told me on more than one occasion. I never knew exactly what that meant but guessed that ladies weren't supposed to have pierced ears.

Back in my dorm room with my roommate in class, I gathered my ear-piercing supplies: a ruler, a large, sturdy sewing needle, a rectangular pencil eraser, my bottle of alcohol, my newly purchased gold earrings, and courage. I measured my earlobes and made a red mark on each lobe by pushing a sharpened pencil into lobe at the correct spot. I bathed the earlobe, the needle and the eraser in alcohol. With the eraser behind my earlobe, I jammed the needle through the lobe on the pencil mark and then wiggled the needle around a bit to make the hole wider. I removed the needle, bathed the hole with alcohol, shoved the earring into my ear lobe and bathed the area with alcohol again. I repeated the process with the other ear. Surprisingly, it didn't hurt as much as I expected and there wasn't much blood. The next step was to twirl the earrings and bathe the area with alcohol as often as I could. When my little bottle of alcohol ran dry, I replenished it with alcohol from the lab. I loved the result, and Mom didn't mention my newly pierced ears when I went home for Thanksgiving.

I was busy with classes and my work in the lab the rest of the semester. I cleaned benches and washed dishes every workday and tried to complete my tasks perfectly. I still ran out of work before my required twelve hours, so the graduate students taught me about their work. I watched while they prepared the culture media using rabbit blood. I learned about every Leishmania species in culture, and they showed me what each species looked like under the microscope. They explained the lifecycles, told me where the infection was endemic and how the infection spread. They pulled out textbooks with illustrations of infected people. These were very scary parasites.

That fall, there were peace rallies and civil rights rallies in cities around the country. I heard that there was a Students for a Democratic Society (SDS) chapter at Nebraska, but I didn't think the militant subgroup, Weather Underground, had a presence. The Weather Underground was planting bombs in buildings on other college campuses. Someone phoned either the local fire department or college administrators to tell them about the bomb, where it was and when it was due to explode. Authorities immediately evacuated the building, disarmed the bomb, and no one was ever hurt. Nothing like that was happening in Lincoln. The true activists on campus called everyone else apathetic and they were right. Most students cared more about Nebraska football than anything else.

I often studied in the basement of the chemistry building, Avery Hall, because the women's lounge was huge. There were the usual toilets, sinks, and mirrors, but also a shower, two large desks, and a cot. There was noise and commotion when large lecture classes were about to begin or after they ended but the rest of the time, it was quiet. One afternoon I was studying at my favorite desk in the lounge, in the middle of a difficult chemistry problem. I was slogging through the math with my slide rule when the fire alarm went off. I ignored it. Fire alarms went off all the time in Abel Hall. Some drunk guy thought it would be fun to pull an alarm and watch as the building emptied. Every time, there was no fire and the men filed back into the dorm after the fire department cleared the building. I was writing the answer to the chemistry problem in my notebook when someone stomped into the lounge. I looked up and there, standing in the doorway, was a very large fireman in full gear. "What are you doing here?" he yelled. "Studying," I said innocently. The guy told me that there was a bomb and I needed to get out. I grabbed my stuff and ran up the stairs and out the door. Dozens of students were milling around in front of the building and someone mentioned the Weather Underground. The Lincoln fire department believed the threat at Avery Hall was valid and they were taking it very seriously. I waited outside with the others and after an hour or so, the fire department gave the "all clear." We trudged back into the building and I went back to the women's lounge.

Since Roy wasn't around to drive me home for Thanksgiving and Christmas, I took the train from Lincoln to Alliance. The Burlington passenger train left Lincoln around eleven at night and stopped at every back-water town along the way before arriving in Alliance the next morning. It was a good way to travel. I took a snack, studied in the dim light above my seat for a while, and then slept. After vacation, I took the train back to Lincoln. The eastbound train left Alliance in the morning and got into Lincoln in the early evening. Since the journey back to Lincoln was in the daylight, I studied for exams and wrote papers. Mom packed a box of food to take back to school, so I ate what I could on the train and saved the rest for later.

SEMESTER #2—JANUARY-JUNE 1968

Girls and their dates still got dressed to go [out] but by 1968 pretty much every representation of hope in the country had been put up against a wall and shot.

—ANNE PATCHETT

The Vietnam War was ramping up. There were ground and air offensives and graphic photos of executions in newspapers and on television. On this side of the Pacific, there were civil rights protests at universities in Wisconsin and South Carolina and there were sit-ins and student strikes at other universities. I started to pay more attention to the world around me. More and more young men were being killed in Vietnam, and arguments to stay the course seemed shallow and irrational. "We need to beat the communists back in Vietnam," the pundits yelled. I thought of my high school history teacher and his belief that we should just nuke North Vietnam. I wasn't buying it. It was clear that the US was propping up one corrupt dictator after another in South Vietnam. This was an immoral war.

In March, Lyndon Johnson announced that he would not seek reelection, so others jumped into the presidential race. Eugene McCarthy declared his candidacy, running on an antiwar platform. The platform resonated with me and I signed up to work in his Lincoln campaign office. For a few hours each week, I stuffed envelopes, handed out fliers, and talked politics at his headquarters. It felt good to be doing something important. I attended the McCarthy rally at Pershing Auditorium in downtown Lincoln. There were a lot of people on the main floor cheering McCarthy's speech, but there weren't many people in the balconies. I was disappointed with the turnout but I loved being there—cheering and shouting and waving a placard.

On April 4, Martin Luther King, Jr. was assassinated in Memphis. The event pushed more students into activism and a series of protests and sit-ins followed. Still, the assassination didn't have the impact in Lincoln that it did on other college campuses and in other cities around the country.

Later in April, democratic candidate for president, Robert Kennedy, held a rally in Lincoln but I was scheduled to work at the McCarthy headquarters. I walked into the headquarters and instead of a roomful of people working at long tables, there was a lone woman answering phones. She looked up, said that everyone was at the Kennedy rally, and told me I should go. I left and walked to the Coliseum on campus. This was a much smaller venue than Pershing, and there were so many people outside that I had to push and shove to get inside. Once inside, there was nowhere to sit. The place was packed with students and adults, and the crowd was loud. A man walked to a microphone, said a few words, and introduced Kennedy. Senator Kennedy was young, handsome, and articulate. He talked about his vision for the country, about civil rights, and about ending the Vietnam War. He was charismatic and persuasive but I was committed to McCarthy. I continued my volunteer work with the McCarthy campaign through that semester. The national conventions for both parties would take place in the summer, so I crossed my fingers and hoped that McCarthy would be the candidate.

Mom and Dad took me home after the semester ended. I planned to spend the summer like every other summer. The only difference was that I watched the news to learn what was happening in Vietnam and in the presidential race. In June, Robert Kennedy was shot and killed after a campaign rally in Los Angeles. It was inconceivable. I didn't understand how so many assassinations could be happening in the US. Assassinations happened in small, corrupt countries with no rule of law. Our country was falling apart.

The policeman isn't there to create disorder;
the policeman is there to preserve disorder.

—MAYOR RICHARD DALEY DURING THE 1968
DEMOCRATIC CONVENTION

Politics lumbered along. The Republicans chose Richard Nixon as their candidate. He seemed a little creepy to me, but I had turned into a left-wing radical, so any Republican would likely have been creepy to me. The Democratic convention in Chicago was a disaster. There were antiwar protests outside the convention center and the mayor of Chicago ordered the police to disperse the protesters. The protests and the police response escalated to the point of rioting. There were many arrests in Chicago and the fiasco galvanized the antiwar movement across the country. The Democrats didn't pick Eugene McCarthy. He was probably too much of a leftist. Instead, the Democrats chose Hubert Humphrey. He was a centrist, not charismatic, and didn't garner enthusiasm among my peers.

Year 3

SEMESTER #1—SEPTEMBER 1968–JANUARY 1969

Mom and Dad took me back to Lincoln again that fall. I was still living at Sandoz, but my new room was one of the larger corner rooms facing Abel Hall. Susan, my roommate from last year, and I had a falling out and Susan moved to Ag Campus. My new roommate, Jo, brought a couple of lounge chairs so we could relax in our huge room.

My work-study grant had been renewed, so I still had my job in Janovy's lab. I was enrolled in zoology, organic chemistry, English, and a sociology course. A few weeks into the semester, I started to feel sick. It wasn't like anything I had had before and no matter how much I tried to ignore being sick, I kept feeling worse. Finally, I went to student health. The doctor did some tests and told me I had mononucleosis. There was no treatment. I just had to get plenty of rest, and in a few months, I would be better. Instead, I got worse and I knew I could not continue with everything. On the last day to drop classes, I dropped sociology, leaving me with eleven credit hours. I called Mom to let her know what I had done and explained that I was now a part-time student. As usual, Mom told me not to worry. "Just take care of yourself." I didn't tell anyone else that I was part-time. I was afraid that the university would take away my work-study grant and kick me out of Sandoz Hall since both were reserved for full-time students. Nothing happened. I suppose that since I originally enrolled as a full-time student, that status stayed on my record through the semester. Enrollment, Student Aid and Housing clearly didn't communicate with each other.

That fall, Nixon was elected president. He had promised to get the country out of Vietnam, but it didn't seem like anything was happening. Marches and sit-ins continued when I was too sick to care. It took all of my strength to go to class, study a little, eat a little and sleep a lot. I managed to continue working in Dr. Janovy's lab per my work-study grant and was getting more responsibility. I prepared blood culture media, moved the microscopic Leishmania from one culture flask to another, and basically kept some cultures growing and healthy.

Well, we'll not risk another frontal assault.
That rabbit's dynamite.

—GRAHAM CHAPMAN, "MONTE PYTHON
AND THE HOLY GRAIL"

Dr. Janovy and the grad students kept rabbits in the locked animal room in the basement. Other professors kept animals for their research, but most of the other animals were mice and rats. (I was happy that Janovy didn't keep mice.) While I wasn't allowed to bleed the rabbits, I did accompany grad students a few times for this unpleasant task. We dressed in old lab coats, took the sterile bleeding supplies, walked downstairs and into the very smelly animal room. The grad student selected a rabbit that hadn't been bled in a few weeks and hauled him out of his cage. The rabbits were feisty and bitey, but no match for a grad student and his helper. We strapped the poor animal down on his back, sterilized the chest area, and the grad student plunged a long needle attached to a large syringe directly into the animal's heart. He filled the syringe with blood, pulled out the needle, and I held gauze over the wound in the chest. After a couple of minutes, we released the rabbit from his restraints and returned him to his cage. The whole process seemed inhumane to me. I had worked with animals my whole life and this was awful. The grad students agreed that it was a wretched process for us and for the rabbits.

They reminded me of the photos of the men, women, and children who had been infected with the parasites. These people suffered horrific pain and many died. They told me to remember the goal: We need to learn as much as possible about these parasites, and someday, someone will expand on the work and find a way to prevent or treat an infection. If rabbits had to suffer a minute or two every few weeks, so be it. I understood the logic and the importance of the work. I just wished that there was a better way.

I took the train home that Thanksgiving and slept most of the way because of the mononucleosis. By Christmas I was feeling better and instead of taking the train home, I rode with Kathy P. She drove to her home in Bridgeport and Dad picked me up at her house. I rode back to Lincoln with Kathy after vacation. I helped pay for gas and we talked the entire trip. The downside of riding with Kathy was that I couldn't sleep and I couldn't study.

Semester #2—January-June 1969

Chemistry is a class you take in college, where you figure out two plus two is ten or something.

—Dennis Rodman

Zoology was turning into a great major. I loved nearly every class, even though I didn't necessarily love (or even like) every professor. I took courses in vertebrate and invertebrate zoology, physiology, herpetology, genetics, and parasitology. I got a few As and Bs but mostly Cs. I wasn't unhappy with the result.

Chemistry was more difficult because it seemed like a foreign language sometimes and there was a lot of math. I learned to depend heavily on my slide rules for the math and had three of them—a main slide rule, a backup, and a second backup if I lost the first two. Organic chemistry was the study of chemicals with carbon-hydrogen bonds. It was a rule-driven science so remembering the rules was the key to balancing equations. We made aspirin in one of the labs. My lab partner asked the lab instructor if we could eat the aspirin we had created. The instructor shrugged and said he guessed you could, so my partner bundled the tiny amount of white powder into a paper towel and stuffed it into his pocket.

Inorganic chemistry was the study of substances that didn't have carbon-hydrogen bonds—basically everything on the periodic table except carbon and hydrogen. The rules were somewhat different but balancing equations was still balancing equations. We created a salt or two in the labs, but nothing as cool as aspirin. I was gaining confidence in my ability to think critically and to solve difficult math problems. But then I enrolled in elementary physics. It should have been an interesting class because the course was supposed to cover matter (the substance that makes up a physical object) and energy (light, motion, gravity etc.) and how matter and energy relate to each other. The course description said we would use scientific method to test the theories of Isaac Newton, Galileo, and others. It turned out to be the worst course of my entire college career, and it did a good job killing my confidence. There were probably two hundred students in the large lecture hall, and the professor clearly didn't want to be teaching an elementary course. He droned on and wrote what seemed to be random equations on the blackboard. Nothing he said made sense and nothing related to what was written in the syllabus. The lectures weren't logical or linear, which made the class doubly hard for me. I decided to just study the chapters that the professor was supposedly covering in each lecture and hope for the best.

The week before the first exam the professor told us that there would be some multiple-choice questions and several problems. He said he would give us two points for a correct answer and subtract one point for each incorrect answer. "Oh my God!" I thought.

The exam was horrible. I studied hard at the expense of all of my other classes but the wording of the questions was convoluted and complex. I was completely overwhelmed and tried not to panic. I attempted the math and wrote an answer to each question. We got the exam results the next week. The average was -23. I got a -30, which wasn't that bad in comparison, but it was still a horrible grade and I needed to pass this class; I absolutely could not fail and have to repeat elementary physics. When the professor discussed the exam in class, he was livid. He ranted the whole hour about what a brainless bunch of students we were. We were all incredibly stupid and didn't know how to think. He couldn't understand how the university could have granted admission to such a bunch of morons and idiots. After more insults, he stormed out of the lecture hall, slamming the door on his way out.

The lab sessions were better. The lab instructor was from India and in his first year of his PhD studies. Some of the guys in the lab (I was the only girl) complained to the lab instructor about the professor. The lab instructor was sympathetic and tried his best to explain what the professor was trying to teach. Using the blackboard in the lab, he retaught every lecture we had had since the previous lab. His method of teaching was helpful to me. I felt a little sorry for the guy because he was walking a fine line. He was desperate to help us, but at the same time wouldn't bad-mouth his major professor or throw him under the bus.

My lab partner was an architecture student who scored a +30 on the first exam so I knew I needed to get some help from this guy. His name was Pete; he lived in Abel Hall and I was grateful that he was willing to help me. We sat in the lounge, reviewed the lab work, and Pete went over his lecture notes. I asked him why he was so good with this stuff and he said it was just logic. He said he never actually did any of the calculations for the multiple-choice questions. He just looked at a problem, looked at the choices, and picked the most logical answer. He said he didn't do much of the math in the problems either; just enough to get a ballpark result. The professor didn't seem to care much about a precise answer, just an answer that was close enough. The two of us studied together that whole semester and with Pete's help, I got a D in the class. It was the only D I ever got but I was glad to escape with a barely passing grade. I called Mom when I was sure that my final grade would be a D just to let her know and also to apologize for not doing better. Mom said that as long as I had done my best, it was OK. I felt better, but it still felt like I had let my parents down.

Like every other semester, I enrolled in an English literature course. I liked these classes and I needed arts credits to graduate. Besides, the classes were easier than the science classes and the instructors on the Arts side of Arts and Sciences were far less rigid and structured. They were, as a group, lenient and forgiving. Many participated in peace marches and sit-ins, so if there was a large event in Lincoln, they canceled class, which allowed me to march as well. (Instructors on the Science side of Arts and Sciences never canceled a class.) The English major students were not as serious as students in the sciences. These folks were laid-back and lighthearted. They didn't take themselves too seriously and it was refreshing.

On a whim I had enrolled in a Black studies class. We read books by W.E.B Dubois, Eldridge Cleaver, and Malcolm X, and speeches by Martin Luther King, Jr. I loved the *Autobiography of Malcolm X*. It was a perspective that was completely new to me. The instructor talked about Freedom Riders, about the four little girls who were killed in a KKK bombing in September 1963, and about the Bloody Sunday on March 7, 1965. We discussed the assassinations of Malcolm X in 1965 and Dr. Martin Luther King in 1968. I don't believe that Malcolm X's death even made the news in Alliance, unless it was a tiny story, buried on the last page of the newspaper. King's death was covered, though, and I remembered my Grandma Jesse, a bigoted woman, telling me the summer after his death that she was glad. She said it was good that someone got rid of another communist (*racial slur*).

There were very few African American students in the class, which was not surprising because there were very few African American students enrolled at the University of Nebraska—except for football players. Even the Black studies instructor was white, so the discussions were skewed since the African American students weren't vocal in class.

My work in Janovy's lab continued and I was still the only female working in that all-male environment. I was treated with respect. There were no off-color jokes, no insinuations, nothing that made me even remotely uncomfortable. There was a lot of chatter on topics that ranged from research grants, national politics, university policies, the Vietnam War, and student protests. My coworkers seemed indifferent about anything political. They had more important things to worry about—like finishing their theses, getting their PhDs and finding a job. They knew where I landed on most of the topics, but they didn't care—at least to my face. They were nonjudgmental about my leftist political leanings. I learned a lot about communication and interaction with others from these guys. I watched when they had heated arguments about their research, arguing about one approach to a problem versus another. Often Dr. Janovy entered the fray, stating his opinion in no uncertain terms. The discussions could be loud and passionate, but the men didn't sink to name-calling or personal attacks. I liked that they had bitter fights but were still friends. They still laughed at each other's jokes, still ate lunch together, and still talked about family life.

One afternoon's discussion was uncomfortable for me, though. I walked into the middle of a heated discussion about birth control pills. Everyone was there, including Dr. Janovy, and I thought, "What can these guys possibly know about birth control pills?" I didn't consider that they may have known something because they were all married. At any rate, one of the guys had heard about a doctor in Lincoln who was prescribing birth control pills for unmarried co-eds. He even knew the doctor's name. Everyone knew this was against the law because birth control pills had been legally available only for married women since 1965 but were not legal for unmarried women. Dr. Janovy said that someone should report the doctor because he should lose his license. One of the guys asked what I thought. I shrugged and said, "I don't know," because that was the only answer I could give. I certainly wasn't going to tell these guys that the doctor they were talking about was my doctor and that I was taking the pill.

I had suffered horrible menstrual pain for years and in the last year, the pain was debilitating. I missed some classes and even considered leaving school, but one of the girls in the dorm told me to see a specific doctor because he had helped some other girls. I made an appointment and the doctor prescribed birth control pills, saying that in just a few months, there should be a dramatic improvement. He advised that I not tell anyone that I was taking the pills because I didn't want any boys to know. I took his advice and didn't tell anyone. After taking the pills for two months, everything was better. For the first time in years, the pain was manageable. If it hadn't been for that doctor, I'm pretty sure I would have left college and moved back home. He had saved me.

Never has our future been more unpredictable, never have we depended so much on political forces that cannot be trusted—forces that look like sheer insanity.

—HANNAH ARENDT

This semester the dress code began to erode. Some girls began wearing pants to the cafeteria and to class—especially on cold days. Interestingly, they didn't suffer any consequences from the dorm RAs or from the dean of women at the university. I walked downtown and bought a pair of slacks at Penney's. I gathered my courage one day and actually wore them to class. Nothing happened. It was amazing and liberating.

In March and April, I marched along with many others through the downtown streets. On one particularly warm, sunny day, there were hundreds of protesters chanting and carrying signs and hundreds of hecklers lining the sidewalks, yelling insults. A few policemen stood along the march route, trying to keep the two groups apart. Some people on the sidewalks threw tomatoes at us and a few people threw gravel and small rocks. The march organizers kept yelling at those of us in the ranks to ignore the hecklers, don't engage, keep moving and keep chanting. My position in the middle of the group changed as we rounded a corner. I found myself on the edge, very close to the sidewalk and the counter-protesters screaming insults and throwing things. One man, about my brother Ronnie's age, stepped off the sidewalk and started walking next to me. I assumed that he was joining the march because at first, he just walked. Then, he turned sideways and yelled, "Go to Russia you commie bitch."

"Who is he yelling at?" I thought. I turned to look at him and he turned and moved so he was facing me, walking backward as he continued to yell. I walked forward, moving toward him, we locked eyes and I knew that he was directing his insults toward me. It was shocking. I kept walking, staring at the guy. He kept yelling, kept walking backward but suddenly stopped and returned to the sidewalk. I turned to look at him before I pushed my way toward the center of the pack and toward the safety of the crowd. The whole encounter only lasted a few minutes and strangely, I wasn't scared. I was more shocked than scared. I couldn't understand why the guy picked me out of the crowd for his tirade. I didn't even know him. I couldn't fathom why anyone would believe I was a communist. It was ludicrous. I was a patriot, doing my part to stop a war and save lives. I was obviously right and he was obviously wrong.

After the march, I ran back to the dorm and called home. I told Mom about the man and what he had yelled at me. I tearfully told her that I was not a communist. I just believed that the Vietnam War was wrong. Mom listened and told me that as long as there are men on this earth, there will be wars. I just needed to accept that fact. I said I didn't believe it. Mom just sighed. At the end of the short conversation, she told me to be good, to stay out of this thing, and stop marching in protests but she knew that that wasn't going to happen. I continued to march, but took great care to stay in the middle of the group.

I was neither a militant nor a zealot. I didn't belong to the Students for a Democratic Society, and certainly not the Weather Underground, but I knew a few march organizers who were SDS. I didn't question the bravery of the Americans fighting in the war, but I believed that it was wrong for Americans to die in jungles half way around the world for a cause that no one could articulate. It was my duty to do what I could to support the antiwar cause.

At the same time, I couldn't waste my parent's money. I couldn't participate in so many activities that my grades suffered. If a march, sit-in, or strike was called on a day when I had a science lecture or lab, I went to class. I was also duty-bound to fulfill my work-study obligations. If I was scheduled to work in Dr. Janovy's lab during an event, I went to work. According to the more militant activists, I was apathetic and not a true believer. Maybe that was true. I considered myself an antiwar activist, but I was a pragmatic activist.

The spring semester ended, but I didn't go home that summer. Jo and I moved out of the dorm and into a cheap furnished studio apartment south of downtown Lincoln. The place was about six hundred square feet. There was one room with a full-size murphy bed on one wall, a small bathroom off the main room, and a tiny kitchen in the opposite corner.

The place suited us—small and cheap. We wouldn't be there much anyway because Jo was taking a full course load that summer. I was enrolled in an algebra class and would be working in the lab. On July 20, we walked to the student union to watch television coverage of Neil Armstrong's walk on the moon. The lounge was packed and the whole crowd cheered Armstrong's first words from the moon.

The last couple of years, I had casually dated a few guys. Terry was an agriculture major and lived in the Farmhouse fraternity. I went to some great parties at his house and I went to his spring formal. Jim was a zoology major and rode a motorcycle. We cruised through Lincoln neighborhoods on his bike, and when he did wheelies, I held on for dear life so I wouldn't topple off the back. I never dated Ralph but we went to many of the same parties. He was in the teacher's college and his goal in life was to go to as many parties as humanly possible. He was charming, charismatic and a very funny drunk. Everyone liked him. After a few beers, he told party-goers that his name spelled backward was Dolf. We just stared at him and shook our heads. The rumor was that he left school after that summer because his grades were bad and his parents were fed up. His friends said he joined the army and went to Vietnam. I hoped that he would make it home.

Year 4

Semester #1—September 1969–January 1970

Jo and I decided to move to a larger place for the fall semester. We were tired of sharing a bed and generally tired of being in each other's face all the time. We found a cheap, furnished, two-bedroom apartment on the second floor of an old house. There was a small eat-in kitchen in the rear of the house facing the parking area and alley and a small bathroom next to the kitchen. A short hall led to the living room at the front of the house where there was a large window on the north wall facing the street. The two bedrooms were on either side of the hallway. I took the room with the east window and Jo took the larger room with a west window. The house was east of campus at Twenty-third and U Streets. It was one block south of Vine, so about seven blocks east of Sandoz. Neither of us had a car and it was going to be a twelve-block hike to get to the center of campus. We would each have our own bedroom, though, so walking a few additional blocks was worth it. We planned to walk to campus in the morning and not return to the apartment until after our last class. We moved into the new place and I took the train home for a couple of weeks before school started in the fall.

I was anxious to start school again. I had done the math and knew that even if I took a class in the summer of 1970, I wouldn't have enough credits to graduate until January of 1971. I was worried that Mom and Dad would balk at paying for an extra summer and an extra semester, but I gathered the courage one night and told them what I needed to do to graduate. "That's fine," was all Dad said. I felt guilty about spending more money but was grateful that my parents were supportive.

Late one afternoon while fixing supper Mom said there was news about a former teacher. Mrs. D's husband had died, killed in the house where they lived. There had been a small explosion and the man's body burned in the resulting fire. The police said it was an accident but Mom said there were some rumors about the unusual circumstances. I remembered Mrs. D's lesson about TNT in science class when I was in sixth grade. I thought about the husband's mysterious death and wondered.

My parents took me back to school, helped me move more stuff into the apartment and they met Jo. I don't think Mom and Dad liked the new apartment. It was not the best part of town, but the house was just a block south of Vine Street, a busy street with plenty of traffic at all times of day and night. Besides, deposits and rent had been paid, so there was no getting out of it. They took Jo and me grocery shopping and out to dinner, and headed home the next morning. I bought books at the bookstore the next day and prepared for the first day of classes and my first day back in Dr. Janovy's lab.

My English class this semester was the best one yet. We studied the poetry of Byron, Keats, and Shelley. There were only ten students in the class, and all but me were either upper-level English majors or graduate students in English. The professor, Bernice Slote, knew her subject backward and forward. Professor Slote was a popular English teacher, a poet, and a literary critic. Her works had been published in *The Atlantic* and *The Yale Review*, but she was most famous for her interpretations of Keats's work and for her research papers and books on Willa Cather, a Nebraska author. She invited the class to her home for pizza one evening and we sat in her Victorian living room, discussing poetry and eating pizza. No one cared that I was a science major. I held my own in discussions and got an A on every paper. Slote told me that I should consider majoring in English because I had potential. I told her that I couldn't change majors because I was too far along in my zoology major. I was on track to earn a minor in English, though, and wondered if I should have worked a little harder on my writing skills.

Having nearly completed my zoology requirements, I decided to branch out and take a botany class. It was a fascinating subject and I allowed myself a regret or two about not majoring in botany. But, as with English, it was a little late.

I may not have gone where I intended to go,
but I think I ended up where I needed to be.
—Douglas Adams, "The Hitchhikers Guide to the Galaxy"

I figured that the first day of the zoology class was going to be like most other first days in most other zoology courses. I walked in the door and realized immediately that it was not going to be the same. I knew a lot of the other students, fellow zoology majors, but one student was unexpected. There was Dennis Lambert. It was good to see him, but I was surprised. He had been a pre-med major and should be attending medical school in Omaha. He was probably surprised to see me, too because the last time we talked, I was a pre-nursing student and should be in Omaha. Dennis told me that he had changed majors and was now a double major in zoology and chemistry. I told Dennis that I had also changed majors, and I was now zoology major with a minor in English literature. We agreed that it was amazing we hadn't run into each other before. The lab section for the class was going to be in the evening, once a week. Nighttime labs were not ideal, but we decided it would be fun to be lab partners. After class, Dennis and I walked to the Union, grabbed a coke and continued our chat. It was like time hadn't passed. Our conversation started where we left off back in the fall of 1966. After a long time, we both needed to head home. Dennis lived in an apartment on Fourteenth Street about fifteen blocks south of the center of campus and I lived east, so we couldn't even walk part way together. It was OK, I was going to see him again in just a couple of days at the next lecture.

It's cliché, but true. My feet didn't touch the ground all the way back to the apartment. I walked in the door and yelled, "You will never believe who's in my zoology class. Dennis Lambert!"

"Who?" was Jo's response. I told Jo the history of Dennis and me and told her about the long conversation over cokes at the Union. Jo listened but frowned the entire time. She told me to be careful. "Don't get involved with this guy. He was bad news before and he will be bad news again."

"We're both older. We're not the same people," I said. "I like him."

"No," Jo replied. "You like your memory. Not him. I don't want to talk about this anymore. It's just too stupid." We cleaned up our supper dishes and went to our respective rooms to study. I studied for a while, but mostly thought about Dennis.

We started dating after that first meeting. We sat next to each other at every lecture, shared class notes, and completed our zoology lab projects together. We ate supper at the Union every week before our lab sessions, ordering roast beef sandwiches with french fries drowned in brown gravy. I paid for supper one week and Dennis paid the next week, back and forth through the entire semester. Why we didn't just go Dutch every week is beyond me. We went to a few movies, but movies cost money, something neither of us had. More often, we spent time at the Union, sitting on a couch, drinking cokes and talking.

If we weren't together, Dennis called me nearly every night or at least he tried to call. Jo was jealous of my relationship with Dennis, and she spent hours on the phone in the evening so Dennis couldn't get through. It made me angry because she was so passive-aggressive, and our relationship suffered. Still, we needed each other to share the apartment expenses. We just ignored each other most of the time, and Jo did her best to keep Dennis away from me.

I went to Dennis's apartment a few times and met his friends. Several lived in his apartment building and most were students. Dennis's roommate was a guy named Jim, and he and his girlfriend Shirley were nice but very quiet. Dennis said that Jim was an engineering student so didn't need to have social skills.

Both Dennis and Jim were in ROTC and would get their army commissions upon graduation. After that, they would spend at least two years in the army, and probably be sent to Vietnam. Dennis was a member of Pershing Rifles (PR) and was pretty high ranking in their military hierarchy. He tried to tell me about his responsibilities with ROTC and PR, but I had a hard time understanding the commitment and more or less tuned him out on the topics. The activities meant little to me. While Dennis was spending his spare time in military-related activities, I was spending my spare time with antiwar marches and anti-establishment protests. It seemed like we were on opposite sides of the debate, except that Dennis eventually confided that he shared some of my opinions about the war and the establishment. He was also a pragmatist. He enrolled in ROTC to get the benefit of being an officer. He said he was there for two reasons: he felt compelled to serve and if he was going to die in Vietnam, he wanted to die as an officer. Yes, he had an obligation to the army after he graduated but he also received a small stipend because of ROTC. The stipend helped him get to graduation.

There were still many days of protest at Nebraska but there was no violence. I participated when I could, but my work and school schedule made it difficult. In November, Nixon called on his followers, "the silent majority," to support him and his war policies. After the speech, there were renewed protests across the country.

In December, the first draft lottery since WW II was held. Any male born between 1944 and 1951 was eligible for the draft. A couple of girls I knew had boyfriends who disappeared from campus in the middle of the night after that first draft lottery. The rumor was that their parents had spirited them off to Canada or maybe the boys had gone to Canada on their own. I knew boys who joined the Air Force, the Coast Guard, and the Navy because they didn't want to get drafted and be assigned to the army. I also heard of boys who became Quakers so they could claim to be conscientious objectors. My brother Roy was classified 4-F because of a medical condition, but there were boys whose wealthy fathers used their considerable influence to secure a 4-F for their sons.

Young men either had a path chosen for them or they chose their own path. No matter the path, there were consequences. Those drafted into the army served as enlisted men in jungles and could get killed. Those who enlisted in a "safer" branch of the service or in ROTC might still die in battle. For those lucky enough to survive, there was no hero's welcome. They faced hostility when arriving back home.

Those who chose to go to Canada could never return home—ever. Those who chose to become Quakers had to obey all church doctrine and live as pacifists for the rest of their lives. Those who were granted 4-F status had to endure skepticism from those who thought they had either faked a medical condition or had their fathers buy their 4-F.

I went home for Christmas break in December and told my parents that I was dating Dennis. I said we were pretty serious, and Mom smiled and said, "I knew he was the one for you." I told her that maybe she was right and would never doubt her again.

SEMESTER #2—JANUARY 1970–JUNE 1971

The war has stretched the generation gap so wide that it threatens to pull the country apart.

—FRANK CHURCH

After an uneventful Christmas break, I went back to the little apartment I shared with Jo and we began the new semester. Nationwide and in Nebraska the uneventful became eventful. In February, the Chicago Seven were found not guilty of inciting a riot at the 1968 Democratic Convention in Chicago. Celebrations and marches followed. Shortly after that, a bomb being constructed by New Jersey Weathermen exploded prematurely, killing three Weathermen. The deaths were celebrated by right-wing politicians and by the conservative public (the silent majority). The country did unite behind the Apollo thirteen moon flight. Things had gone horribly wrong but in an amazing engineering feat, the astronauts landed safely after six days. The nation also seemed to unite around the first

Earth Day on April 22. Marches in cities and on campuses around the country celebrated the planet.

In May, Nixon ordered additional US forces into Cambodia, expanding the Vietnam War. There were more protests across the country than ever before. A group protesting the escalation into Cambodia met on the north steps of the Nebraska Union. A subgroup marched from the Union to the draft board office in downtown Lincoln. Twelve students were arrested. I didn't participate in these protests because I had to work. That evening, about fifty students walked into the ROTC building on campus to "occupy" the building until demands were met. The student newspaper, *The Daily Nebraskan*, described the event: *"After a few minutes the number of students swelled…to an estimated 500 students. The atmosphere of the sit-in was like a carnival as a four-man band was brought in to entertain the demonstrators."* Late that evening, university administrators and police met with the demonstration leaders and the event was de-escalated. I didn't attend the "occupation" but Dennis did—not as a demonstrator, but as a protector of the building's assets and the ROTC equipment and documents.

This summer I hear the drumming. Four dead in Ohio.

—Neil Young

The next day, we learned that on May 4, nine student protesters were injured and four students were killed at Kent State University in Ohio when National Guardsman opened fire on them. This was a sobering and shocking turn of events. Who would have believed that citizen-soldiers in this country could shoot and kill university students? A one-day strike was called for May 6 to mourn the loss of fellow students and to continue the protest of the Vietnam War and the escalation into Cambodia.

[In 2020 while living in Ohio, I watched television every day when Governor Mike Dewine delivered his daily coronavirus pandemic update. On May 4, Dewine stepped to the podium and said that he would delay the update with one minute of silence to honor the students killed at Kent State on May 4, 1970, fifty years ago today. He and everyone on the dais bowed their heads for one full minute. It was a poignant gesture that took me back to those horrible days. I struggled to hold back the tears.]

Dennis and I were practically inseparable even though we didn't share any second semester classes. In March we decided to get married. There was no proposal and no engagement ring. We just mutually decided to get married, randomly chose August 22 as the date and started to make plans. I called home and told Mom. She was excited but since we couldn't talk long, I told her I would write to let her know more details when I knew more. There were decisions to make. Dennis was graduating in June and would get his army commission at a ceremony following graduation. If he started his army career immediately, he would go on active duty in the summer. In that case, I would stay in Lincoln until I graduated in January 1971. This was the socially acceptable option. A man was supposed to start his career quickly so he could take care of his wife and family. But Dennis said that there was a second option. He could apply for a nine-month deferment and go on active duty in March 1971. If he got the deferment, we would both stay in Lincoln, Dennis would work and I would finish my degree. In March, we would go together to his first assignment. We both liked this option so he applied and actually received the deferment. He immediately rented the top floor apartment in his building for $45 per month, with the lease beginning on August 1. Dennis was going home after graduation because he could make a lot of money working for the Greyhound bus line. I would stay in Lincoln to go to summer school and work in Janovy's lab. Dennis planned to return to Lincoln in early August and move into our apartment. I would join him immediately after the wedding.

We hadn't decided where to get married. The customary choice was the Methodist Church in Alliance because a bride was supposed to get married in her home church. My parents would like this option, but I didn't relish the idea of planning a wedding from afar even though I knew Mom would do everything perfectly. The other option was to get married in Lincoln where I could be in total control—a better option for me.

Since I was a member of the Methodist Church, I knew we could get married at the Wesley Foundation on campus, but I hadn't attended services there for a few years and I was reluctant to talk to the minister. Dennis was a member of the Lutheran church and his parents were friends with the pastor at Grace Lutheran Church in south Lincoln. He called to set up a meeting. The pastor was friendly at first, but when we asked about getting married at Grace Lutheran, he was suddenly less friendly and told us that he wasn't in the marriage business. It was good that Dennis was a Lutheran, but the only way he would marry us at Grace Lutheran was if I converted to Lutheranism and joined Grace Lutheran. Dennis offered to transfer his church membership from his home church in Maryland to Grace Lutheran. That way, we would get married in a home church. The pastor declined and said that as the bride, I needed to be the member. We probably should have said, "never mind," because we had another option. I could have transferred my Methodist membership to a church in Lincoln but we didn't consider this. Instead, we agreed with the Lutheran pastor's request, and I made an appointment for my first Lutheran lesson in late June. I would have five or six lessons before I took an exam and became an official Lutheran. Luckily, our August 22 date was available for a wedding, so the church secretary put us on the calendar. Now, I just had to tell my parents that I was going to be a Lutheran and was getting married in Lincoln. I made a collect call home that night. I'm sure that Mom and Dad were disappointed that I was getting married in Lincoln, but they didn't seem to care that I was going be a Lutheran. After all, Mom had left her home church, First Baptist, when she married Dad.

Mom was going to start a list of everything that needed to be done for a wedding and I was going to buy a bride's magazine that had a list of things to do. Between us, we were sure we could cover everything. I asked Dad and Mom if they could come to Lincoln in June to attend Dennis's graduation and meet his parents. They agreed and Rick and Sharyl would come along for the ride. Since there were two weeks between graduation and the beginning of summer school, I asked if they could stay in Lincoln long enough for us to go wedding dress shopping. I knew that Mom could sew a beautiful wedding dress if I asked, but I didn't think that would work since I'd be in Lincoln and the dress would be in Alliance. It would just be too difficult to manage all the fittings necessary for a hand-made gown. Besides, Mom loved to shop.

After we found the dress, Mom, Dad, Sharyl, Rick, and I would leave for Alliance. I wanted to spend a few days at home before taking the train back to Lincoln for summer school. Dad said I wouldn't have to take the train. Roy wasn't using the 1964 white Dodge Dart anymore, so he and Mom were giving the car to Dennis and me as a wedding gift. I was very surprised and couldn't wait to tell Dennis. It was a good, solid car and had an automatic transmission with push buttons next to the steering wheel instead of a gear shift. It would be the first time I had a car in Lincoln, but I couldn't drive to class because I didn't have a campus parking permit. I planned to leave the car in the parking lot behind the apartment most of the time but would have the car for my wedding-related errands.

Since we had confirmed our wedding date, Dennis and I went to a local jewelry store to pick wedding rings. We selected simple, matching wedding bands. The rings were 14 karat gold with diagonal lines etched around the circumference and we had the rings engraved. Dennis's ring said, LLJ to DLL 8-22-70. My ring said, DLL to LLJ 8-22-70. I arranged to pick up the rings when the engraving was complete.

I gushed when I told my friends in Lincoln about Dennis and about our wedding plans. Kathy P, whom I had known since the early days at Sandoz, wanted to host a bridal shower in Lincoln. The shower had to happen before the spring term ended so she picked May 17. Kathy sent an invitation to Mom and Sharyl, but since they would be in Lincoln for Dennis's graduation in June, they couldn't come for the shower. Mom was upset about not being able to come to my shower but I told her not to worry. It was OK because the only people at the shower would be school friends. Mom did mail her shower gift to Kathy, though. She even wrote a sweet poem to accompany the gift:

> *Leah*
> *To say I'm thinking of you*
> *Especially today*
> *And that I'd be there with you*
> *If I could have my way.*
> *—V. Jesse*

Summer—June 1970

Mom and Dad arrived the evening before Dennis's graduation. We went to supper and I noticed that Mom was wearing pierced earrings. I told her that her earrings were very pretty. She thanked me and said that she loved having pierced ears because she didn't have to endure clip-on earrings that were heavy and pinched her earlobes. I didn't mention the number of times she told me that only gypsies had pierced ears.

Dennis's parents came from Maryland for the graduation and the commissioning ceremonies, both at Pershing Auditorium. It was a beautiful warm day in Lincoln and the commencement was wonderful. I sat with my family and watched Dennis get his Bachelor of Science degree. I was jealous. I wished I had taken additional classes every semester so I could be graduating too but was resigned to the reality. I would graduate in January and our life together would be on track. The commissioning ceremony followed commencement. Dennis asked me to pin on his second lieutenant bars but I think that Dwight, Dennis's dad, was a little disappointed. He was an army reservist and would have loved to pin on Dennis's bars.

There were dozens of men getting their commission. (Women weren't allowed to enroll in ROTC). I was caught up in the pageantry of the commissioning ceremony, but I was conflicted. My fiancé was going to be an army officer, something I never imagined. I cared deeply about the antiwar movement and I was about to find myself on the other side of the fence. The thought of being married to an army man made me a little uncomfortable, but I believed that I could reconcile the two sides. More important to me at that moment was the fact that Dennis might get assigned to Vietnam and might not come back. That possibility far outweighed anything else.

Dennis and I hosted an engagement party at his apartment after graduation and commissioning. We bought a cake and cookies and borrowed a punch bowl. It was a very small and very happy event. I talked to Dwight for a while. He was warm and kind and welcomed me to the family. He said he couldn't be happier for his son because Dennis was marrying a country girl with common sense and a work ethic. I talked to Dennis's mom, Helen, for a time also. It was clear that she was trying very hard to be nice to me, making every effort to be friendly and pleasant. I so wanted her to like me.

Dwight and my dad got along famously, which, at first blush, didn't seem likely. Dwight was highly educated with a bachelor's degree from Nebraska and a master's degree from South Dakota State. He lived in a city apartment just outside Washington D.C. and worked for the US government. My Dad had a high school diploma and a business certificate. He lived in a small house on a ranch in the Sandhills of western Nebraska. He was self-employed, working cattle for a living. Still, the two had a lot in common. Both were smart; both were articulate, and both were extroverts who could talk to anyone. Both had grown up in the country in Nebraska and both had served in WW II. It seemed like they talked and laughed through the entire party.

Mom and Helen also had a lot in common. Both had grown up in a small town in Nebraska with many siblings. Both graduated from high school and worked after graduation. Both married their sweethearts in the early 1940s. Helen worked hard for twenty-five years to become a trusted secretary and assistant to powerful men. She had responsibilities to ensure the success of her office and her department. Mom had worked full-time on the ranch alongside Dad for twenty-five years. She had responsibilities to ensure the success of the ranch. Both women were introverts—opposites of their extrovert husbands. The two just didn't connect. Helen and my mom talked for a bit, but were clearly uncomfortable. After the party, Mom asked me what I thought of Dennis's parents. I told her that Dwight was great but I didn't think that Helen liked me. Mom said that sometimes, when people are nervous, they don't seem friendly. "Helen was just nervous to meet you and your family. She'll like you when she gets to know you. Don't worry."

The day after the party, Dennis and his parents left for Maryland. He planned to work all summer at the Washington DC Greyhound bus station, making as much money as possible before coming back to Lincoln. He and I had tape cassette players and we agreed that instead of writing letters, we would record our "letters" on tape, mail the tape, listen to the taped message, then record a new message and mail it back. We couldn't talk on the phone because it was too expensive but with taped messages, we could at least hear each other's voices.

Dad, Mom, Sharyl, Rick, and I went shopping after Dennis left. The first stop was Miller and Payne, a large, upscale department store in downtown Lincoln. We took the escalator to the bridal shop and I told the bridal consultant what I was looking for. She picked several gowns for me to try and Mom and I went into the dressing room. I tried on a couple, showing each to Dad as he and my siblings waited patiently on soft sofas just outside the dressing room area. I tried on a third gown and I fell in love with it. It was beautiful—the most perfect dress I had ever seen. It was off-white organza with a high neckline and the lace bodice had a bolero silhouette. The sleeves were lace and were gathered into cuffs. The skirt was floor length and the back fell into a chapel-length train.

I walked out and modeled the dress for Dad. He liked it and I told him that this was the one I wanted. "Wait a minute," he said. "This is the first store. We should walk down the street to Gold's first. They might have something even better."

"No," I said. "This one is perfect. This is the one. Please?" Of course, Dad agreed. What could he do?

Mom and I chose a small lace Camelot-style headpiece and a floor-length silk veil. I modeled the veil with the dress and it was indeed perfect. I asked the clerk about shoes, and she told me to go to a shoe store and buy a pair of off-white fabric dress pumps with a low heel. They should be plain with no embellishment. She told me to wear sheer stockings, definitely not white or off-white. My earrings should be small and simple.

Next, we needed to find Sharyl's dress. The consultant picked a few off the rack for Sharyl to try and we all liked the last one. The dress fit Sharyl well and the style was similar to my dress. It was floor length, had a high neckline, and the bodice had a bolero silhouette. The sheer sleeves were gathered into a tight cuff. The clerk said she could order the dress in just about every color under the sun and asked what my wedding colors were. I had never considered wedding colors and no one had asked that question before. I thought about it and I didn't actually have a favorite color. Well, the dress that Sharyl was wearing was a lovely shade of aqua, and she looked good in that color. I told the clerk that the colors would be aqua and white. Mom and Sharyl liked my choice. As luck would have it, the clerk produced an aqua hairpiece with a short veil for Sharyl to wear. I thought it was great and bless her, Sharyl didn't complain even though it kind of looked like a big aqua spider caught in a net while clinging to Sharyl's blond hair.

It only took a couple of hours for us to find a wedding dress, a veil, and a maid of honor dress. Sharyl and I left our dresses at the bridal shop for alterations. Next, Mom, Sharyl, and I stopped at the lingerie department because Mom said I needed a beautiful nightgown and cover-up for the wedding night. We browsed for a while and found the perfect floaty, sexy duo in aqua. It was beginning to look like aqua was indeed my color. Mom stopped by the women's department and looked for a mother-of-the bride dress, but couldn't find anything. We walked to Gold's, the other large downtown department store, and Mom looked for a dress there. She asked me if I wanted to look at bridal gowns, but I emphatically said that I already had the perfect dress. Mom didn't find a suitable dress at Gold's either but said she would find something in Alliance or Scottsbluff.

We left for home the next morning, and the following day Mom, Sharyl, and I reviewed Mom's wedding to-do list. We used the magazine to help us identify tasks and work out the sequence. I knew girls who had planned their entire wedding when they were in high school. They knew the location, the style of the wedding dress, the number of bridesmaids, the music, the number of tiers on the cake and on and on. Not me. I had certainly thought about getting married, but hadn't planned the event because I wasn't sure that I would ever find the right guy. I think Mom had given my wedding a lot more thought though. She told Sharyl and me that she had always wanted to have a big, white wedding with a floor-length lacy gown. She dreamed of walking down the aisle of a church decorated with flowers. Mom said that when she and Dad decided to get married, she begged her mother to make her a long wedding dress, but Grandma refused, even after Mom reminded Grandma that she wore a long lacy gown on her wedding day. Grandma's refusal was final so Mom wore a skirt and blouse on her wedding day. Mom's white wedding wish came true though. She probably started planning Sharyl's and my white weddings when we were babies. She even clipped and saved Betty Crocker coupons for years, sending them away for the stainless-steel tableware that she would give us as wedding gifts. As soon as she had a full set for me, she continued saving coupons for Sharyl's tableware.

The three of us sat in the kitchen, looking over Mom's wedding to-do list and the list published in the bridal magazine. The first step was to pick out the invitations and get them ordered. Mom and I wrote and rewrote the invitation text until it was perfect. We also wrote the text for a card to be enclosed with the wedding invitations. The card was specifically for friends and relatives who lived in and around Alliance. These people wouldn't drive to Lincoln for the wedding, but would definitely attend a reception in Alliance. Mom wrote her wedding invitation list, and I waited for Helen to send me the Lambert invitation list so I could order a sufficient number of invitations. I told Mom that I would look up printers in the Lincoln yellow pages and take my friend Carol with me to pick out something simple and elegant. After that, Carol and I would tackle the cake, the flowers, the photographer, and the rest of the list. I promised to write home every week to let Mom know how I was doing with the wedding plans.

I'm not sure how I met Carol, but it was probably at some party. She was from Lincoln and lived in an apartment off A Street in south Lincoln. She wasn't a college student, but worked at Gold's department store as a window dresser. She had her own car but often drove us around Lincoln in her brother's 1965 Ford Mustang. Carol was a great friend, always there when I needed something. The situation with my roommate, Jo, was not getting better. She was getting more and more jealous of my relationship with Dennis. She hated him and hated me because I loved him. It wasn't a good situation, but it only had to last through the summer. Besides, with Dennis gone, Jo was a little less hostile. It also helped that she drove home to Omaha nearly every weekend.

I planned to drive the car back to Lincoln on Sunday because summer classes started on Monday. Jo called me early Thursday morning and asked me what was going on since summer classes started today. I was stunned and said that I thought classes started on Monday. She smugly told me that I was wrong. I said that I would leave as soon as I packed the car so I'd only miss one day of classes. I hung up and told Mom that I read the class schedule wrong. Classes started today, so I had to get ready to leave.

It was a mad rush to get everything into the car. It was pouring rain, and since I had barely driven, let alone driven in the rain, I was in a panic. Finally, Mom said, "Sharyl can ride with you to North Platte. You can drop her off at Roy and Cherie's house. You'll have company half way and only have to drive alone the last half. You can still be in Lincoln before it gets dark." Mom said that she and Dad would go to North Platte on Sunday to pick up Sharyl and bring her home. I don't think anyone asked Sharyl if she wanted to ride to North Platte, but she seemed willing.

I drove in the rain with Sharyl riding shotgun to North Platte. Mom called ahead, so Roy and Cherie knew we were on the way. Sharyl and I got to Roy's house and we ran into the house while the rain poured. We stayed awhile and ate a snack. Finally, I decided that I should drive on and Sharyl took her suitcase out of the car. I started off again, on my own, with no partner to keep me company. I stopped at Bosselman's to buy gas before I got back onto Interstate 80. I had stayed at Roy's too long because I ended up driving in the dark, in torrential rain for what seemed like an eternity. I was driving 45 mph, and trucks flew by me, throwing gallons and gallons of rainwater onto the windshield. My wipers couldn't keep up with the deluge. I kept an eye on the center line, an eye on the side of the road, and just kept moving. I finally made it to the apartment and waited for a lull in the rain before I took my suitcases up the stairs and into the apartment. Jo was there and she made me feel like an idiot, which was justified. I was just grateful to be back but I had missed one whole day of my new botany class. I planned to talk to the professor on Friday, give him my story and apologize.

I was too wound up to sleep that night, so I left very early for class on Friday. I caught the professor and apologized for missing the first class. He didn't seem too concerned and told me that it happened a lot and that I could catch up very easily. He gave me the name of another student who took good notes. After class, I secured the notes so I could copy them, and I dropped by Dr. Janovy's lab to say hello to the guys. I told them before the end of spring semester that I was getting married, and they asked how the wedding plans were coming along. I relayed details about wedding venues, wedding dresses, and my upcoming Lutheran lessons, but I'm not sure they were all that interested.

Nothing exists except atoms and empty space;
everything else is opinion.
—DEMOCRITUS, CA. 400 BCE

I went to my botany class, went to work at Dr. Janovy's lab, and started my Lutheran lessons. I realized that it was good I had a car because I wasn't sure how I could have walked to Grace Lutheran and back to the apartment at night without it. Pastor B. was a little nicer than at that first meeting, but he was still humorless. He had very strong opinions about religion in general and Lutheranism in particular. He began the whole discussion with a lecture on the difference between Lutheran beliefs and Methodist beliefs—which might have been a useful lesson if I had cared. The lecture continued with a review of Lutheran beliefs about the Eucharist vs. Methodist beliefs, which veered into a sermon about consubstantiation vs. transubstantiation. I think he saw my eyes glazing over and returned to the basics of

Lutheranism. I was a little offended by his apparent refusal to accept anything related to my Methodist upbringing as an acceptable belief. I likely mistook his zealous instruction as arrogance. It ended up being a six-session discussion on Lutheran theology, with side trips into some very obscure ideology. Maybe the pastor thought that since I was a university student, he had to make the course challenging and interesting. I should have paid more attention because I might have learned something.

Tis the privilege of friendship to talk nonsense, and to have her nonsense respected.

—CHARLES LAMB

Carol and I picked out the wedding invitations and I ordered enough to cover the Jesse list, the Lambert list, Dennis's list, and my list. As soon as I had the invitations in hand, I began addressing them. The deadline for mailing was July 22, thirty days before the wedding.

The wedding was going to be a small affair with one maid of honor (Sharyl) and one best man (Dennis's brother Frank). Roy and Dennis's good friend Bruce would be ushers. My little brother, Rick, would light the candles and Barbara, Dennis's sister, would manage the guest book. Our three-year-old nieces, Brenda Lambert and Veronica Jesse would be flower girls. I engaged the church organist to play the organ and asked my cousin Tommy Dill, who had a beautiful singing voice, to be the soloist. I talked to several ladies in the church women's group to make arrangements for the reception in the church hall. They had several good suggestions about logistics, florists, and bakers.

I made an appointment with the florist, and Carol and I leafed through his book. The florist asked what my favorite flower was. Not again! I didn't have a favorite flower but since my dress and veil had little appliqués of daisies, I decided that the bouquet should be daisies. It was a good choice because daisies were in season in August and would not be expensive. I now had to figure out who else needed flowers and the size and style of flowers for the church altar. I chose the style of my own bouquet first: daisies and flowing aqua ribbons. Sharyl's bouquet was similar but smaller and the bouquets for the two little flower girls were smaller still. We picked boutonnieres for Dennis and Frank, the dads, the ushers, the soloist, and the organist. We picked corsages for the mothers and grandmothers. Finally, we picked a lovely floral arrangement for the altar. All of the flowers would be delivered to the church around noon on August 22.

Next, Carol and I met with the baker at his pastry shop. I didn't want anything too fancy and certainly didn't want little dolls depicting the bride and groom on the top tier. I picked a fairly simple, four-tier white cake with white frosting, embellished with aqua flowers and piping. The cake would be topped with white and silver wedding bells trimmed with white netting. The bakery promised to deliver the cake to the church at noon on the twenty-second.

Last, Carol and I met with the photographer to discuss the types and number of photos for my wedding book. We looked through some examples before picking about ten photos. With the wedding plans humming along, I was beginning to feel a little less stressed.

Summer—July 1970

Mom had been talking to friends and relatives about my upcoming wedding and about the wedding plans. Aunt Lois and Mom's friend Jo decided to host a bridal shower for me on July 18 at Aunt Lois's house. At my shower, there would be games and gifts, cake, and punch. I loved this and asked Carol to drive to Alliance with me for the shower. We left late in the morning of July 16. It would take about eight hours to get home. We made it through Sidney and, at dusk, just north of Sidney, a deer ran across the road in front of me. I slammed on the brakes, but not before I hit a second deer, a doe, that flew into the air and landed in the ditch. I was shaken but we were OK. I was worried about the deer but more worried about the car so we turned around and drove back to Sidney. I parked in front of a little diner. There was a pay phone inside and I called home to tell Mom and Dad what had happened. Mom panicked because everyone knew stories of people who died when their car hit a deer. I assured Mom that Carol and I were OK. "The windshield doesn't even have a crack," I said. "I'm going to try to find someone to look at the car." Dad was on the phone by then and said that he and Mom would start for Sidney immediately. "We'll figure it out when we get there."

A county sheriff was sitting at the far end of the diner's counter, drinking coffee and smoking a cigarette. I walked over to him and told him about my collision with a deer. He asked if we were hurt and when I said no, he grabbed his hat and we went outside to look at the car. He told me the car looked fine and if it drove OK, I could go ahead and drive on to Alliance. First, though, he wanted to know where the deer was and asked that I lead him to the spot.

Carol and I drove slowly until I got to what I thought was the right place. I stopped, got out of the car and pointed to the ditch. "It should be about there." The sheriff grabbed his flashlight and started walking along the side of the road. He came back and said the deer was dead but he would call a friend, an Indian (Native American), who could butcher a deer that size in just a few minutes. He said the deer would be in someone's freezer in a few hours. I thanked him for his help. He wished us luck and Carol and I headed north. I asked Carol to watch for my parents' car coming toward us. It was a big Dodge with license number 61-B55. We hadn't gone too far when I saw Dad's car and stopped. Dad must have seen us at the same time because he turned around and drove up behind us. Everyone piled out of cars—Carol and me, Mom, Dad, Sharyl, and Rick. Dad had a flashlight and he looked at Carol and me and then at the car. He said the car looked fine and I told him that a sheriff thought it was OK, too. Dad said he would drive the Dart, so Carol and I got in with Mom and Sharyl. Rick got in the Dart with Dad and we drove home.

Carol and I rested the next day, ate Mom's home-cooked meals, and strolled around outside. Carol didn't want to venture too far from the house because the country was a little scary to her. I wanted to ride horses but Carol was unwilling. She thought the "beasts" were just too huge. I decided that there would be another time for horseback riding.

We relaxed the morning of the shower, then drove to Aunt Lois's house in the afternoon. When we arrived, there were a couple dozen women and girls packed into the Ravert's small living room. My grandmothers and many of my aunts were there along with friends and neighbors that I had known since childhood. Aunt Lois and Jo told everyone that I needed absolutely everything, so most of the gifts were kitchenware and kitchen tools, serving dishes, sheets, towels, and tablecloths. The hostesses also asked everyone to bring a copy of their favorite recipe, and these were a treasure. It was a wonderful party. The gifts were great, but the best part was spending an afternoon with these women who were an important part of my life. I couldn't wait to tell Dennis about the shower.

After the shower, we piled the gifts into Mom's car and left for home. Once home, we moved the gifts from Mom's car to the Dart, had a nice supper, and relaxed. Mom gave me her gift—a small blue glass vase and a poem that she had written for me:

> *When you are feeling*
> *forlorn*
> *Really tired and blue*
> *Hold up this little piece*
> *of glass*
> *And let the light*
> *shine through.*
> *It too, is blue*
> *and cold*
> *not really much*
> *account.*
> *But your touch of*
> *warmth & love*
> *Will let its beauty*
> *out.*
> *Then you will know*
> *the touch of friends*
> *of Dear ones near*

and far
And know their light
will shine for
you
No matter where you
are.

—V. Jesse

Carol and I left for Lincoln the next day, and thankfully the return trip was uneventful. Carol helped me unload the car and we piled everything we could into my little bedroom. We stacked the overflow in the corner of the living room. I didn't like that because I knew Jo would be annoyed, but I had to put my stuff somewhere.

From ghoulies and ghosties and long-leggidy
beasties and things that go bump in the night,
Good Lord deliver us.

—Scottish Prayer

The next Saturday evening, I picked up Carol and we went to my apartment. I parked in front of the house, not wanting to go around to the back alley. Jo had gone home to Omaha, so it was just the two of us. We sat in the little kitchen talking and laughing while we ate sandwiches and chips, drank cokes, and listened to music on the radio. It was after nine o'clock when I thought I heard a noise coming from the living room. "Did you hear that?" I asked. Carol said that she didn't hear anything, so I shook my head and decided that I was hearing things. We talked for a few minutes more and I heard something again. It was a strange sound—not rustling like a scurrying mouse, not muffled voices like a radio turned down low, not even human whispers. The sound was more like a low growl but not quite animal. I got a chill, first up my spine and then down my arms. The hair on the back of my neck stood up. I turned to Carol. "You heard that, right?" Carol nodded. "Is Jo in the living room?" she asked. "No, she's in Omaha until Monday morning." We sat there for a few minutes more, afraid to move and afraid not to move. It was quiet. Finally, I said that Jo probably left her radio on and we heard radio static. I got up and walked into Jo's room but the radio was off. I went back to the kitchen and sat down. "Her radio's off," I said. "Probably just a car driving by the house with the radio turned up loud."

"You're right," said Carol. She turned up the volume on our radio and said, "We'll just drown those guys out."

We talked a little longer, polished off the bag of chips and heard the noise again, louder this time. It was definitely in the house and definitely coming from the living room. "Well, shit," said Carol getting out of her chair. I got up too and we tentatively started down the hall toward the living room. The lights in the living room were off, but it was dimly lit by the light coming down the hall from the kitchen and from the street light just outside the living room window. For the second time I felt a chill up my spine and the hair on the back of my neck stood up. I had a sick feeling in my stomach. We got to the living room door and looked into the room. Nothing. We both peered around the corner to the right side of the room. Nothing. Next, we looked to the left. There, in the corner close to the door, where my shower gifts were stacked, was a broad, smoky silhouette. It looked to be about seven feet tall and a good three feet wide. The top was narrower and rounded, sort of head-shaped. Below the head, there were "shoulders," dropping away into the rest of the smoke. There were no eyes, no mouth, nothing but this transparent, foggy silhouette and I could see my stacked gifts through the fog.

I think I screamed but I couldn't move. Carol grabbed my arm and yelled, "Get out! Get out!" My legs still wouldn't move and I kept staring at the fog. "Come on!" Carol yelled. "Get your keys. We have to go!" My legs started obeying the commands my brain was sending and I turned around. I tore into my room and grabbed my purse and keys. Carol and I flew down the stairs and out the door. We ran to the car and I got in on the driver's side while Carol jumped into the passenger seat. We sat there, breathing heavily for a minute before we looked up toward to the living room window. There, in the window, the silhouette hovered. It looked like it was peering down at us, but there were no eyes. Carol and I both screamed again. I tried to put the key into the ignition, but my hands were shaking so badly that my fingers didn't work. I told Carol that I couldn't drive. We stared at each other for a second and she said, "I'll drive." We opened our doors at the same time, ran around the car and traded places. Carol's hands weren't shaking as much as mine. She put the key into the ignition and started the engine. We looked up at the living room window again. Our ghost was still there, hovering. Carol punched D, hit the accelerator hard and she peeled out. We raced east, toward Carol's apartment.

Carol had the remains of a six-pack of cheap beer in her fridge. We finished the six-pack and fell asleep on the couch. Carol and I talked about the ghost the next morning but we didn't know what to make of it. I didn't go back to my apartment that day. Jo would be back to the apartment on Monday morning, so I decided to wait until then before I went back.

I got up early on Monday and drove to the apartment to get ready for class and for work in the afternoon. I entered the apartment tentatively, but everything was fine. Nothing was out of place. Jo had been there but had gone to work. Her unopened suitcase was lying on her bed. I walked very slowly into the living room. There were no remnants of a smoky presence. My shower gifts were stacked on the floor, undisturbed. I sat on my bed for a few minutes then took a bath, put on clean clothes and walked to class. After class, I ambled into the lab and started to wash the glassware. Ellis, one of the grad students, was the only other person there. I was not talkative like I usually was because I was still thinking about Saturday. Ellis asked if I was OK. "I'm OK," I said, "but something weird happened on Saturday night." Ellis asked me what was going on, so I sat in a chair opposite him and I relayed the whole story. I told him I was scared because I thought the ghost was going to hurt Carol and me. Ellis didn't say anything for a few minutes, just looked at me. I was sure he was going to tell me that I was being hysterical and that ghosts don't exist. Finally, he said that I was looking at this all wrong. He said that I had lived in that apartment for over a year and nothing like this had happened before. He thought something was going on in the house or in neighborhood. The ghost wasn't there to hurt me but was there to watch over me. It wanted to scare me because I needed to get out of the house for some reason. Maybe it was frustrated because I didn't leave after those first few noises, so it had to do something dramatic. Ellis said that I didn't need to be scared going forward because the ghost was my protector. I just needed to be more aware and if there were unexplained noises, I shouldn't wait. I should get out of the house. "Maybe you're right," I said.

"We'll see what happens next." Nothing happened next and nothing happened the rest of the summer. I never told Jo what had happened that Saturday night because I didn't think she would believe me.

I didn't tell the Lutheran pastor about the ghostly encounter either. He didn't seem like the type to take me seriously, so I just continued with my Lutheran lessons until the end of July. The final exam was take-home, so I looked up all of the answers in the confirmation booklets that the pastor had given me. I got 100 percent on the exam so that meant I had passed muster and was now a full-fledged Lutheran. With that hurdle cleared, the Lutheran wedding was officially on.

Summer—August 1970
A WEDDING, TWO RECEPTIONS, AND A CHIVAREE

The best thing to hold onto in life is each other.
—AUDREY HEPBURN

After working all summer, Dennis was back in Lincoln the first week of August. He settled into the little apartment, and I started moving some of my belongings and the shower gifts into our new place. It was a thrilling time for both of us and it didn't seem quite real.

Mom, Dad, Sharyl, and Rick arrived in Lincoln on August 20 and so did Dennis's parents and his sister Barbara. The rest of the wedding party arrived on the twenty-first for the rehearsal. We welcomed Dennis' brother Frank, his wife Norma, and their three-year-old daughter Brenda; Roy, Cherie, and their three-year-old daughter Veronica and six-week-old son Brian; and my oldest brother Ronnie. The other relatives included my grandparents, Dennis's grandmother and various aunts, uncles, and cousins. It wouldn't be a big wedding, but it would be perfect.

The rehearsal went well but my cousin Tommy, the soloist, was nervous. He had a hard time staying on key until the organist intervened. Instead of playing the accompaniment, the organist offered to play the melody. This worked well for Tommy and after that, he sang beautifully. Dad and Mom left the mints, nuts, and punch ingredients in the church hall before we left the church that evening. Dwight had arranged the rehearsal dinner at a large American Legion Hall on O Street. I don't remember what was on the menu but it was likely Nebraska beef. I imagine that there were toasts and speeches, but I don't remember any of that either. I just remember sitting next to Dennis, holding his hand. After the dinner, Mom and Dad dropped me at my apartment and went to a motel for the night. Dennis took our car and went to his bachelor's party. There was a fierce thunderstorm and torrents of rain during the night, lasting until the early morning of our wedding day. It finally cleared, leaving behind a typical summer day in Lincoln—very hot and very humid. Mom always said that having rain on a wedding day was good luck, so I decided that rain was an excellent omen.

Mom, Dad, Sharyl, and Rick picked me up and off we drove to the church. Mom's dress, a street-length, pale-pink number with sheer sleeves, was beautiful and she looked lovely. Dad was handsome in his black suit. Sharyl and I took our dresses, shoes, and hair pieces into the church so we could dress in a classroom/makeshift dressing room.

When we got to the church, the flowers and the cake had already arrived. The ladies' group had placed the cake on the head table in the reception hall along with nuts and mints, cups, and saucers. They would prepare the punch and coffee during the wedding so the drinks would be fresh for the reception. The florist positioned the wedding centerpiece on the church altar, and the remaining flowers were in a large box in the dressing room. The flowers were gorgeous, better than I had imagined. We began sorting flowers, setting aside my bouquet, Sharyl's bouquet, Mom's corsage, and Dad's and Dennis's boutonnieres. We put the rest of the flowers into piles on a large table—flowers for everyone in the wedding party. Everything was accounted for and that was a relief because I had this fear that someone important wouldn't have flowers. With Mom and Dad's coordination, Roy, Cherie, Frank, and Dennis's friend Bruce took care of the flower delivery. They just needed to know who got which flowers.

Sharyl and I got dressed, taking care not to mess up our hair and makeup. We looked at ourselves in the full-length mirror and we looked great. I had my traditional bride accessories: something old (the handkerchief that my mom had carried at her wedding), something new (my dress), something borrowed (Carol's pearl earrings), something blue (my blue and white garter). The photographer was anxious to get some dressing-room photos, so he lurked in the hallway outside while Sharyl and I primped. He took photos of Sharyl and me and of Mom and me and then said that he was going to find the groom so he could take photos of the groom and best man. I asked the photographer if Dennis was at the church. Mom said, "Of course, he's here. I saw him a few minutes ago. You worry too much."

Dad walked me down the long aisle of the church to an organ version of "Trumpet Voluntary." Mom had asked why I wasn't walking down the aisle to "Here Comes the Bride," but I told her that I couldn't stand that song: "Here comes the bride, big, fat and wide." It was a horrible processional song. I couldn't believe brides still used it.

I don't remember much of the actual ceremony, except that I was so emotional that I had a hard time holding back tears. I was incredibly happy. After the wedding, there were photos of the wedding party and then it was on to the reception in the church hall. The reception line was short. Mom was at the beginning, then Dwight, Helen, Dad, me, Dennis, Sharyl, and finally Frank. About sixty people were at the wedding and the reception in Lincoln. We had cake, punch, coffee, mixed nuts, and aqua and white mints. It was a small, quiet, intimate celebration. We opened our gifts and talked to friends before it was time to go on our honeymoon. When my older girl cousins were married, they changed into a going-away dress before they left the church with the new husband. The dress was typically street-length and the same color as the bride's wedding colors. The bride wore a corsage, similar to the ones worn by the mothers of the bride and groom. I didn't want a going-away dress because I wanted to wear my wedding dress as long as possible. I loved the dress and figured I would never wear it again.

Dennis and I left the reception in our wedding finery, and as we walked out the door, we were pelted with handfuls of rice. We ran to our waiting car that had been decorated with shaving cream, and when we opened the car door, our guests emptied bowls and boxes full of rice into the car. We went to Carol's apartment and changed into our traveling clothes. I left my bouquet in Carol's refrigerator. I thought I would retrieve the flowers when we got back to Lincoln and press them as a keepsake. Unfortunately, when we got back to town, the flowers were long gone.

We left Mom and Dad at the church for cleanup. They packed our gifts into Carol's car so she could deliver them to us later and they left the altar flowers at the church for Sunday services the next day. They packed the extra cake, mints, and nuts into their car to take home. The church ladies cleaned the fellowship hall and washed the dishes.

Dennis and I drove to Kansas City that evening and checked into a nice hotel. The next day we toured the city. Dennis drove to his old neighborhood and then to the important Kansas City landmarks. We walked around Country Club Plaza and window-shopped. That night, we ate at a steakhouse and went to the Starlight Theater to see *Fiddler on the Roof*. It was the first time I had gone to a musical since grade school when I went to Chadron State College's performance of *Brigadoon*. This performance was spectacular—what a difference between a college and a professional production. I sang the songs in my head for days afterward.

We left the next day and drove to Manhattan, Kansas, where Frank and Norma lived in a small, two-bedroom, limestone farmhouse just outside town. We ate dinner together, Norma put little Brenda to bed in her room, and the four adults talked into the night. Norma and I had a lot in common. She had grown up on a farm in rural Kansas and had gone to a one-room school for the first eight years. She had graduated from Kansas State University with a degree in library science and had a good job at Kansas State. Frank had also attended K-State and worked at a local store. There was a pull-out sofa bed in the living room so I assumed that Dennis and I would sleep there, but Frank and Norma gave us their bedroom on the second floor. They slept on the pull-out bed. It was a kind and thoughtful gesture. Norma made pancakes, eggs, and ham for breakfast the next morning, and then we were on our way west.

We left Manhattan early because it was a long drive to Alliance. I think we took Highway 77 north out of Kansas to Lincoln and from there west on Interstate 80. We got off at Ogallala and took Highway 81 north to Hyannis. This was the most direct route home, but 81 is a long, lonely road. It's about sixty miles through the Sandhills with only one small town, Arthur, smack in the middle. In Hyannis, we took Highway 2 west about fifty miles to Dad and Mom's turnoff. I don't think Dennis was happy with this route because it was desolate and there were absolutely no other cars on the road. He asked more than once if we were going the right way but we finally got home. I was happy to be there and Dennis was happy that we actually made it.

The next day after lunch, Dad brought two saddlehorses into the barn and saddled the horses for us. Dennis and I left the corrals and rode into the south pasture. We rode to the windmill southwest of the house and then into those hills that were so familiar to me. Since it was late summer, the grasses were khaki, auburn, lavender, and mauve. From a hilltop, I showed Dennis how the hills rolled away in every direction, folding into one another until they met sky. I pointed out my house, Uncle Vern and Aunt Lois's house, Jesse Lake, my little school house, and even Alliance, ten miles to the west. After exploring the pasture and looking at some cattle, we rode home and put up the horses. I don't know what Dennis thought of his ride through the hills, but I wanted to show him my home, the most beautiful place in the world. I hoped he liked it.

Silently, one-by-one, in the meadows of heaven, blossomed the lovely stars, the forget-me-nots of the angels.

—Henry Wadsworth Longfellow

After dark, we went outside and gazed into the night sky. We found the North Star, the Little Dipper, the Big Dipper and the Milky Way. I told Dennis that on some nights you could see the Northern Lights dancing on the northern horizon. It was a perfect night for star-gazing but it wasn't long before the mosquitoes chased us inside.

Mom made all of the arrangements for the second reception at the Methodist Church. There were bouquets of flowers on the tables, corsages for Mom, Sharyl, my two grandmothers, and me. There were boutonnieres for Dad, Dennis, and my grandfather. Mom bought a beautiful wedding cake at the local bakery, along with a couple of sheet cakes. There was nothing for Dennis and me to do but show up. Dennis wore his suit and I wore a white, street-length dress and matching street-length navy jacket. For the second time, we stood in a reception line and welcomed family and friends. For the second time we cut the wedding cake and sat at the head table eating our cake, nuts, and mints. For the second time, we opened gifts. Toward the end of the party, Jo, the woman who helped Aunt Lois with my bridal shower and who had driven Roy and me to school in Alliance for years, took Dennis aside. She told Dennis that she would be getting him later. Dennis had no idea what this strange woman meant by the strange remark. He hadn't even met her before the reception.

After the reception, we packed the gifts and left-over cake, nuts, and mints into the car and took everything home. We relaxed the rest of the day and Dad did his evening chores. Mom suggested that we put together something for supper so Sharyl and I walked with her into the kitchen. Suddenly there was a commotion outside in the yard and then loud pounding on the windows and doors. I looked at Mom in terror, then out the kitchen window. There were faces staring in the window, but not scary faces. These were the faces of laughing friends and family. Everyone was holding a pot or kitchen pan and they were banging the pans with wooden or metal spoons. Some people were blowing on toy horns and others were wildly swinging cowbells. Mom laughed and said, "Don't worry. It's a chivaree!"

[A chivaree is a noisy "serenade" performed by relatives and friends of a newly married couple. The relatives bang on pots and pans and use other noisemakers. The goal is to interrupt the newly married couple on their wedding night. The chivaree is a tradition in parts of the Midwest, and was a long-standing tradition around Alliance. As a child, I went to several chivarees with my family. I had no idea what was going on, just that it was okay to make as much noise as possible.]

The chivaree for Dennis and me wasn't typical because it didn't take place on our wedding night, but it was still a grand surprise and a good excuse for a party. After the outside noisemaking, the group streamed into the house with sandwiches, salads, cakes, cookies, lemonade, iced tea, and snacks. The guests also brought card tables and chairs and we set up tables all around the dining room and living room. Everyone ate supper and then divided themselves into groups of four to play cards. In the middle of the merriment, Jo took Dennis aside again and said, "See, I told you I'd get you!" Dennis laughed. "You certainly did."

The next day, we went to church services at the Methodist Church with the family and on Monday drove with Mom and Dad to Rushville, the county seat of Sheridan County, to handle some official business. We took our birth certificates, our driver's licenses, and our marriage certificate. First, Dennis needed to establish residency and register to vote in Sheridan County. I needed to officially change my name to Lambert on my driver's license, and since I was now 21, I could register to vote. We established Mom and Dad's address on Hickory Route as our permanent home address and licensed the car in our names. We drove back through Alliance on the way home and stopped at First National Bank to close my savings and checking accounts and to set up new joint accounts. We added Dad's name to the signature cards because he could take care of bank-related business for us when needed. On the signature line, I wrote, Leah L. Lambert, because the notion of writing 'Mrs. Dennis Lambert' was ludicrous. It was still early, so we dropped by the insurance office to transfer the insurance on the Dart to our names. After that, it was back to pack our gifts into the car. Dennis and I left for Lincoln early on Tuesday morning. The week had been filled with merriment and a series of parties with Dennis and me as the guests of honor. We had great fun, but now it was back to school and work.

Year 4.5

SEMESTER #1—SEPTEMBER 1970–JANUARY 1971

I would not wish any companion in the world but you.

—WILLIAM SHAKESPEARE, "THE TEMPEST"

Our third-floor apartment on South Fourteenth Street was converted attic space, so at six hundred square feet, it was much smaller than the other apartments in the building. The landlord gave us a reduced rent of forty-five dollars a month if we kept the stairs clean, swept the sidewalk in good weather, and scooped the snow in the winter There was a living room in front, a kitchen, bathroom, and bedroom in the back. The bedroom was just big enough for a double bed and a small dresser, and the fire escape was outside the kitchen door. We had a small gas furnace in the living room but didn't turn it on often. The apartments below us had hot water radiators and all of that heat rose into our apartment. The floors were especially toasty.

There was a coin-operated laundry and a small mom-and-pop market across the street on the corner. The rest of the neighborhood was mostly apartment buildings but there were a few single-family dwellings. The closest grocery store was several blocks away.

Dennis had a job at Campbell's Nursery, the largest nursery in Lincoln. It was manual labor. Dennis and the other men on the crew provided the muscle to plant trees, bushes, and shrubs, and install hardscape for projects in and around Lincoln. He rode in the back of a truck with the other laborers to the nursery's tree farm, dug up and transported trees and shrubs to the job site. Once there, they dug holes and transplanted the plants into the new location. It was back-breaking work, but Dennis said that it would keep him in shape for army duty beginning in March. Dennis eavesdropped on landscaper discussions whenever he could. He learned where specific trees would thrive and where they wouldn't, learned which plants needed sun and which ones needed shade, learned how to plant, how to water and how to fertilize. He figured the information would come in handy if we ever had a real house, a real yard, and a real garden.

Before classes started, I took my old social security card and my marriage certificate to the social security office to get my name changed and to get a new card. I also took my wedding certificate to the university registrar's office to change my name. They would make the adjustment on my records and I would graduate with Lambert as my last name.

Since we had a car, getting to and from school and work was easy. Dennis dropped me at campus on his way to work and picked me up on his way home. There were plenty of places to study on campus between classes so I had most evenings free to be with Dennis. I was enrolled in fourteen credit hours, just enough to complete the requirements for graduation. Since I was only four hours short of a chemistry minor, I enrolled in quantitative chemistry.

Unfortunately, I lost my work-study grant that semester. I never knew exactly why, but I suspect it was because I was a married woman. Dr. Janovy was disappointed with this turn of events, but he pulled some strings and got me a teaching assistant (TA) job for a first semester zoology class. Dennis McLaughlin, a graduate student working on his PhD, was the professor teaching this beginning class. I didn't know McLaughlin, but I knew who he was because he sometimes hung out with the grad students in Janovy's lab. In the orientation program for the teaching assistants, I learned that

I was assigned to teach one lab section with fifteen students. McLaughlin handed out a detailed lab syllabus that specified the tasks to be completed each week. We had to strictly follow the syllabus, pick up lab materials and specimens before the lab section, set up the lab before the students arrived, and clean up after the students left. Lab quiz dates were also listed. We just had to pick up the questions the day of the quiz and return the papers to McLaughlin's office after the quiz. The whole thing seemed straightforward. If I liked teaching, I figured I could get a teaching certificate for high school science after Dennis got out of the army. I didn't actually have a career plan for my degree in zoology, but teaching seemed like a logical choice. Besides, if you already had a degree, you didn't have to take PE classes.

Unfortunately, I hated every minute of my teaching experience. I didn't like the preparation, the cleanup, or the testing. I didn't like needy students or arrogant students. So, if teaching was a calling, and it probably was, it wasn't my calling. I could scratch another career option off the list.

In mid-semester, I ran into Dr. Janovy and he asked me how it was going. I told him that the job was going great (a lie), and that McLaughlin was a good guy (not a lie). Janovy said that if I ever thought about getting a graduate degree in zoology, I should let him know. I could study parasitology. "I'd love to have you as a grad student," he said. I told him thanks, but since Dennis was going into the army for a few years, I couldn't plan too far ahead. Secretly, I was intrigued with the idea of getting a PhD, but I also knew that getting a PhD would require teaching. So, another career option was off the list.

The only other woman in my chemistry class was a couple of years older than me and she was a young wife too. We learned that we had a lot in common and we became friends, chemistry lab partners, and study partners. When talking one afternoon after we finished studying, she told me that she was transferring into the medical technology program at the University of Nebraska, Omaha. She would complete one last year in that program and then have a bachelor's degree in medical technology. I asked some questions about the program because I had never heard of it. She told me that medical technologists worked in medical labs and when doctors ordered tests for patients, the techs performed diagnostic testing. I told her that the job sounded interesting but Dennis and I were moving in March and I couldn't make any career decisions for a while.

"Just think about it," she said. She suggested that I research the career since I clearly liked working in a lab. She said there are schools everywhere, and because I would already have a bachelor's degree in science, I would qualify for enrollment. The course work took ten to twelve months, and when I passed the certification exam, I would get a national registry number. After that, I could get a job at any hospital, anywhere in the country. I tucked the information away for future reference and moved forward to finish the semester.

With school and work and being newlyweds, Dennis and I didn't pay too much attention to protests and politics. We didn't vote in the 1970 elections. Roman Hruska was running for senate again and everyone knew the Republican would win. On the national stage, antiwar activists (maybe Weather Underground) bombed a building at the University of Wisconsin in August, and there had been a huge antiwar rally in Pennsylvania in September. In October, peace talks with North Vietnam fell apart and in November, Lt. William Calley went on trial for the My Lai Massacre. Marches and sit-ins continued at Nebraska, but, as always, the Nebraska activists were neither violent nor all that committed. Students, including the activists, WERE committed to Nebraska football though, and everyone was ecstatic when Nebraska won the national title.

When Christmas break rolled around, we chose to go home to Alliance. Dennis's sister Barbara was going home to the Lambert's in Maryland and Dennis's brother, wife and daughter were going to Norma's home in Tipton, Kansas. We drove to the Sandhills to spend a few days before Dennis had to be back at work and I had to be back at school. It was nice to be home for the holiday. We spent Christmas Eve with Grandma Woodworth, opened gifts on Christmas morning before eating cinnamon rolls for breakfast, and then drove to the typical Jesse Christmas with all of the relatives. Much to their credit, the Jesse's welcomed Dennis into the fray. It helped that Roy knew Dennis, and Roy could run interference as needed. It also helped that Dennis was a regular guy. I'm sure the family feared I would fall for a long-haired hippy type but Dennis wasn't that guy. After dinner, he landed in the middle of the men's card games that were fast-paced and ruthless. Fortunately, Dennis is a fast learner and could hold up his end. After supper we went home but stopped to gaze at the stars before going inside.

Once back in Lincoln, I returned to the final two weeks of school and Dennis returned to work. I took my last final exams and got ready to graduate. Winter commencement was held at Pershing Auditorium on Saturday, January 13, 1971. Mom and Dad drove to Lincoln on Friday and left on Sunday morning. I was happy that they could come to my graduation even though Dad was busy feeding cattle. At least the cows hadn't started calving yet. Mom and Dad gave me a portable Kenmore sewing machine for college graduation.

I didn't look for a job because we were leaving for Dennis's first assignment, in San Antonio in February. Dennis continued work at the nursery until two weeks before we left. We made a quick trip to Alliance and stayed only a few days. I was worried about Dad. He didn't feel well, looked pale, and was very tired, but he said he was fine. The night before we left, it snowed heavily and there was no way we could get to the highway. Dad said that the only option was for him to pull us to the highway. He hooked a chain from a tractor to the frame of our car and it was time to say goodbye. I cried and cried because I was already missing Mom. I would soon be a thousand miles away from home and I didn't know when we would be back. I climbed into the car with Dennis and Dad pulled us all the way to the highway before sending us on our way. When we got to Lincoln, Mom called and said that Dad had appendicitis. He had surgery and spent the rest of the winter convalescing.

Dennis and I finally got serious about packing for our trip to Texas. We knew we would only be in San Antonio for three months before Dennis got his permanent assignment, so we decided the take the bare minimum with us—clothes, Dennis's uniforms, sheets, towels, pots and pans, kitchen necessities, a radio, and some miscellaneous items. We decided to store everything else at Dennis's uncles' house in Walton, a little town outside Lincoln. The bachelor uncles had room in their basement for our possessions, and everything would be safe and sound until we could retrieve our stuff. After we moved our boxes to the uncles' house, we packed the car, said goodbye to our friends and left the apartment key with the landlord. We were on our way to a new adventure.

CHAPTER 11

The Army

*If you don't get out of the box you've been raised in,
you won't understand how much bigger the world is.*

—ANGELINA JOLIE

San Antonio

MARCH–JUNE 1971

The drive from Lincoln to San Antonio was the longest road trip I had ever been on. It was exciting at first because we were setting off on a great adventure. The excitement wore off by the time we got to Oklahoma City and when we got to Dallas, not only was the excitement gone but we were driving through pouring rain. Dennis, being the Good Samaritan, picked up a hitchhiker on the outskirts of the city. "Are you crazy? You don't know that guy," I said when he stopped the car on the shoulder. Dennis just said, "Its pouring. He's cold and wet and needs a ride. If it was me, I hope someone would stop. You worry too much."

"He sounds like my mother," I thought.

The guy ran to the car and tried to open the back door, but I rolled down the window and told him he would have to ride in front. I scrunched as close to Dennis as I could and eyed our passenger warily. The man thanked Dennis for stopping and apologized for getting the car seat wet. "It's OK," Dennis said, "It's an old car. Where are you headed?" The guy said there was a gas station about ten miles ahead, and we could just drop him there. He would call someone from the pay phone. It was slow-going that ten miles because traffic was backed up in the heavy rain and we were creeping along. Our hitchhiker turned out to be a nice guy. He asked what we were doing with our car loaded down, driving in the hard rain. Dennis told him that we were headed to San Antonio because he was going into the army. The two of them talked about the army the rest of the ride to the gas station. When we arrived, Dennis pulled up to the door, the guy thanked Dennis for the ride and wished us good luck. With that, we went on our way. We found a hotel and spent the night south of Dallas.

We arrived in San Antonio the next day and I was stunned. I had never seen such a beautiful city. Everything was green, the weather was wonderfully warm, and the people were friendly. The grass was different. The flowers were different. The trees were different. The houses were different. The city even smelled different. It actually "smelled" warm. I decided that I was going to like our first venture into unfamiliar territory. I thought of Dorothy. This was definitely not Kansas.

Dennis was assigned to Ft. Sam Houston and at the housing office, he located a little, furnished duplex on Claremont Drive, just a few blocks from the post. The duplex was a little bigger than our apartment in Lincoln and it felt comfortable. We had a carport out back and there was a small garden area with a pergola that I thought would be perfect for sunbathing. The woman who owned the duplex was peculiar, but she was nice to us and, after all, she was willing to take on short-term renters. She was about forty-five years old, wore much too much makeup, wore her blouse much too tight and her skirt much too short. A cigarette dangled from her bright red lips.

We moved our belongings into our side of the duplex, went to buy some groceries and then to the phone company to get a phone. I wrote letters to my parents and to Dennis's parents, giving them our new address and phone number.

Dennis was scheduled for two months of Officer Basic training and then one additional month of Advanced Training to learn to run an aid station and help as a medic as needed. He told me that he was being trained for deployment to Vietnam. I tried not to think about it.

Since we would only be in San Antonio for three months, it made no sense for me to get a job. If Dennis was deployed to Vietnam, we would have to decide where I would live while he was away. I could stay in the duplex in San Antonio, close to Ft. Sam Houston, but I didn't know anyone. I was much more likely to go back to Lincoln or back home to Alliance. We would cross that bridge when we got to it.

On Dennis's first day of Officer Basic, he was nervous when he left the apartment but he was very handsome in his uniform. His first day went well because Dennis, like his father, is an outgoing, social extrovert. He made friends and decided that the assignment would be good and would go by quickly.

While Dennis was at work, I passed the time in the duplex. I cleaned house, organized, re-organized, cooked, and sat on the front porch beside the palm tree and watched traffic. I decided to get a tan while we were in Texas, so

I bought a bathing suit on one of our trips to the Post Exchange or PX. I watched out the window and after our landlady finished sunbathing in the back garden, I went outside with my little transistor radio and sat in the sun. I used baby oil and iodine as my suntan lotion, just as I had done when I sunbathed on the ranch. There was room in the garden for the landlady and me to sunbathe at the same time, but I didn't want to get to know her. She was weird.

Dennis had an ID card confirming that he was on active duty and I had a dependent's card. With our cards, we could get on post, buy groceries, merchandise, and gas at the PX and liquor at the Class 6 store. We often spent hours roaming through the PX, looking at the products and the fantastic prices. It was strange for me to be in the PX where over 80 percent of the people were dressed in an army uniform. It was a long way from my days as an antiwar protester, even though my last march had been less than a year ago. This was a strange new reality and I knew I had to keep my opinions to myself.

I listened to music while I worked around the house or sat outside in the sun, but the music was interrupted with news reports on the hour. In late March, Lieutenant William Calley was found guilty of murder in the My Lai massacre. In May, peaceful antiwar protesters tried to interrupt government proceedings in Washington DC, and about twelve thousand people were arrested. In June, Southwest Airlines began operations with short flights between Dallas, Houston, and San Antonio. This was huge news in Texas. Everyone was proud that a Texas airline was competing with the big national airlines. Also in June, the *Pentagon Papers* were published. Those leaked government documents revealed that the US had been involved in Vietnamese affairs through the presidencies of Truman, Eisenhower, Kennedy and, of course, Johnson and Nixon. The Papers also disclosed that President Johnson had secretly expanded the war with raids on North Vietnam, something that was never reported to the media. The government tried to stop the publication of the papers, but the Supreme Court upheld the rights of the free press. Lots of people suspected that there was something questionable and underhanded about the handling of the Vietnam War, and now the truth was out. The deceptions had gone back further than anyone could have imagined. Still, the war continued.

I was one of the only wives accompanying her husband to Officer Basic. We met one couple who had a baby named Andrew. We both liked that name and decided that if we ever had a baby boy, we might name him Andrew. All the rest of Dennis's classmates were either unmarried or their wives had not accompanied their husbands on this short assignment. While I was often the only female at gatherings, I was never uncomfortable. Everyone was kind, courteous, and respectful. San Antonio was in Bexar (pronounced Bear) County and Bexar County was dry. Beer and wine sales were allowed at county-sanctioned stores but only during specific daytime hours and never on Sunday. The sale of distilled spirits was restricted even further. Restaurants and bars sold setups like tonic, cola, or 7-Up, and customers brought in their liquor bottles in paper bags or in small flasks tucked into a breast pocket. Customers drank a little of the setup, and then filled the glass with whatever was in the paper bag. All in all, it was so much trouble going out for a drink in San Antonio that we just went to the Officer's Club, which was on US government property and exempt from local liquor laws. Dennis and

I also ended up hosting parties at our duplex because the Officer's Club was a little expensive and most of the guys lived in the BOQ (Bachelor's Officer's Quarters) so couldn't have parties. We crammed as many people as possible into the duplex, where we ate snacks, drank beer, listened to the radio, or watched TV on our small rented set.

Dennis and I bought a San Antonio map and started hitting some tourist spots. We went downtown and visited the World's Fair Pavilion and Space Needle, we went to the Alamo and the other missions, and went to the Riverwalk and La Villita. Since it was springtime, we met Dennis's friends downtown for A Night in Old San Antonio. This was a highlight of San Antonio's Fiesta, a tradition celebrating the Battle of the Alamo and the Battle of San Jacinto. We had a wonderful time at the celebration. There were masses of people eating street food, listening to mariachi music, and smashing cascarones (hollowed out eggs, filled with confetti) over each other's heads. Several of the guys had flasks of liquor in their pockets, so we bought setups, drank a little, and filled the glass with liquor. We partied from early in the evening until early the next morning.

We took a couple of road trips to Laredo, Texas, where we left our car in the parking lot and walked over the bridge to Nuevo Laredo, Mexico. (Passports were not required.) We made our way through the markets and bought souvenirs from vendors in tiny shops. We even bought a heavy onyx chess set because Dennis wanted to teach me the game. When we were loaded down with treasures, we walked back over the bridge, stashed everything in the car and drove north to San Antonio.

We drove to Corpus Christi and Padre Island another weekend. I had never seen an ocean (or a gulf) before and I loved the beach. The sand was soft under my feet, the breeze smelled of salt, and the sound of the waves was mesmerizing. I decided then and there that we would own a house at the beach one day.

Dennis said when we first got to San Antonio that the time would go by quickly. He was right. After Advanced Training, the army would assign Dennis to a permanent station and they asked all of the soldiers to list their top three geographic areas for assignment. Dennis listed East Coast, West Coast, and Germany, but the army was trying to be more accommodating and decided that soldiers would be much happier if they were stationed close to home. Since our official home was Nebraska, Dennis was assigned to Ft. Riley, Kansas, home of the First Infantry Division (The Big Red One). We were a little disappointed, but there was no arguing with the army. At least it wasn't Vietnam. We decided to live in Manhattan, which was only about fifteen miles from Ft. Riley. Dennis's brother Frank and his family lived just outside Manhattan and his sister Barbara attended Bethany College in Lindsborg, Kansas. It would be nice to be close to family. A fair number of Dennis's friends from basic were also assigned to Ft. Riley but one guy was assigned to Vietnam. The rumor was that he didn't show up for deployment because he was in Canada.

With another move facing us, we realized that we had acquired a lot of stuff during our short stay in Texas, and there was no way we could get everything to Kansas in our little car. It had been a great car, but we needed something bigger. Dennis's parents drove a Buick so he wanted to look at Buicks. We shopped the used car lot at the dealership but didn't see anything we liked—either too beat-up, too old, too expensive or too conservative.

Finally, the salesman showed us a 1968 Buick Skylark that had been traded in that morning. The car was pale-yellow with a white vinyl top, four doors and a V-8 engine. It was sportier, bigger, and heavier than our Dodge. Dennis test drove the car and liked the power so we traded in our small Dodge for that big Buick.

Even with the bigger car, we still had too much stuff, so Dennis bought a trailer hitch at the PX and he installed it at the post's self-serve garage. We rented a small U-Haul trailer, loaded it up, gave the duplex key to the landlord, and said goodbye to San Antonio.

Manhattan, Kansas
June–December 1971

Until you step into the unknown,
you don't know what you're made of.

—Roy T. Bennett

We drove our pretty "new" Buick, towing the U-Haul trailer northward toward Kansas and into another adventure. We arrived at Frank and Norma's house outside Manhattan after an uneventful trip but only stayed with them a few days before we found a house to rent. The house's former owner, a woman who had immigrated to Manhattan from Sweden decades ago, had recently died. Her daughter was sentimentally attached to the house and didn't want to sell it for a while. Instead, she decided to rent her mom's home, fully furnished, to a young couple. The rental rate was cheap and the house was conveniently located on Moro Drive, several blocks east of Aggieville, the main hangout for Kansas

State University students. It was a huge place, probably two thousand square feet. There was a front porch, a large living room, a sun room, a formal dining room complete with chandelier, and a huge country kitchen at the rear of the house. The basement stairs were off the kitchen, next to a tiny half-bath, and a grand staircase in the living room led to the upstairs bedrooms. On the second floor, there was a screened-in sleeping porch above the sunroom, three large bedrooms, and one full bath. The bedroom in the back had been converted into a small kitchen because the previous owner had taken in boarders (students) who rented one bedroom and the makeshift, second-floor kitchen. The boarder shared the bathroom with the home owner. We decided that we would use the upstairs kitchen for storage, although we didn't have a lot of stuff to store. We took a weekend and drove to Lincoln to pick up our belongings from Dennis's uncle's basement. Most of our wedding gifts fit in the cupboards in the large kitchen, but we stored some extra linens in the second-floor kitchen.

The first time Frank and Norma came for a visit, they were amazed that we could rent such a big house for so little. We were leading a charmed life, they decided. Norma told me that she was sorry she hadn't been watching the paper for rentals because she and Frank would have nabbed the place before we found it. We laughed at Norma's bad fortune, but a few months later, Frank and Norma bought a lovely two-story house fairly close to the university campus. Dennis and I helped them move from the farmhouse to their new home in town.

When Dennis started his job at Ft. Riley, he was assigned to the First Medical Battalion in the First Infantry Division. There were about two hundred people in his battalion, and the battalion's job was to support the division when it was in the field. Within the battalion, there were three companies, each with a captain and three lieutenants. In the battalion headquarters, there was a lieutenant colonel who was the commanding officer, a major who was the chief executive officer and three more staff officers for personnel, operations, and supply.

The division's setup seemed strange to me at first, but it actually made sense, given the state of affairs in the world. Dennis described it as a "Division minus." Two-thirds of the division was assigned to Ft. Riley and one-third was assigned to West Germany. In the fall of every year, the Ft. Riley two-thirds went to Europe to join the Germany one-third, and the reassembled division went on maneuvers with NATO forces in Europe. The effort was called Reforger and it was a major component of NATO's Soviet deterrence. The remainder of the year, when the division was split, the Ft. Riley two-thirds had to be ready to deploy to Germany in two to three days if there were problems with the Soviet Union or as Dennis said, "If the balloon went up."

Initially, Dennis was a platoon leader for A Company. Each of the three companies was assigned to set up a clearing station. The soldiers in the company had jobs like medics, mechanics, and drivers. If an infantry soldier in the field was hurt, he was taken to the closest clearing station, where there were medics and doctors. When in the field, the medical battalion had tents, tent stoves, and cots because they were set up to take care of wounded soldiers. The rest of the men in the division slept on the ground, even in very bad weather. To stay in good graces, the medical battalion sent tents, stoves and cots to the general's office so the top brass could sleep in a warm tent on cots when they were in the field.

Dennis's job as platoon leader for A Company lasted about four months and then he became the assistant adjutant for the battalion. The adjutant was the personnel officer and he maintained the battalion's personnel records. Dennis said as assistant adjutant, he did some personnel work but mostly he was the colonel's gopher.

After Dennis and I were settled into our house, I asked Norma, who worked at the K-State library if she thought I could get a job at the university. Norma said that there were always a lot of openings because it was a big campus with many departments. She told me to go to the hiring office and see what they had available. I dressed up, walked to the office on campus, and filled out an application. The recruiter reviewed my application and compared it to job openings. She handed the application back and told me to take it to Dr. Stanley Leland, a professor in the Department of Veterinary Medicine. She gave me directions and off I went. I walked into the receptionist's office and introduced myself to Dr. Leland's secretary. She told me to go right into Dr. Leland's office. Apparently, the woman in the hiring office had already spoken to Dr. Leland because he knew a lot about me. He looked at my application and he asked me a few questions about my background. I told him about growing up on a cattle ranch, about course work at Nebraska, and about working part-time in Dr. Janovy's lab. He asked why I was in Manhattan, and when I told him that Dennis was in the army, he frowned and asked how long we would be in Manhattan. I told him approximately two years and he seemed happy with that answer. After that, he had dozens of questions about my work in Janovy's lab, about the parasitology research, and about the kinds of work I did in the lab. Leland then told me about his own research. He was also a parasitologist, but he studied a bovine nematode, a parasite named *Cooperia punctata*. He was studying the efficacy of anthelmintic drugs that had been developed by different veterinary pharmaceutical companies, and his research was funded by those companies. My role would be to work with the other research assistant to help with those efficacy studies. After about an hour, he asked me when I could start work. I said I could start the following Monday. We walked to his lab and he introduced me to the research assistant, Carol, and to a couple of graduate students. With introductions complete, he told me to come back on Monday at eight in the morning, and I would get started. First, I had to take my application back to the hiring office to finish the paperwork.

When Dennis got home, I told him that I had a job. We had only been in Manhattan a few weeks and I had had only one interview. We decided that we were indeed lucky. The actual luck was that I had worked in a parasitology lab for a few years and knew my way around a microscope and sterile methods. Sure, instead of rabbit blood, I would be working with cow poop, but that certainly didn't bother me. I dealt with cow poop for the first seventeen years of my life.

On my first day at work, Dr. Leland walked me to the lab. I met Carol again, and Leland gave me a quick lecture. A cow ate *Cooperia* eggs that were in the grass and the eggs went to the cow's small intestine, where the larvae stayed and grew into adults. The adult females laid millions of eggs that were shed in feces onto the pasture. If an animal had a large parasite burden, the animal had diarrhea, weight loss, and small intestine damage but no anemia since these nematodes didn't feed on blood. The parasite was easily treated with anthelmintics and Leland had developed specific protocols to test the efficacy of the drugs. My job was to work with Carol and follow the protocols. Leland published papers all the time with the results of his studies, and his goal was to continue testing drugs and continue publishing papers in scholarly journals. With continued publishing, he kept his tenured status at the university, kept getting lucrative grants from pharmaceutical companies, and kept hiring research assistants.

We walked around Leland's lab. It was huge—five or six times the size of Dr. Janovy's tiny two rooms. There was equipment of all types, shiny new microscopes, a walk-in incubator, a water distiller, an autoclave, and glassed-in offices for the PhD students. It was clear that grants for pharmaceutical research were lucrative. We walked out the back door of the lab and down a long hall to the rear of the building where the livestock were housed. There were no rats or rabbits but several large stalls housing steers and horses. I heard Dorothy in my head, "We're not in Kansas anymore," but this time Dorothy was wrong. I *was* in Kansas.

The steers were all infected with *Cooperia* and the eggs had to be harvested from the feces. The graduate students collected the feces but a few weeks after I started work, Carol and I discussed this delegation of duties. We told Leland that we could collect feces, leaving the graduate students to do more important work, but Leland declined our offer because he didn't think this was a task for women. So the grad students brought us a pan of poop and we washed it to separate poop from eggs. We cultured the eggs, allowing them to hatch and grow into adults. After that, we titrated smaller and smaller doses of a drug to be added to test tubes containing thriving adult colonies. The goal was to learn the lowest drug concentration needed to kill the adults. While not difficult, the research did require precision and meticulous record-keeping.

The first couple of months in Manhattan went well. Dennis drove to Ft. Riley every day with other lieutenants, and I rode my bicycle to work at the university. I was one of only a few second lieutenants' wives with a job. Staying home, managing the house, and participating in army wife events was the best option for many women, but I wanted to work and I was lucky to have a good-paying job.

Dennis and I connected with Kerry and Barb soon after we arrived in Manhattan. Kerry had been in Officer Basic with Dennis in San Antonio, but Barb didn't accompany Kerry since she was back home in Illinois teaching school. The school term ended, Barb didn't renew her contract, and she moved to Manhattan to be with Kerry. Barb was the first wife I met and I was glad that she was a regular person. Barb looked for a teaching position in Manhattan, Ft. Riley, and Junction City, but had no luck. She finally decided that she would just spend the time in Kansas as a stay-at-home wife. At first, Barb and Kerry lived in an apartment in Manhattan, but put their names on the post housing list. Eventually, they moved into a small house on post. Dennis and I liked their house and even talked about putting our name on the list to get a house there. Dennis could walk to work and I could drive to work in Manhattan, but, in the end, we liked our giant house. We had elbow room, something that we hadn't had before.

At first, Dennis's job on post didn't affect me and my job at the university. Dennis and I worked during the day and enjoyed each other's company at night and on weekends. After a few weeks, Dennis told me that there was going to be an event, a Change of Command the next week. The event was scheduled in the afternoon and the officers' wives were invited. Dennis told me about the invitation and I said that I couldn't possibly go. I had just started my job and I couldn't ask for an afternoon off. At work the next day, Dennis told the adjutant that because of my job I wouldn't be able to attend the event. The adjutant told Dennis that it didn't work that way. The invitation wasn't an optional invitation. It was mandatory. Dennis broke the news to me that night. He told me about his conversation with the adjutant and said that I had to go to the event. There was no other choice.

"What if I lose my job?" I asked through tears.

"Then, that's what happens," Dennis said. "You have to go. Just ask Dr. Leland. Maybe he's not as strict as you think. Maybe he'll give you permission to be gone for an afternoon."

The next day, I asked for the afternoon off next week for a work thing at Dennis's job. Leland said, "No. You haven't been here long enough for time off." I explained that my attendance at the event wasn't optional. If I didn't go, it would affect Dennis's army career and I couldn't do that to him. Still, Leland told me no. In desperation, I told Leland that I had no choice. I had to attend the event at Ft. Riley and if he didn't allow me to attend, I would have to resign. I was teary because I didn't want to leave my new job. Leland stared at me for what seemed like a full minute and then told me that he would give me permission this one time. He would not, under any circumstances, give me permission to attend an event at Ft. Riley during the day ever again. I thanked him over and over and promised that it wouldn't happen again. When I told Dennis the good news, he replied casually, "See, you worry too much. Things always work out."

The morning of the event Dennis caught a ride to work so I could have the car. At lunch, I rode my bicycle home, changed clothes and drove to the place on the post where Dennis told me to park. I met Dennis at our prearranged spot, and he escorted me to the open field where the event was to take place. He dropped me with the other wives and went to take his place with the other officers. I was dressed in smart trousers, stylish shoes with a chunky one-inch heel, and a dressy blouse. As soon as I saw the other wives, I realized that I should have called Barb to find out what she was wearing. Every other wife was wearing a dress and either low heels or stiletto heels. I could feel everyone's eyes on me. They were judging me as a hick who didn't know how to dress. I was embarrassed, actually mortified, and just wanted to get out of there. Unfortunately for me, after the event, the new lieutenants had to introduce their wives to the senior staff. I was incredibly uncomfortable because of the way I was dressed. I knew I was an embarrassment to Dennis but I tried to be gracious and charming to prove that I wasn't a hick, even though I dressed like one.

When we got in the car, I told Dennis that I was sorry that I wasn't wearing the right clothes. Dennis said, "You do worry too much. You look great. The best-looking wife in the bunch." I felt better I but knew Dennis was just being nice. I decided to research appropriate apparel by studying what other women wore to various events. In the meantime, I would dress up more when I went to events on post. I remembered the old dress code at Nebraska, and it occurred to me that wives of army officers were probably stuck with an old code like that. I was also bothered that there wasn't one woman officer at the event. I asked Dennis about it and he said this was a combat unit, a unit supporting combat troops, so there couldn't be women in the ranks or in leadership roles. I didn't think this was right but I kept my thoughts to myself.

I began to receive invitations to tea from the colonel's wife, the major's wife, and captains' wives—all spouses of officers in the battalion. These teas were mandatory but were scheduled on Saturday afternoons because a few of the wives worked outside the home. The first tea was hosted by the colonel's wife to welcome the wives of officers who had just been assigned to the First Medical Battalion. I wore a knee-length pencil skirt, a dressy blouse and my black pumps with two-inch heels. I looked at myself in the mirror and decided that this outfit should be okay. Off I drove to the colonel's house on post that sunny Saturday afternoon.

I rang the bell and the colonel's wife opened the door. She was gracious and welcoming. There were already many women in the living room and I joined them. I looked at everyone's attire and decided that I was dressed appropriately this time.

After everyone was assembled, tea and coffee were served. I had to balance a cup and saucer, while politely nibbling tiny sandwiches and petit fours. (I was grateful for my mom's and my aunts' etiquette lessons.) While we sipped tea, the women described their experiences as army wives and discussed expectations and proper etiquette to those of us who were new to the army or new to Ft. Riley. If we hadn't already, we were to purchase calling cards at the PX. The calling card was the size of a standard business card and our name would be centered on the front. The colonel's wife gave each of us one of her cards as an example. My calling card would have my name printed in the center. Well, not my actual name, but Mrs. Dennis L. Lambert. We were to carry our calling cards everywhere and when we attended an event, we would discreetly place a calling card in the small, silver tray on a table near the front door. It was clear that this was an elaborate attendance system. I assumed that someone kept track of attendance, but I wasn't sure what happened if you didn't attend. I certainly didn't want to find out. I wasn't happy with the name format on the calling card. After all, I wasn't Mrs. Dennis L. Lambert; I was Ms. Leah L. Lambert. I was losing my identity—or maybe it was already gone.

Several other women had jobs and couldn't always attend events during the week. One of them asked if this would be a problem. The colonel's wife told the woman that it was generally okay to miss events during the week because of work, but it was important not to miss events on the weekends. An army officer's wife was expected to demonstrate her support of her husband by being invested in all activities.

Another woman asked how she would know what to wear to an event. The major's wife said that if the wife was attending an event with her husband, the required dress would often be included in the invitation, but if not, we should ask our husbands to inquire for us. As a last resort, she told us it was okay to call her and ask. She said she was always happy to help and that it was important to dress for the occasion. We didn't want to arrive at an event wearing the wrong clothes because it reflected badly on our husband. (I felt even worse about my error in judgment at the Change of Command ceremony.) As a rule of thumb, our dress should mirror what our husband was wearing. If he was wearing his duty uniform (green fatigues), we needed to dress casually in a dress or a skirt and blouse. This also applied if it was summer and our husband was wearing his khaki summer uniform with short sleeves. If our husband was wearing his Class As, it was dressy, and we should dress like we were going to church. If our husband was wearing his dress blues, it was a formal event and we should wear a formal or cocktail dress. There was at least one formal every year on post, so the women recommended that we shop for a formal dress soon to be prepared. For women's events like teas or luncheons, the "dress code" was skirts or dresses, but definitely not slacks. If we were invited to a casual cocktail party, dressy slacks were acceptable, but a skirt and blouse or a dress were always the best choice.

There was a general discussion about military hierarchy in the medical battalion and in the division—basically a discussion of the tiers of influence. General's wives were the most influential, then colonel's wives, and on down to second lieutenant's wives, who were the lowest members on the totem pole. This rule was strictly applied at the division level because that was a systematically structured, rigid environment. The rule wasn't followed as strictly among wives at the medical battalion level, though. There, all of the wives were treated a bit more like equals.

There was a discussion about Reforger. We were reminded that in the fall, the men would be gone six weeks for maneuvers in Germany. During that time, there would be additional events to keep wives from feeling out of touch and lonely. It was a way to provide support. I could be excused from events during the week because I had a full-time job.

The weekend after the tea, Dennis and I went to the PX. I bought a floor-length skirt, a lacy blouse and ordered my calling cards. When the cards arrived, I stashed a dozen or so in my purse so I would have them every time there was an event.

In the late summer we received an invitation to a cocktail party at the colonel's house. The invitation stressed casual dress, so Dennis wore slacks and I wore a skirt and blouse. I didn't know what to expect at that first party. College parties had kegs of beer and fruit punch spiked with Everclear. I assumed, correctly, that this wouldn't be like that.

We were greeted at the door by the colonel. He took our coats and I covertly looked for a silver tray for calling cards. There was no tray, so I guessed that attendance at a cocktail party was not mandatory or tracked. Dennis and I stepped into the living room, filled with men and women with a mixed drink in one hand and a cigarette in the other. There was a stereo playing in the background. Dennis walked up to some guy and introduced me. The guy introduced Dennis and me to his wife. We talked awhile and the colonel came by to ask what I wanted to drink. I didn't know the names of drinks, but had heard of Seagram's and 7, so said that. "Very good. What about you, Dennis?" Dennis said, "Just scotch." Off the colonel went and within a couple of minutes, he was back with our drinks. We stood around talking, holding our drinks for a while, and then the colonel's wife told us to help ourselves to the canapés. So just like the tea party, I had to balance my drink and a small plate of canapés on my knees while looking sophisticated. My two goals here were not to drink too much and not look like a hayseed. I succeeded with the first but I'm not so sure about the second.

A month later, another invitation to a cocktail party arrived. This one was at the major's house, also on post. When we walked in, I saw Barb, sitting in the living room, nursing a drink. I sat next to her while Dennis and Kerry hovered nearby. The major asked what I wanted to drink.

"Maybe a martini," I replied. The major said he made a mean martini and returned quickly with a martini glass filled to the brim with a dry martini. It was a great martini. I ate a couple small sandwiches and had some chips and dip from the buffet table, but every time my martini glass was half empty, the major filled it up again from his glass pitcher. I'm not sure what Dennis was drinking that night, nor do I know how many drinks we had. All I remember is that I was woozy and I tried very hard NOT to act drunk. Dennis drove us home—very carefully, trying hard not to look like he was driving under the influence. We made it home, stumbled up the stairs. and fell into bed.

We didn't go to bars or pubs in Kansas because Kansas liquor laws were even more restrictive than those in Texas. A statewide prohibition of alcohol sales had been in effect since the 1800s. Kansas law had been eased a little, and the new law allowed distilled beverage sales in private clubs, but not liquor by the drink. Patrons had to buy a bottle of booze from the club and buy their setups separately. It was expensive and too much trouble, so we went to someone's house or we went to the Officer's Club on post. While laws were strict regarding distilled beverages, anyone eighteen years old or older could buy 3.2 percent beer. It seems that in the late 1930s, some clever entrepreneurs convinced the legislature to reclassify 3.2 percent beer as a "cereal malt beverage" so it could be sold legally. This was a boon for both college and university towns and small border towns in Kansas. Marysville, Kansas, was on the Nebraska border, directly south of Lincoln on Highway 77. Marysville liquor stores had a thriving business selling to college kids who drove to Kansas, bought cases of 3.2 beer, and carted them back to Nebraska for resale at exorbitant prices.

In September, the division was making plans for Reforger in October. I dreaded Dennis's departure, but there wasn't anything I could do about it. At least Frank, Norma, and Barbara would be around to keep me company and I would have the car. In early October Dennis got word that he wouldn't be going on Reforger. The adjutant planned to leave the army at the end of the year and he wanted to go to Europe one last time. That meant that the assistant adjutant (Dennis) needed to stay behind. Neither Dennis nor I complained about this turn of events.

My job was going well. It was a busy lab, but the workload was manageable and Carol and I got along famously. The atmosphere was similar to the one in Dr. Janovy's lab. Carol and I were the only women working with male graduate students, but we were treated with respect. One unmarried student got flirtatious a few times, but Carol and I ignored him. We were both married and couldn't be bothered. There was the usual lunchtime chatter about politics and campus affairs, but mostly the grad students were too busy for anything but their research. That left Carol and me to discuss politics, movies, music, or fashion.

Dr. Leland was still busy penning scholarly papers and one afternoon he asked Carol and me for help. He wanted us to read a draft to identify issues with spelling, structure, syntax, or grammar. This was in my wheelhouse so I jumped at the opportunity. Carol and I spent a lot of time on the project and did such a good job that Leland continued to ask for our help.

Several times, a grad student needed a unique piece of glassware for an experiment. Carol and I took a sketch to K-State's glassblower, Mitsugi Ohno. He looked at the sketch, asked a question or two, and then told us when the glass would be ready for pickup. Mr. Ohno had worked as a glassblower at the University of Tokyo before being hired by K-State, where he set up his glass blowing shop in the chemistry department. He made glass equipment for researchers in veterinary medicine, biology, chemistry, and physics. His real job, though, was as an artist. He was a renowned glassblower and created beautiful glass sculptures. He was famous for his blown-glass Klein Bottles.

[A Klein Bottle, in mathematics, is a non-orientable surface. It's a one-sided surface, which if you could travel on the surface, would take you back to the point of origin while you flipped upside down. In space, the inside of the bottle turns into the outside and the outside turns into the inside.]

Since a real Klein Bottle doesn't exist in three-dimensional space, Mr. Ohno's bottles were not perfect Klein Bottles. They were excellent three-dimensional representations, though. I bought a bottle for Dennis that Christmas.

The year 1971 was flying by. I was lonely for family so Dennis and I invited my parents, Sharyl, and Rick for Thanksgiving. Our big old house had lots of room for everyone to sleep, and we had a huge kitchen so I could help Mom prepare the meal. The family was there for a few days and I loved every minute. I missed my family, but I especially missed my mom. It was ridiculous since I hadn't actually lived at home since I left for the university in the fall of 1966. It was different now. I had so much to tell Mom and so many things to ask but there just wasn't time. I was miserable when they got in the car and left for Nebraska. I think I cried for hours.

We spent Christmas by ourselves because neither Dennis nor I could get time off. Frank and Norma went to her parent's house in Tipton, and Barbara spent her Christmas break in Maryland with Dennis's parents. My parents were celebrating in Nebraska. It was nice to be together, just the two of us, but we were lonesome and a little sad. We had both grown up spending every Christmas with large extended families. We decided that we would never spend another Christmas alone.

January–December 1972

Dennis's first boss left Ft. Riley in January and a physician arrived to take his place. Besides being the medical battalion commander, he was also the division surgeon and on the division commander's staff. With that change, some of the medical battalion's tasks changed. In addition to setting up clearing stations during division maneuvers in the field, the battalion began operating three troop medical clinics around the post, and each clinic was staffed with doctors and medics. In March, the adjutant left and Dennis got the job of S1/Adjutant, or personnel officer. The job was a good fit because Dennis liked working with people.

In February, Dennis's grandmother, Pearl Lambert, died. We drove to Davenport, Nebraska for the funeral and spent time with Lamberts who came from around the country. In March, Dennis's Aunt Donna called and said that the family was cleaning out Pearl's house. There was a lot of furniture that no one wanted, and she asked Dennis if he wanted to come and have a look. If he liked something, he could haul it away. That night, Dennis talked to Frank and they decided to rent a U-Haul truck the coming weekend to retrieve whatever they could from their grandmother's house. Frank came home with a few items but Dennis came home with a windfall. There was an oak buffet, a matching oval dining room table with four leaves, eight oak dining room chairs with leather seats, a bed with oak headboard and footboard, and his grandfather's sturdy rocking chair. Dennis's grandparents purchased the furniture in the 1920s and Dwight told us that he slept in the bed the entire time he lived at home and that he would always remember the dining room set from his parent's little dining room. Dennis said that he took the rocking chair because one of his fondest memories of his grandfather was the one of him sitting in that rocking chair, smoking cigars. Our house on Moro was fully furnished and we didn't need more furniture, but we thought everything would come in handy someday. We stashed it all in the basement until we moved into an unfurnished house.

Because we had a huge house, Dennis and I began hosting parties for the other officers and their wives or girlfriends. Everyone brought their own liquor and an appetizer, snack, or dessert to share. We always invited Frank, Norma, and Barbara and her friends. Barbara had transferred from Bethany College to Kansas State, and she was living in an apartment with friends just off campus. Barbara usually arrived early to eat supper with us and then help with party preparations. One evening, our guests started to arrive before I had cleaned up after supper. Barbara told me she would stay in the kitchen to clean up, but I told her that we would just stash the dirty dishes, pots, and pans in the oven, wipe off the counters and no one would be the wiser. Barbara stared at me, not believing that I was doing this, but when I started shoving dishes into the oven, she just laughed and helped with the cleanup. Lucky for me, no one brought food that needed to be warmed in the oven.

*Maybe all the people who say ghosts don't exist
are just afraid to admit that they do.*

—MICHAEL ENDE

We had heard unexplained sounds in our house as soon as we moved in, but that March the sounds came more frequently. The chandelier in the dining room started to move and clink while we were in the living room or sunroom. With the windows closed, no forced-air heat, and no one walking through the dining room, there was no real explanation. We also began to hear footsteps on the stairs. At times, it sounded like someone was walking up the stairs and other times like someone was walking down. We poked our heads out of the sunroom toward the stairs but no one was there. Often, after the footsteps going down, the chandelier moved and clinked. It was as if someone had walked downstairs and into the kitchen. We decided that it was the ghost of the little lady who had died in the house, going to the kitchen to get something to eat. We laughed about it. We weren't frightened. We were taking good care of her house and we were sure she was happy.

One evening, our friends Barb and Kerry told us they were going to have a baby. Barb couldn't find a teaching job and besides, having a baby in the army was cheap. I think they ended up paying a few hundred dollars for everything—pre- and postnatal care, delivery, and nursery. Dennis and I were very happy for them and even considered having a baby of our own because it seemed like everyone was having a baby. This certainly was the conventional choice. Normal couples had babies within a year or two of getting married, and normal military couples had babies because it was so much cheaper than on the outside. But we weren't a normal couple and decided we had other options. We could have a baby like the rest of our friends, enjoy parenthood, and make our parents very happy. Or, for the next year, we could save all the money I earned in Leland's lab and live off Dennis' salary. After he was discharged, we would have enough money to go to Europe for a couple of months and see the sights. The Europe option won. There was another, less positive reason for postponing parenthood. Neither of us expected to live to see age thirty. The world was falling into chaos and no one was trying to stop it. In January, on Bloody Sunday, British troops killed about fifteen unarmed civil rights marchers in Northern Ireland. In February, there were riots in Ireland, the British embassy in Dublin was burned, and bombs exploded in Belfast and Londonderry. The war in Vietnam was unending. In March, the North Vietnamese crossed the DMZ into South Vietnam, and in retaliation, the US started bombing Hanoi. If nothing improved, we weren't convinced the world could be saved.

In the near term, Dennis decided the time was right to visit his parents in Maryland. He missed his mom and dad and he wanted me to see Washington DC. I was more than willing to go on another adventure, so we packed the car and drove east in early April. We spent the night in St. Louis, a large, beautiful city, but there was no time to see the sights. We got up the next morning and continued driving east. Once at Dennis's parents' apartment in Silver Spring, we started our vacation. Dennis's parents worked the first part of the week, so the two of us saw as many DC sites as possible. Dwight got tickets for us to tour the White House and the Capitol building. We saw memorials, toured part of the Smithsonian, and drove through DC neighborhoods. I fell in love with Georgetown with its tall townhouses and thought it would be a wonderful place to live. We saw a movie at Dennis's favorite theater and went to a coffee house, tucked away on the lower level of a row house. It was small, smoky, and dimly lit, with tiny tables scattered around the room. We picked a table toward the back and Dennis ordered espresso and shortbread cookies. I was captivated by the atmosphere and the clientele and told Dennis that we should definitely open a coffee house in Lincoln. I thought it would be such fun, but Dennis just shook his head and told me that nobody would pay for coffee in Lincoln. He was right. A tiny, dark coffee house wouldn't fly in Lincoln.

Dennis's parents took us to Baltimore where we toured Ft. McHenry and Old Ironsides. Dwight drove to a small restaurant on the outskirts of Baltimore and ordered crab cakes for everyone. It was the first time I had eaten crab and it was delicious. The Jesse's were meat and potatoes people, and if we ate fish, it was fried perch or crappy.

The weekend before we left for home, Dwight drove us through the Smoky Mountains. It was a cold and icy day and the mountains were shrouded in a thick mist. It was beautiful because the trees were coated in ice and everything seemed so otherworldly.

Our vacation passed quickly and it was hard to leave, but we were soon back in the car, heading west. Not long after we got home, the terrorist group Red Army planted a bomb in a US Army barracks in Germany and several soldiers were killed. Dennis was going to Germany on Reforger that fall, and I was afraid there might be more bombings. I didn't tell Dennis about my fears. He would only worry about me, and he couldn't do anything about Reforger anyway.

Dennis and I talked about our European vacation now and then, but the spring of 1973 seemed far in the distance. We lived day to day and hoped for better times ahead. In June, five White House operatives were arrested for burglary at the Democratic National Committee offices at the Watergate Hotel in DC. In July, President Nixon was taped talking about using the CIA to obstruct the FBI's investigation into the break-in. On one hand, it was hard to believe, but on the other, it seemed like something "Tricky Dick" would do. I didn't like the guy.

That fall, a young lieutenant was assigned to the medical battalion from Vietnam, and he brought his new Vietnamese bride with him. The wife seemed to be much older than the young man, and some of the officers' wives discussed whether or not she had entrapped the lieutenant. I listened to the chatter but didn't participate. It seemed to me that if the woman had trapped the young man, we couldn't blame her. She was probably desperate to get out of her war-torn country and would do anything to escape. I might do the same.

The couple didn't have anywhere to live when they arrived in Kansas. They wanted to live in post housing but no housing was available. There weren't any affordable apartments available in Manhattan or Junction City either, so the colonel asked Dennis to take in the couple. They should stay with us in our big house until post housing was available. Dennis agreed because he didn't have a choice. Dennis told me the news that night and said that the couple would move in that weekend. When they arrived, they were grateful to Dennis and me and thanked us over and over. The wife told me that since I had a job and she didn't, she would cook the evening meal every night. She would do the shopping and the cooking because it was the least she could do to express her gratitude.

I showed the couple to the guest room and gave them sheets and towels. I told them that they could store anything that wouldn't fit in the dresser or closet in the small makeshift kitchen next to their room. They would have to share our bathroom, though.

We only had two keys to the house and our landlord didn't want us to make additional ones. I gave the couple my key and asked that they lock the doors when they left. They agreed and the wife said she would always return to the house before I was due home from work. That way, I would never be locked out. They seemed pleased with the entire arrangement and promised to not be any trouble. We told them that we were very happy that we had a large house and could accommodate them until post housing was available.

Everything went well at first. The wife was always there when I got home from work, sometimes in the kitchen cooking, sometimes upstairs in her room. We ate some Vietnamese food, but she also made every effort to cook American food like spaghetti or meatloaf and potatoes. Then things changed. The wife became distant, arrogant, and passive-aggressive. There were times when I arrived home from work, the house was a mess. The living room furniture had been moved, and there were magazines and newspapers strewn on the floor. There were wet towels on the bathroom floor, dirty dishes on the dining room table, and dirty pots and pans stacked in the sink. I was left to clean up before I started supper for Dennis and me, and I resented the extra work. We also noticed that our friend, the ghost, was no longer active.

One evening after work, I rode my bike home in a pouring rain. I was soaked to the skin and cold. I tried to open the door but it was locked so I pounded on the door. There was no answer. I walked to the rear of the house and pounded on the back door, but again, there was no answer. I went back to the front and sat on the front porch, waiting for the wife to come back and let me in. She didn't come back, but finally Dennis got home and let me in. The house was a wreck. We cleaned up the mess, cooked and ate supper, and while we were washing the dishes, the couple came through the front door. The wife scurried upstairs and the man walked into the kitchen. He apologized for being so late. Dennis reminded him that I didn't have a key and couldn't get into the house. I had to sit on the porch, soaking wet. The guy apologized over and over and promised that it would never happen again. I accepted the apology and told him I appreciated his understanding.

For the next week, Dennis and I didn't see much of the couple, which was fine with us. Every time I came home, the door was unlocked and the wife was upstairs. She didn't cook supper for the four of us, but we didn't care.

The final straw came when I arrived home on a very chilly evening, anxious to get inside and warm up after my bike ride. The door was locked. It was a repeat of the previous time, but it was cold outside, getting colder and I was freezing. I sat on the porch shivering for over an hour and still no one came. Finally, I walked several blocks to a friend's house. I told them that I was locked out of my house and needed to call Dennis to find out when he would be home. Dennis answered and I tearfully told him I was locked out of our house and I was at a friend's house. Dennis was angry. The colonel had asked him to work on a last-minute project and it had taken much longer than he thought it would. He was about finished, would leave Ft. Riley in fifteen minutes or so and come by to pick me up. In the meantime, my hosts fed me supper and warmed me up with hot chocolate. When Dennis arrived, my friend answered the door and there was Dennis, framed in the door, looking handsome in his fatigues. He took off his cap, tucked it under his arm, and stepped inside. He told me he was sorry he had to work late and thanked the couple for letting me stay at their house. They asked if Dennis wanted supper, but he declined, saying he just wanted to get home. I thanked them over and over for taking me in and feeding me supper. When we got home, our guests were there, watching TV. "Where have you been?" the guy asked. "At a friend's house because I couldn't get into my own house," I replied sarcastically. While the guy apologized, I ran upstairs and got ready for bed.

The next day was Saturday and the couple left early. Dennis and I decided they had to go but we couldn't ask them to leave. We were their reluctant hosts, and there was no going back on our word. We devised a plan. We would tell the two that our landlord found out other people were living with us and that was not part of our rental agreement. If the extra people didn't leave, she would evict us. We told our story to the couple when they came back that evening. They said that they would pack and move out the next day. We were solemn and thanked them for understanding, but of course we were thrilled. I have no idea where they went after they left our house but I didn't really care. I wanted to get back to our peaceful life, and Dennis and I hoped that our ghost would return to keep us company.

When preparations for Reforger began that fall, I was fretful about Dennis being in Germany for six weeks. The bombing at the army barracks in Germany still haunted me, and in September, a dozen Israeli Olympic athletes in Munich were murdered by the terrorist group Black September. Germany didn't seem safe. Then, in late September, Dennis told me that, once again, he was staying behind at Ft. Riley. The army was downsizing and as the adjutant, he had to process out about 150 men. This was great news to me. I couldn't believe our luck.

In October, we wrote and requested absentee ballots for the November election. Nixon was running against George McGovern, a democrat and antiwar candidate. We mailed our ballots to Rushville and hoped that Tricky Dick would lose. But, supported by his silent majority, Nixon won in a landslide. At least we had voted.

Later in November, we drove to Kansas City to attend Barbara's wedding. It was a beautiful event and Dennis was handsome in his dress blues. He had wanted to wear a civilian suit, but decided that his dad would prefer the dress blues.

Soon after we got home, the landlord told us that she had decided to sell the house, and she asked if we wanted to buy it. We thanked her for the offer, but told her we wouldn't be staying in Manhattan after Dennis was discharged in March of 1973. We started looking for another place, found a duplex, and gave notice to the landlady. She asked if we wanted any of the furniture in the old two-story house because she wanted to clean it out before putting it on the market. We bought the sofa, a side chair, a dresser, a mattress and bed frame, and the camel-back trunk that the woman's mother (our ghost) brought with her when she immigrated from Sweden.

In early December, just before we moved, Dennis's friend Bruce came to Manhattan for a visit. We walked through Aggieville, visited a few college hangouts, and generally had a great time. The three of us talked about the latest news: authorities had found ten thousand dollars in cash in a handbag that belonged to the wife of one of the Watergate conspirators. It was looking bad for Nixon, but we couldn't have cared less about him.

We hadn't told anyone about our ghostly housemate, but when she walked down the stairs one night, Bruce heard her. He asked if our house was haunted, and we told him that the lady who had died in the house still walked around at night. Bruce was fascinated and actually tried to talk to her, but there was no response—we thought. After Bruce left, our house seemed quieter than normal. A couple of days later Bruce called and said he thought our ghost had traveled with him back to Lincoln. His apartment had always been quiet at night, but now, he heard footsteps wandering through the place. He said it didn't bother him, but he thought it was weird. We told him that we hadn't heard our ghost since he left and we laughed that the lady had formed such an attachment that she left her home just to be with Bruce. "Oh my gosh, you have a girlfriend," Dennis laughed. A few months later Bruce moved to another apartment, but he didn't think the ghost went with him because it was quiet in his new apartment. We thought that maybe she stayed in Bruce's old apartment or maybe she caught a ride back to her house in Manhattan. Since we had already moved, we didn't know. We hoped that wherever she was, people were kind to her.

Our new place was a duplex on McCollum Drive, just a few blocks from campus. The duplex was a lot smaller than the big house, but it had a good-sized living room. The furniture from Dennis's grandmother's house and from the Moro house fit well. The kitchen, a small bedroom, and a full bath took up the rest of the first floor. There was also a large bedroom, a storage room, and a full bath in the basement. We chose to use the basement bedroom as the master bedroom because it was so big.

We celebrated the Christmas holiday in Manhattan. Dennis's Mom and Dad stayed with Frank and Norma, so we spent most of the time at Frank's, eating, drinking, talking, and completing a large jigsaw puzzle. It was certainly better than being alone for the holiday, but I missed my own family.

January–March 1973

Tell me what it is you plan to do with
your one wild and precious life.

—Mary Oliver

There was fabulous news in January. First, Nixon announced a Vietnam peace agreement and the peace accord was signed in Paris. I was ecstatic. The antiwar movement had actually worked! Second, the Supreme Court overturned state bans on abortion in a case known as *Roe v. Wade*. This was an amazing turn of events and hard to believe. The ruling confirmed that women had rights. We were recognized as sentient humans who could control our own bodies. Forced pregnancy was a thing of the past.

Time was slipping away and we needed to start planning our trip to Europe. We also needed to start planning for our futures. I remembered my friend from chemistry class. She was going to be a medical technologist and she thought that I would like that job. It seemed like a suitable career choice, so I started my research. There were medical technology schools conveniently located in Kansas City and in Lincoln. At all of the schools, I would take classes for twelve months, pass the national exam and then get a job in any hospital. Still, I had had good luck finding a research assistant job at Kansas State, so an alternative was to get a research job wherever we moved. Having my salary dependent on a professor and his ability to secure grants seemed risky though. I could also apply for graduate school at Nebraska, but I still didn't find that option appealing. In the end, I chose two med tech schools in Kansas City and one in Lincoln. I requested applications and spent hours making my applications perfect. I mailed the three applications with my return address in Alliance. I had done my best. All I could do was cross my fingers and hope for at least one acceptance letter while we were in Europe.

At the same time, Dennis was trying to decide what he wanted to do after he was discharged. One of his superiors wanted him to stay in the army. Dennis was offered a position at Walter Reed in Washington, where he would learn how to operate a new piece of medical equipment called a heart-lung machine. The machine was used for heart surgeries, so it was a chance to get in on the ground floor of the new technology. It was a new job in the army and Dennis would get a promotion after he completed training. We would move to Washington DC and be close to his parents. I was enamored with DC when we visited, so I liked that option. The downside was that Dennis had to re-up and stay in the army. He said that there just were too many *(expletives)* in the army, so he declined the offer. Dennis decided his best option was to go back to the Nebraska and get a PhD in zoology. He completed the required documents and applied, using our Alliance address as the return address. He also hoped to hear back while we were out of the country.

With that done, we started to make plans for our grand tour of Europe. I don't think that our parents actually thought we would go through with it, so they were surprised when we started making plans. We obtained our passports and began talking to people who had been to Europe—mostly Dennis's fellow soldiers who had either had a tour of duty in Europe or who had gone to Germany on Reforger. The cheapest airline flights were on Icelandic Airlines, and Icelandic flew out of New York's JFK. We wrote for information but decided that we needed a travel agent's help. On a Saturday morning, we dropped by Travel Unlimited, an agency on Poyntz Avenue in Manhattan. We explained that we wanted to spend a couple of months in Europe, with no particular agenda. We told her that when Dennis separated from active duty we would drive to Alliance, spend a few days there, then fly from Denver to Baltimore. We would spend a few days with Dennis's parents then fly from New York to Europe. We had studied a calendar and selected March 31, 1973 as our departure date from New York. Our tentative return date was going to be May 23, but we wanted to be able to change the date if we decided to stay longer. Everything had to be "on the cheap."

The travel agent was a great help. First, she reserved our flights. We would fly United from Denver to Baltimore and Icelandic Airlines from JFK to Luxembourg. Icelandic required a stop in Reykjavik, Iceland, but that was fine. On the return, we would fly from Luxembourg to JFK (with a stop in Reykjavik), spend a couple of days in New York, and take the train from New York to Washington. Dennis's parents would pick us up at the train station, and after a couple of days in Maryland, we would fly from Baltimore to Denver. My parents would pick us up and take us to Alliance to pick up our car.

When in Europe, we planned to travel by train using Eurail passes. The agent told us that the Eurail passes were valid across Western Europe, but not in the United Kingdom, so we would have to purchase separate train or bus tickets there. She didn't have any recommendations but thought that bus tickets would likely be cheaper. She purchased everything on our behalf and we picked up the airline tickets and the Eurail passes just before we left Manhattan.

We were too old to qualify for accommodations in youth hostels because most hostels were reserved for travelers under twenty-one. We decided we would stay in pensions and third or fourth class hotels where we would secure a room with a sink. The toilet and bathroom would be shared with other travelers in the hotel. Breakfast was included much of the time, so that was one less meal we would have to purchase. We went to a bookstore and bought a book listing the lower-class hotels in cities across Europe. The book included notes about each hotel (English-speaking staff, friendliness, cleanliness, etc.) We also bought a journal so we could document our trip and finally three phrase books (French, Italian and German) so we could have rudimentary conversations while traveling. We went to our bank and requested more money in American Express traveler's checks than we ever imagined we would need. The plan was to cash checks for local currency at American Express offices and go to an exchange office at the railroad station as needed to exchange one currency for another. Our goal was to bring home as much money as possible. Along with the traveler's checks, we received a small handbook that listed approximate exchange rates and the street addresses of American Express offices in every large European city. We knew that this little book would come in handy.

We promised our parents that we would stay in touch by sending postcards as often as we could. We also told them that if they needed to send us news from home, they should write to us in care of the American Express office in Rome because we would be there in April or to the Dusseldorf office because we would be there in May. We would pick up our mail when we arrived in those two cities. Those two cities were the only places where we could be contacted.

We planned to travel light—one bag each because we would each have to cart our own luggage on and off the train. I started making a list of everything we needed to take with us, knowing that we could buy toiletries and sundries everywhere. People told us that we needed to "dress up" in Europe if we didn't want to look too conspicuous. Most American tourists wore clothes that were much too casual, so it was easy to pick them out of a crowd. I packed skirts and blouses, and chose to wear 'hush-puppy' shoes that were comfortable but not too casual. Dennis packed trousers, shirts, and his comfortable boots.

Barbara sewed lined, dark-olive-green coats for us. Dennis's was thigh-length and mine was knee-length. The coats were going to be a godsend because we read that the weather could be chilly and rainy in early April, and they would serve double-duty as bath robes when we walked down the hall to the shared bathroom at our hotels.

When Dennis's discharge date was close, we watched the news more closely. The Irish Republican Army bombed Whitehall and the Old Bailey in London and there were bombings in Ireland. We decided against visiting Ireland and would substitute Scotland. Even though there were bombings in London, we decided to visit London anyway. We also agreed to visit several cities in Germany in spite of bombings and terrorist attacks. There was no way we could stay clear of danger, so we would trust our luck.

In March, the last soldier left Vietnam. But at home, the big news was that one of the Watergate burglars admitted that he and the others had been pressured into keeping quiet by the former Attorney General, John Mitchell. Mitchell was apparently the boss of the whole break-in operation, and Nixon had been behind the sordid mess. I was not surprised by the news.

We made arrangements for the army to relocate our personal belongings from the duplex in Manhattan to a storage locker in Lincoln. The only thing we packed were some winter clothes for Nebraska and Maryland and our two suitcases for Europe. The moving van came, the men packed our household and hauled it away. We stayed with Frank and Norma for a day before we left Manhattan and the army behind. We were excited about our upcoming big adventure, but I was a little scared. As planned, we drove to Alliance and visited with family. We made a quick trip to Rushville so Dennis could register his army discharge papers with the county clerk. After another day with family, we left our car at the ranch and my parents drove us to Stapleton Airport in Denver. We said our goodbyes, and at noon on March 23, 1973, we boarded our plane to Baltimore. Dennis's parents met us and we spent a few days in DC before they took us to New York's JFK International. On March 31, we arrived in plenty of time for our flight so the four of us sat at the gate and waited. Our departure time, eight thirty in the evening, came and went and still we sat. Dwight was annoyed and nervous. We told him that it was okay and they should just leave, check into their hotel, and get some rest. Dwight refused. He said that he didn't trust that the plane was actually going to arrive. The agent assured us that the plane was in the air above JFK and would land as soon as the pilot had clearance. Dwight asked Dennis if we had hotel reservations in Luxembourg, but Dennis told him, "No. We'll find something when we get there." Dwight just shook his head and walked away. Finally, the jet arrived. We anxiously waited while passengers deplaned and the jet was cleaned and refueled. It was just after midnight when we hugged Dwight and Helen goodbye and, holding hands, boarded the jet. Our European adventure was starting.

Images

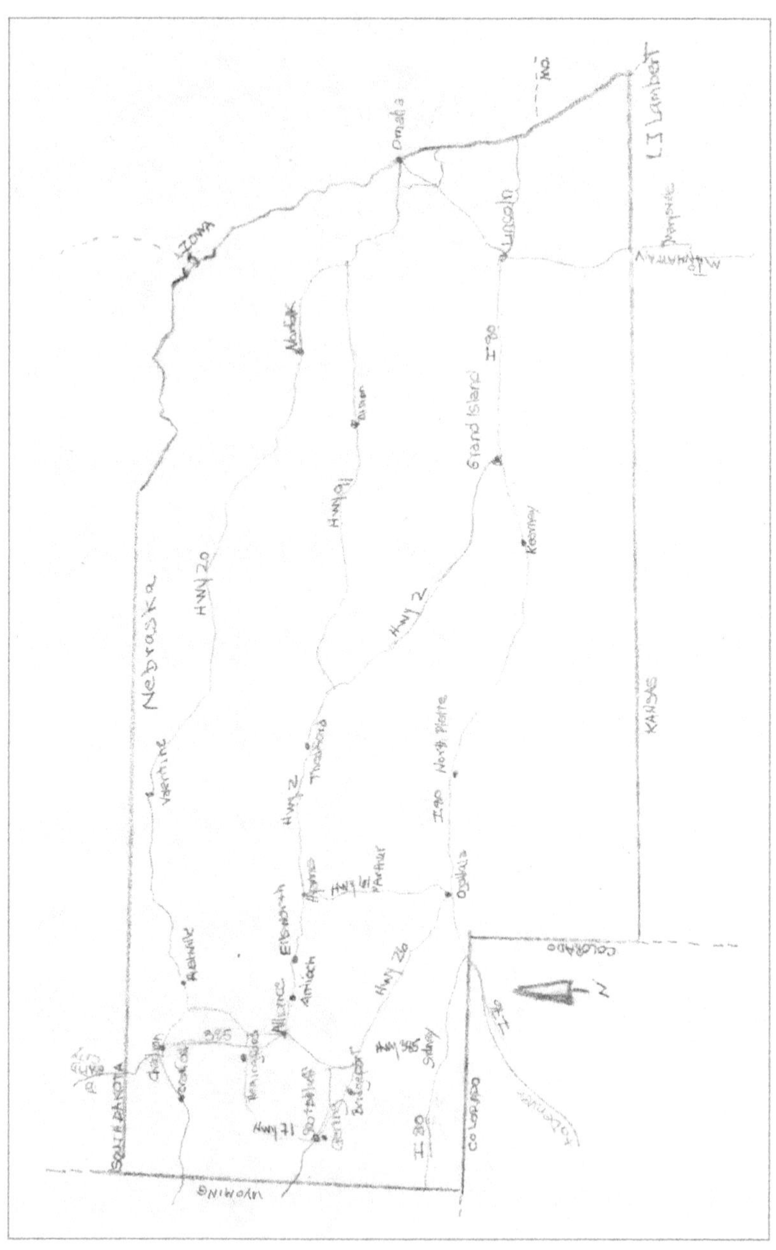

Nebraska Map

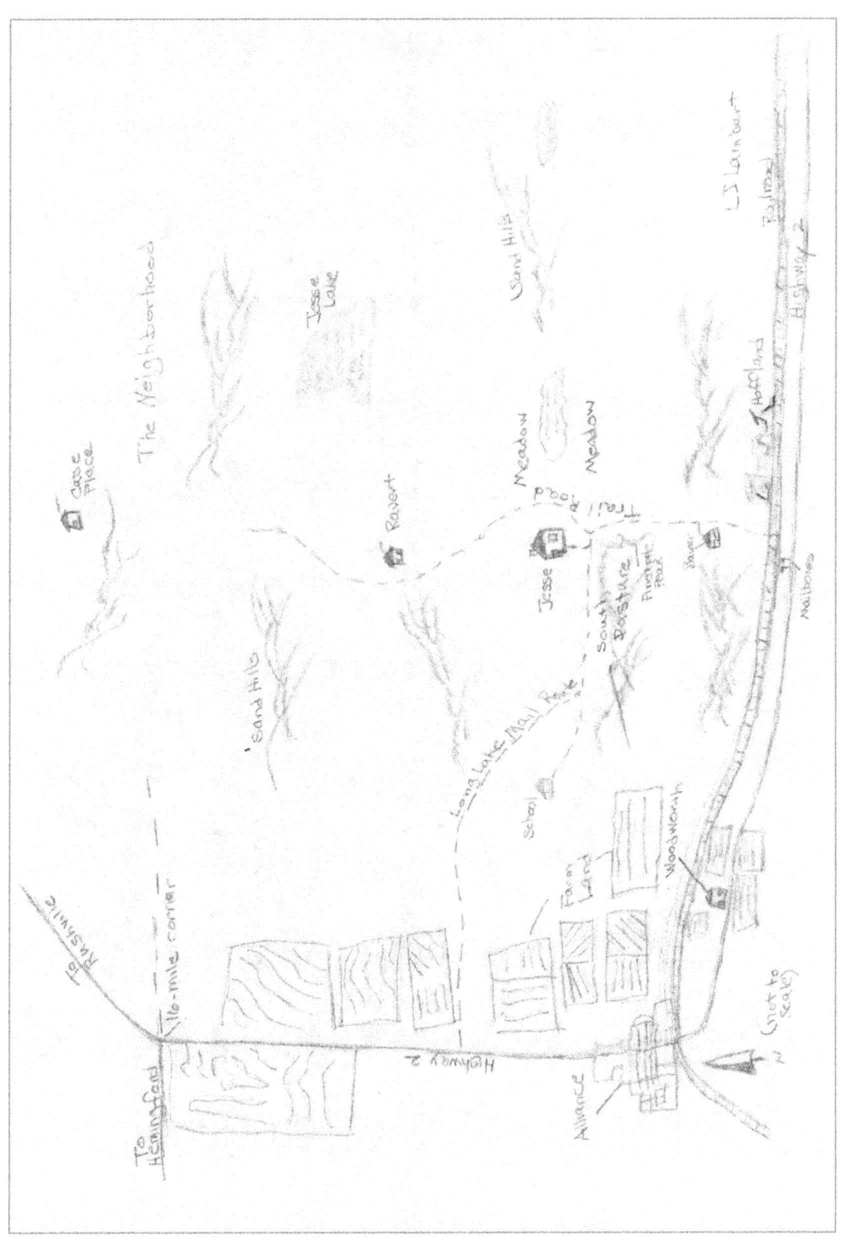

Neighborhood Map

Aerial map of the home place, circa 1949.
Photo taken by WWII pilot flying his single-engine plane

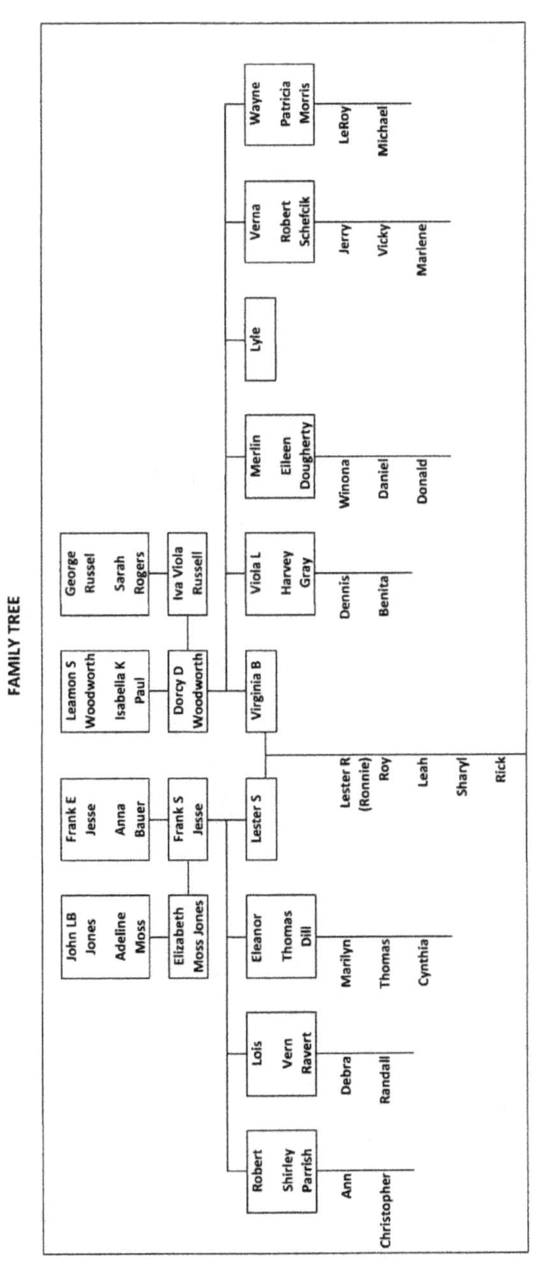

Leah's family tree including great-grandparents

University of Nebraska campus circa 1966

About the Author

Leah Jesse Lambert grew up on a cattle ranch in the Sandhills of western Nebraska. She attended a one-room school through eighth grade before moving on to high school and then to the University of Nebraska. After avoiding science classes at all costs in high school, she ended up with a major in zoology and a minor in chemistry at the university. She enjoyed a successful career in the sciences before moving into management positions and earning an MBA from Southern Illinois University at Edwardsville.

Leah and her husband, Dennis have been married over 50 years. They lived in Nebraska, Kansas, North Dakota, Texas and Missouri before settling in Hilliard, Ohio. The couple loves spending time with their three sons, three daughters-in-law and six grandchildren. They also have a weakness for travel and have visited nearly every state and over twenty countries.

Leah's first book, *Remembering Nebraska,* is a collection of her parents' and grandparents' stories about their lives in Nebraska.